Baseball in 1889

Baseball in
1889
Players vs. Owners

Daniel M. Pearson

Bowling Green State University Popular Press
Bowling Green, OH 43403

Sports in Culture
General Editors
Douglas Noverr,
Lawrence Ziewacz

To Eldora

Contents

Acknowledgments

I would like to thank all of the people in the following libraries who patiently and efficiently aid researchers: The Huntington Library, San Marino, California; The Library of Congress; The Doheny Library, University of Southern California; The Amateur Athletic Foundation of Los Angeles Library; The National Baseball Library, Cooperstown, New York; and Clemson University Library. I began research in The Huntington and completed it at Cooperstown and The Amateur Athletic Foundation. The Los Angeles Dodgers, Inc. gave me an invaluable research grant that enabled me to sojourn in Cooperstown for four weeks during the summer of 1989.

Tom Heitz and Bill Deane provided an excellent work environment at The National Baseball Library. Tom Heitz also invited me to participate in the Leatherstocking Baseball Club's practices and games. It proved to be one of the most purely enjoyable and educational experiences in my life, and I met some unforgettable people. I learned from the way that William "Old Clothes" Arlt approached the game and life. He and Michael "Bring 'Em Home" Jerome taught me the inside town ball game, and Mike was the perfect host at his Inn at Cooperstown. Pat Kelly, Director of the Photo Department at the NBL, helped me confirm identifications of 1889 photographs.

Janice Knight introduced me to W. P. Kinsella's work, and she also gave generously of her late husband's personal sports library. Her interest in my research has been of inestimable value.

William E. Unrau, Professor of History at The Wichita State University, gave me important directions through the publication thicket after he had read the original manuscript. He and Gerald L. Shannon, former Chairman of The Social Science Department at Bethany College, Lindsborg, have encouraged me ever since they introduced me to history in the early 1960's.

My father and mother, the late Everett and Doris Pearson, blessed my siblings and me with a full and free life in the sunlight of Lindsborg, Kansas. They taught us so much, especially the best elements of what some social historians refer to as plain-folk American values. My mother once emphasized one of these values by saying about her experience as a young girl in the depression: "I don't know how we made it, it was such a struggle during those years, but we never gave up." Both of our parents inspired us to try a variety of endeavors, and both enjoyed our interest and participation in all sports. My father's uncle, the late Emil Wistrand, showed me how he could "play catch" in his seventies, thereby demonstrating the fielding techniques of late nineteenth century players. I am thankful that Emil and Ted Palmquist, representing Swedish immigrant and first-generation American groups, shared with me their youthful experiences in baseball.

I thank my wife, Eldora, for everything that we have shared these past thirty years, especially our two daughters, Rachel and Sarah. Both have learned to appreciate baseball in their own ways, and they regard a game at Dodger Stadium important for each homecoming.

Introduction

When I first became interested in the 1890 National League baseball players' revolt, I logically delved into its origins. The research that I began in the early 1980s eventually led me to concentrate on the developing conflict between players and owners during the 1889 season. My original intent was to highlight the players in their year of planning revolt from "the system," to describe their working environment, and to provide some perspective on the relationship of their revolt to the labor unrest of the period. Early on, I also thought that the tight pennant races in both major leagues could serve as a natural framework and let the players, most of them of working class origin, speak with their feet. The rivalries among the major contenders (Brooklyn, St. Louis, New York, and Boston) and their star players provided a good story base, since such well-known (even to people living now) stars as King Kelly, Charlie Comiskey, Buck Ewing, and Monte Ward were at their peaks that year.

Two eminent baseball historians, Harold Seymour and David Quentin Voigt, have shown that baseball had achieved its designation as the national game by the 1880s. As the United States was becoming more nationally oriented politically and economically during that time, this highly popular professional sport aided in the nationalization process by providing a much needed spectator sport for the rapidly urbanizing nation. Not surprisingly, as urban workers tried to organize themselves to cope with the corporate system, so National League baseball players had formed a Brotherhood of Professional Baseball Players by 1885. Baseball team owners made more profits as the '80s progressed, and players began demanding higher salaries. With two competing leagues, a "world's championship" between the two instituted by 1884, creative experimentation in rules heightening public interest, and with innovation and improvement in playing techniques, the American sporting public was primed for the great season of 1889.

In that year, both the National League (founded in 1876) and American Association (founded in 1882) staged two close, exciting

1

pennant races which represented a fitting culmination to baseball's expansion in the 1880s. Baseball captured the imagination of thousands of urban dwellers as it never had before. It had definitely become the national game by 1889, and it had become recognized, especially in New York City, as a valuable and necessary feature of modern urban culture. In some ways, the 1889 season was modern baseball's borning cry.

Team rivalries that already had a fairly long history greatly enhanced the public's interest by 1889. The National League's New York Giants, Boston Beaneaters, and Chicago White Stockings had developed fierce, competitive traditions that involved numerous followers in all three cities. In the American Association, the St. Louis Browns, Brooklyn Bridegrooms, Cincinnati Redlegs, and Philadelphia Athletics played each other with equal zeal and the same sort of loyal followings.

By 1889, the growing conflicts between the owners and players received wide publicity. St. Louis Browns' President Chris Von der Ahe would clash with his players more than any other owner, but New York Giants' President John B. Day had early salary disputes with two of his stars, John Montgomery Ward and Tim Keefe. Boston's James B. Billings almost caused his manager to quit because of an injudicious telegram in the heat of the pennant race, and Louisville's early-season owner, Mordecai H. Davidson, alienated his players to the extent that they briefly went on strike. Players' basic rights in relation to the reserve clause, salary limitations, and player sales became major topics of conversation in 1889, with Brotherhood President John Montgomery Ward leading the players in the National League. His primary opponent was the millionaire Chicago White Stockings owner, Albert Goodwill Spalding. In the American Association, St. Louis Browns' players Yank Robinson and Arlie Latham incurred Von der Ahe's wrath, but they also asserted their rights through impromptu, ad hoc actions that were widely criticized and, in Latham's case, never fully understood nor investigated.

Owners were plagued with other problems. John B. Day struggled throughout 1889 just to find a proper playing field for his world championship team. Gaining the valuable support of *New York Times* editorial writer Edward Cary, Day still lost money because of poor or newly developed sites. In Cincinnati, Redlegs President Aaron Stern finally gave up on the American Association when Sunday baseball was banned in that city, and Brooklyn's Charles H. Byrne had to rebuild Washington Park after a disastrous fire. Crowd control, especially on

Sunday in the American Association, was an ongoing concern as the pennant races became hotter and tempers became shorter.

More women attended baseball games in 1889 than ever before. Encouraged by this development, owners and baseball publicists sought to further improve baseball's image with more attention to quality of play, ethics, new rules and players' drinking habits. However, disturbing questions about gambling made the 1889 season a fitting capstone to a turbulent, innovative, experimental, rip-roaring decade.

Sadly, professional baseball tore its structure apart after 1889 and would not recover for over another decade. But baseball cranks (fans) would remember the glorious 1889 season for a long time. As late as 1931, John Kieran encountered two old men recalling the glory days of the 1880's Giants: "They were the people, just as Jim Mutrie used to say" (*Times*, 17 January 1931). This sort of identification and fellow feeling among the spectators and players was possible because there was not, as yet, a great separation between them. As players like Mike "King" Kelly, Buck Ewing, Charlie Comiskey, and Darby O'Brien stretched and broke rules to win at all costs, as they railed at baseball's authority figure, the umpire, as they drank and celebrated boisterously, and as they played skillfully and creatively, the common people in the sixteen major league cities cheered them lustily because they defined the people as many of them would have wanted to be, had they a chance. Not only upper class and professional middle-class Americans sought definition in the rapidly changing American society during the 1880s. The New York Giants' slogan, "We Are The People," had real meaning for those yearning to be heard, to be known, to make good. Baseball was an escape but also a validation for lower-class and middle-class Americans. We are the people. We are great.

Ultimately, what drew so many people to baseball games in 1889 was the high quality of play and the colorful players, many of whom were at their career peaks. Of the four top teams in the two leagues, the New York Giants had the most star players. Eventually, six of them would be elected to the National Baseball Hall of Fame, and a strong case could be made that a seventh, Mike Tiernan, should join them. Boston boasted of four future Hall of Famers, although both Mike "King" Kelly and Hoss Radbourn were in decline. Nonetheless, Kelly helped draw large crowds wherever Boston played and Radbourn pitched effectively through mid-season. Although not in the Hall of Fame, Charlie Bennett provided

Boston with one of the great catchers in history, and Hardie Richardson impressed everyone in the outfield and at second. The St. Louis Browns had lost some of their top players because of Chris Von der Ahe's player sales after 1887, but they still claimed four recognized stars, and two others, Arlie Latham and Yank Robinson, enlivened games and drew crowds. In Brooklyn, the Bridegrooms impressed people with their playing ability, but they could only claim one true shining light, Bob Caruthers.

All four teams had managers with strong personalities, and the Giants' Jim Mutrie was easily one of the most remarkable in history. Primarily a promoter, he left the field strategy to his captain, the great catcher, Buck Ewing. Brooklyn's Bill McGunnigle was quieter than Mutrie, but was known throughout the American Association for numerous idiosyncrasies. Charlie Comiskey was one of the great playing-managers in the history of baseball and at the top of his game. Boston's Jim Hart struggled manfully in trying to channel the considerable energy of King Kelly and Hoss Radbourn in the right directions. Usually, this meant away from bars.

To tell the story of 1889, newspapers across the country had attracted a talented, articulate group of sportswriters. (Fullerton 18, 184) Four of the best, William Ingraham Harris, William D. Sullivan, Joseph C. Pritchard, and J. F. Donnolly, wrote about the four top teams for Francis C. Richter's sports weekly, *Sporting Life*. They effectively communicated how the players of 1889 played baseball in a vigorous, rollicking, urgent, rough and tumble, even violent, style that matched the spirit of the times.

Perhaps Ren Mulford, Jr. best defined the players' motivation when he wrote of Buck Ewing after the latter's death from Bright's disease in 1906: "During his boyhood, he played ball because it was in him to play, and it had to come out." (*Cincinnati Enquirer*, 21 October 1906) Much the same sentiment was expressed by the late Ted Palmquist, who played baseball in his youth around my hometown of Lindsborg, Kansas. During the 1920s and 1930s, Ted would sometimes skip supper to practice. He once said with some feeling, "If we had a dime in our pockets for gas, we'd drive to a game." Spanning the decades, these player-workers demonstrated the carefree, joyful, yet extremely competitive play that typified so many.

In sum, I have sought to provide, through this study of a specific year in baseball, some insight into the sporting aspect of working class culture in the late 1880s. I believe that looking at baseball from the "inside out" in this manner is essential to our understanding of what Stephen Hardy refers to as the sport product. In his superb article, Hardy emphasizes the three-fold quality of the sport product (the activity or game form, the service, and the sporting equipment) but never mentions players in connection with this product. (Hardy, "Entrepreneurs" 14-19) Of course, Hardy was exploring possible research topics that dealt primarily with entrepreneurial and organizational developments. In that connection, I must admit that the following account of the 1889 season would suffer without attention to baseball owners' trials relative to the players' revolt.

Nonetheless, I have chosen to focus on the players and have tried to let them tell their story as much as possible. Some players of 1889 earned salaries that compared favorably with mechanical engineers and Harvard professors. Since most of them traced their origins to working class backgrounds, they recognized their good fortune. Some organized their finances wisely, but others did not and had nothing left after their careers ended. But while they could, they played the game they loved. They fought their wars on the baseball field. They won the attention of thousands of urban dwellers and made baseball a topic of conversation as it had never been before. Some lost their money and some lost their health. But while the sun shone or enough sawdust could be poured on the muddy fields, they played the game that best reflected the environment of late nineteenth century America.

Chapter One
Growing up with America and Baseball

The United States seethed in the 1880s. They had emerged from reconstructing their union in 1877 after defining civil rights for all males through the 14th and 15th amendments. Blacks were still not allowed to attain their rights, however. This contradiction between constitutional theory and practice would not be reconciled until the end of the century, at the expense of Blacks' rights. The economy exploded. Railroads expanded into all parts of the country, opening the great vastness west of the Mississippi for its final settlement. Land speculation flourished as immigrants poured into the rural and urban magnets. Corporations organized on a scale which insured renewed attempts to organize labor, with attendant corporate opposition and violence. Many urban dwellers simmered in abysmal tenements. By the end of the 1880s, Southern and Great Plains farmers were poised to initiate what one historian, Lawrence Goodwyn, has called the last major democratic movement in the United States. The United States had begun to modernize its navy by 1889 and in the next decade would redefine its relationship to the rest of the world. Demographically, economically, politically, and diplomatically, the United States experienced a primary transition in the 1880s. Regional, rural, parochial America was becoming national, urban-industrial and imperial. New political, social, and economic institutions imposed standardization, order, regulation and authority as American society grew more complex.

Northeast and Midwest urban governments adapted with difficulty to the rapid growth of population and business. Major cities in the 1880s had altered dramatically from the pre-Civil War era and, in some cases, had become major urban centers only since the Civil War. Through this process of accelerated urban growth, entertainment, quite naturally, became one of the most important facets of daily life for all urban social classes. Gunther Barth, in his book *City People,* eloquently described the importance of the department store, vaudeville house, and the ballpark as a means of occupying people's leisure time. With equal articulation and eloquence, Stephen Hardy (*How Boston Played*) demonstrated how urban sports and recreation developed during the late nineteenth century both because of observed needs and creative economic and technological developments. Hardy also analyzed sport and recreation's relationship to the complex socio-psychological processes of what he termed city-building in Boston (Hardy 14-20). Steven A. Riess (*City Games*) contributed greatly to our understanding of the complex relationships between urban society and sports in the late nineteenth century. Barth, Hardy and Riess have shown that a primary feature of urban popular culture in the 1880s was the growing attention paid to a profession relatively new since the Civil War—playing baseball. The people most responsible for baseball's increasing importance and popularity, the players, managers, owners, sports reporters, and influential newspapers editors, provide a fascinating explanation for professional baseball's rise within the context of their unique working environment. For purposes of studying a specific time period, the 1889 season is particularly worthy of attention since it represented the culmination of the baseball's first decade of growth and increased public attention, featured the most exciting pennant race to that time and caused the first organized players' revolt against baseball owners.

Why did attendance at major league baseball games increase all through the 1880s, culminating in the 1889 Brooklyn Bridegroom record of over 350,000? (Betts, *Sporting Heritage* 96) Why was baseball so popular in the 1880s? A primary reason for the burgeoning attendance was that many people wanted to watch highly skilled players who had gained a wide reputation (Hardy 9-10,17; Betts 97, 115-116). In 1889, the four pennant contenders in the National League and American Association all boasted of well-established star players.

Manager-first baseman Charlie Comiskey led the St. Louis Browns to four American Association pennants from 1884-1888 with his innovative tactics in the field and on the bases. "Commy" revolutionized first base play during the 1880s by playing off the bag and teaching his pitchers and second basemen to cover first when necessary. The major innovation was the second tactic, since other first basemen had played away from the base before the 1880s and did so during Comiskey's time (Seymour 61-62; John J. McGraw 50). He held special morning practice with his pitchers for the necessary tutelage. Sam Crane, New York sportswriter and 1880s player, recalled, perhaps a bit inaccurately, the sensation Comiskey caused

The incomparable Buck Ewing in 1888. Ewing batted .327 in 1889 and led the National League catchers in putouts and assists. Photo credit National Baseball Library, Cooperstown, N.Y.

when he first played in New York in 1883. When he took his position far back of first base, "the amazed spectators jeered and hooted the tall, gawky, lanky youngster who dared to make such an innovation." However, when Commy quickly demonstrated how he could still take throws at first, "the fans broke into loud and long applause and Comiskey became a hero" (*New York Journal*, 29 January 1912). Crane also praised Commy for his daring base running, especially his ability to slide head first or feet first. Mobile on the base paths, Commy instituted more movement among his infielders by shifting them according to the batter and pitcher. Commy attracted crowds with his playing and managerial abilities.

The New York Giants featured numerous star players, but the greatest was probably their catcher and captain in 1889, Buck Ewing. One of the Giant pitchers, Hall of Fame member Mickey Welch, reminisced in 1939 about his great teammate: "From his haunches, looking innocently at his pitcher and without moving his head, he could throw side-armed to first base with a rifle-shot pickoff throw" (Ewing file, NBL). Ted P. Sullivan, manager and baseball scout of the late 1800s, humorously recalled that Ewing "could throw from any position and he did not require a derrick to straighten him up before he got the ball out of his hand" (Sullivan 17-19). Sam Crane cited Ewing's cat-like reactions to passed balls, "lightning fast" movements, and "quickness in getting the ball away" as the key elements of his greatness. Ewing, like Comiskey, became an inventive field leader. Crane said that "he did all the signaling for base plays, and his snappy, gingery methods kept all of his players right on their tiptoes all the time, and woe betide the player who missed a sign, for Buck, after giving a signal for any particular play, would let the ball go every time, and any slow-thinking player would be shown up horribly" (Ewing file, NBL). Buck, an excellent runner, perfected the "hook" slide, and pitchers feared his clutch hitting ability. Ewing excited crowds with his catching, running and hitting; some say he was the greatest catcher of all time.

In Boston, the faithful had been entranced with the great Mike "King" Kelly since 1887, when Beaneater owners bought the King from Albert G. Spalding for $10,000. The general opinion about Kelly's playing ability emphasized his running skills. Kelly himself said that as a young player for the 1882 Chicago White Stockings: "I had India rubber in my shoes then. I was like I was on springs" (Spalding 265). Baseball experts euphorically lauded Kelly for his quick thinking, both as an outfielder and as a catcher. Not a strong fielder at either position, Kelly still made things happen even when he was on defense. On the base paths, his daring enabled him to run freely even as alcohol took the spring from his legs. Hugh Duffy, Hall of Fame outfielder who played with Kelly briefly in the early 1890s, thought him the greatest player and base runner (Kaese 42-45). Tom McCarthy, another Hall of Fame outfielder and Duffy's compatriot, assessed the King's base running succinctly:

> In the first place, he always took plenty of room, more room than the average man of his time did...No man guarding a bag ever had more of Kelly to touch than his feet. He never came into a bag twice in the same way. He twisted and turned as he made his famous "Kelly slide," and seldom was he caught. He was a regular boxer with his feet when sliding into bases. (Spink 103)

Baseball historian Robert Smith vividly described the anticipatory glee that animated crowds when Kelly reached first base: "When at last he did start for second, a roar would go up as if a dam had let go" (Smith 1947, 88). Truly, Mike Kelly was the king of crowd-pleasers by 1889 even though his skills were diminishing. Many questioned his ability to continue playing much longer.

Boston's regular 1889 catcher, Charlie Bennett, drew raves for his throwing ability. Bennett was said to be as great a catcher as Buck Ewing although not as quick in getting rid of the ball. The Beaneaters also boasted of hard-hitting first baseman Dan Brouthers and utility man Hardie Richardson. At pitcher, Boston featured John Clarkson, the most dominant hurler in the National League during 1889. Clarkson had a superb change of pace, a sinker, and magnificent control. A handsome man, Clarkson attracted women in large numbers when he pitched. He would tuck an immaculate, white, silk handkerchief in the front of his spotless uniform. John Clarkson also pitched with an exceptionally graceful delivery.

Brooklyn cranks surged to the ballpark in record numbers not because the Bridegrooms were so famous but because they played so well together. (Gerald Cohen, a modern-day expert on baseball etymology, has decided that the term "crank" was "the standard term for a baseball fan" from 1888 through 1890. The term was first used by *The New York World* in 1882, according to Cohen. Quoted in Paul Dickson, ed., *The Dickson Baseball Dictionary* 114.) Charles H. Byrne, Brooklyn's first President, had recruited his brother-in-law Joseph J. Doyle and gambling proprietor

Ferdinand A. Abell to finance and organize Brooklyn's first major league team in 1884. Entering the American Association in that year, Byrne and his co-owners spent rather freely in 1884, 1887 and 1888 to build a solid pennant contender by the spring of 1889. Purchasing the Cleveland National League team in 1884 and the American Association New York Metropolitans in 1887, Byrne achieved a major coup when he bought three key St. Louis Browns' players after the 1887 season. Browns' owner Christian (Chris) Von der Ahe had expressed dissatisfaction with his team's performance in the 1887 World Series loss against Detroit. Unfairly blaming his great pitcher-outfielder Bob Caruthers for carousing, Von der Ahe decided to sell him, pitcher-outfielder Dave "Scissors" Foutz, and catcher Doc Bushong to Byrne for approximately $18,000. Caruthers' sale price, said to be $8,500, approached the astounding sum that Boston paid to Albert G. Spalding for King Kelly. Consummation of such a deal with the hated enemy, the St. Louis Browns, proved doubly appealing to Brooklyn's followers. Brooklyn-St. Louis games became unusually intense in 1888, with Caruthers, Foutz, and Bushong concentrating all of their considerable skills on defeating the hard-driving Commy and his team. Foutz and Bushong had suffered broken fingers during 1887, and the Browns reasoned that neither would be as effective again. Bushong never did regain his old form. Foutz, also called "The Human Hairpin" because of his extremely slender physique, became a dependable, hard-hitting first baseman. Caruthers particularly enjoyed defeating his old teammates. By 1889, the established rivalry between the Browns and Brooklyn Bridegrooms contributed greatly to record attendance in Brooklyn.

King Kelly, in his book *Play Ball,* stressed the need for team and player rivalries to draw good crowds, citing the great Boston Beaneater-Chicago White Stocking rivalry that grew from his sale to Boston in 1887. Both cities displayed great spirit in their cheering, especially Boston's cranks led by General Arthur Dixwell. His piercing "Hi! Hi!" became the rallying cry for Boston rooters. Kelly reasoned that such strong rivalries helped players perform better and generally, "it adds interest to the games." By 1889, the main rivalry in the National League was that between the Boston Beaneaters and New York Giants. Like Byrne in Brooklyn, Boston owners James B. Billings, William H. Conant, and Arthur H. Soden spent liberally to acquire a winning team. They bought Kelly and Clarkson from Spalding for 1887 and 1888. For the 1889 season, they acquired four Detroit stars: Charlie Bennett, Charlie Ganzel, Dan Brouthers, and Hardie Richardson. Boston cranks thought that their team was a sure thing for the 1889 pennant even though the Giants had one of the strongest teams in history.

In some respects, the great interest shown by baseball spectators in established team rivalries paralleled the voting public's support of the two-party political system. White males dominated the political process in the 1880s, and they trooped to the polls in large numbers when the issues attracted them and when parties competed vigorously for their support.

Baseball contained other elements which mirrored important developments in American society. The United States was rapidly becoming a major industrial power, with resultant urban growth in the Northeast and Midwest. Dramatic changes in business organization, the number of business transactions, transportation, housing, labor-employer relationships, availability of city services and mere numbers of people in urban areas led to a feeling among all classes of Americans that they were charting new courses and breaking the bonds of old methods and traditions. Rural, regional, parochial America began to alter noticeably. Accompanying the vitality and innovation in American society by the 1880s, a certain degree of anti-authoritarianism or opposition to outside interference lent tremendous force to the pell-mell growth that the United States experienced at this time. Professional baseball, inaugurated during the 1860s, grew rapidly with the economic expansion after the 1870's depression and drew a large number of spectators from the laboring and middle classes. Both groups had many reasons to oppose the numerous new restrictions that were imposed on them as employees of medium and large-scale business. The average work week was 10-12 hours per day, six days per week, and unskilled workers labored at very low pay with little job security. Urban living conditions were atrocious for a large majority. Dislike for the foreman, the boss, the superintendent, the "cop", and the landlord was a common feeling among urban Americans, and at times they disliked intensely. What better entertainment than to go out to the ballpark to watch players like King Kelly and Charlie Comiskey stretch and/or break the rules, while the umpire, the baseball authority symbol, was harassed and harangued by players and crowd?

Mike "King" Kelly, the Babe Ruth of the 1880s, said in his 1888 baseball promotional book, *Play Ball*, that baseball's popularity was based on its excitement, and part of the excitement was "kicking."

"People...want good playing, with just enough kicking to make things interesting thrown in." "Kicking" in those days meant arguing with the umpire. Kelly was one of the most demonstrative kickers though he noted that spectators enjoyed variety in umpire baiting. Praising Buck Ewing for his playing ability, Kelly mentioned that Ewing also pleased crowds with his good-natured kicking which never left a sting behind. St. Louis Browns' manager-first baseman Charlie Comiskey became one of the most notorious and articulate questioners of umpires' eyesight, while the great Chicago first baseman Adrian "Cap" Anson developed a whining style that earned him the nickname "Cry Baby." Ted Sullivan told of Commy's fierce competitive nature: "He had a volcano fire burning inside him to make himself famous" (Sullivan 26). Umpires were obstacles to overcome for Commy and most players of the time.

Charlie Comiskey also strongly advocated stretching the rules as much as possible. He openly criticized baseball players who acquired gentlemanly reputations in the April 27, 1889 issue of *The Sporting News*. "I go on a field to win a game by any hook or crook. It is the game we are after, not reputations as society dudes." Commy abjured ruffianism, leg-breaking or profanity but thought players should "turn a trick" whenever the chance arose. It was not taking advantage, but merely "getting away with it." Crowds' cheers reached the heavens when noted base-runners like King Kelly and Arlie Latham would steal second and then, if a ball was hit to right field which required the umpire's attention, would "cut" third by ten to fifteen feet and slide home triumphantly. Clearly, if such acts were done away from home, cranks would object strenuously and sometimes stream onto the field to present their argument. Sam Crane said that "the air of injured innocence that Kel would put on in such squabbles was worth the price of admission alone" (Kelly file, NBL). Outfielders on every team would hide balls in strategic locations in the outfield so that if a ball would roll under a grandstand, they would be able to "field" the ball and hold the runner to fewer bases or throw him out. They would also secret balls in their uniform pockets so they could use them if the need arose. A famous Kelly story tells of the King making a fantastic catch under darkening skies for the final out. Responding to his celebrating teammates, Kelly confessed that the ball had sailed into the stands. Knowing that no one could see it, he had faked a catch. Commy would have been deliriously proud. Cranks applauded this sort of rule-breaking and were enthralled that it could be done in the open, especially when it was perpetrated by one of their own kind, a son of the working classes like Kelly, Darby O'Brien, Yank Robinson, or Buck Ewing.

Perhaps this social class link, even for middle-class males who had risen from the working class, was one of the most important reasons for baseball's growing popularity. Consumption of beer and whiskey had grown to astounding proportions by the 1880s, and saloons dotted every urban landscape. For poor tenement dwellers, beer provided a relatively inexpensive escape. Jacob Riis in *How The Other Half Lives*, published in 1890, asserted that New York's Lower East Side had so many saloons because they provided "the one bright and cheery and humanly decent spot to be found." Stark statistics tell the importance of the saloon for New York's poor. In 1889, over 4,000 of New York's 7,884 saloons could be found below Fourteenth Street. They outnumbered churches by forty to one. People drank to get drunk, to flee, to have an excuse to leave the teeming tenements.

Not surprisingly, drinking was not limited to the urban lower classes. William F. Mulhall tended an elegant bar in the Hoffmann House at 25th and Broadway during the 1880s and 1890s. Recalling "the golden age of booze," Mulhall noted that the bar was "very well known and very popular with a long line of great men, for great men, or nearly all great men, drank in those days." Some young scions of wealth were known to spend two or three hundred dollars in an afternoon at the Hoffmann by treating others (Quoted in Henry Collins Brown, ed., *Valentine's Manual of Old New York* 126, 135- 36). Of course, after such a "wine spree," great men retreated to dwellings substantially different from those of the lower and middle classes.

By 1889, New York and Brooklyn residents could also be entertained by two excellent baseball teams. Brooklyn sportswriter Dan Parker once said, "If the truth were known, baseball was probably invented by a Brooklynite in search of an excuse for getting home late for dinner" (Fitzgerald 5). Baseball and beer provided the urban lower and middle classes excuses and havens from stultifying environments. For many, suds and strikes meant freedom.

Among baseball players, drinking was sometimes their worst problem. The most notorious inebriate of them all was the King, Mike Kelly. Albert G. Spalding once hired a detective to trace his path through the Chicago nights. Whenever confronted with such evidence, Kelly always freely admitted his wrongdoing but as easily stated his unwillingness to change his habits. He took his wife with him on road trips, and she often accompanied him on his nocturnal patrols. While touring England, Kelly gloried in the public houses. When asked by an Englishman if he ever drank during a game, the King replied, "It depends on how long the game is." Yet, he was a great player. He challenged authority and propriety and still played extremely well. Common people were attracted to Kelly because he reacted to life's trials as many of them did. However, his escape through booze was celebrated before thousands. He resisted all attempts to control him and "made good." The ultimate child-man, wholly guileless, Kelly seemed to glory in the shedding of responsibility. He was completely free.

Mike Kelly was popular among all kinds of cranks, especially young boys and men from a similar working class background. They could see themselves in him, drinking the nights away yet fooling the umpire and using every trick in his fertile imagination to triumph. And all was done in the clear light of day. He drank openly and broke/stretched rules openly. He had nothing to hide. Orphaned at a young age, Kelly also needed to be admired, wanted, accepted, loved. Possibly recognizing this need, most baseball people condoned his tippling and resented any criticism of his escapades.

Another reason for his popularity was that Kelly admitted his weakness. He could not stop drinking and he never tried. In *Play Ball*, he gave advice about proper training but never used himself as an example since he could not. For success in life, Kelly told young boys, "Never do anything that you wouldn't have your mother know." He also advised others not to drink. One of the most beautiful Kelly stories is that told by George Reese, a University of Pennsylvania pitcher in the early 1890's (Lieb, *The Baseball Story* 79). Reese decided to ask Kelly's advice after playing in an exhibition game against the great King. He wanted Kelly's opinion of whether he should continue studying to be an M.D. or pursue a baseball career with Boston. The Beaneaters had made Reese an attractive offer. Kelly listened carefully, advised Reese to stay with medicine and then, putting his arm around the young pitcher's neck, Kelly said, "and I want you to promise me you'll never take a drink." George Reese was moved by the King's advice and by the retelling. Kelly knew he had erred and so did those who came to see him. They saw themselves at their best and worst in Kelly. Americans idealized spontaneous action. Kelly embodied it. He was so great and yet so human, so famous and yet so close to the people.

Other players like Pete Browning and Toad Ramsey of Louisville struggled with alcoholism but none with so many cheering as the great King Kelly. This celebrative nature of baseball, the pomp, the noise, and the excitement also brought out crowds. Late nineteenth-century Americans were attracted to a certain amount of display and glitter. Kelly recalled a parade that he had witnessed in Washington D.C. as a young boy. "So much gold and lace I never saw before. They [Generals McClellan and Kilpatrick] were simply magnificent. For years, I remembered them, and it was the ambition of my life to go and do likewise." But the King only made war on the baseball field. Even as a youth, he hungered for baseball symbols of authority and recognition. In 1874, playing with his boyhood team in Paterson, New Jersey, Kelly got the right to wear the one cap that the team possessed. "The day I wore it was one of the happiest of my life." He also recalled his great desire for recognition as a team leader. "When I was a boy, playing ball, it was the ambition of my life to wear a white belt, on which was to be marked in vermilion letters 'captain'." Kelly proved not a good captain since he was not disciplined enough. As he said in 1888, "I've grown older since" (Kelly, *passim*).

Another famous baseball personality, St. Louis Browns' owner Chris Von der Ahe, easily recognized the importance of showmanship for attracting crowds. Baseball historian Fred Lieb (*The Baseball Story*, Chap. 13) said that while Von der Ahe was a bit clumsy, he had a knack for getting necessary publicity. In 1887, Vondy transported his players to the home grounds in open barouches. Horses were covered with brown blankets proclaiming the 1886 champion Browns. Opening games of the season in St. Louis would find Vondy leading his team onto the field behind a marching band. Players with working class roots greatly valued such public display and recognition and none more than Mike Kelly. He wrote of being overwhelmed by the special gifts given him when he first came to Boston in 1887, even though he eventually pawned or lost most of them. He recollected in detail the "pomp and pageantry" of the 1887 opening game in Chicago, with the floral tribute for him. Like the King, cranks were lured by the ceremony surrounding baseball, the "color" that accompanied it. Besides Vondy's parades in open coaches, silk foul flags, banquets, endless medals, watches, diamonds, and monetary gifts all surrounded baseball with an aura that helped bring the people to the game.

Among those who inhabited baseball parks, young boys were quite numerous. In the 1950s, St. Louis resident L. A. Paule fondly remembered his boyhood days in St. Louis during the 1880s. He and other school boys used to play hooky to attend games at Sportsman's Park. Bennie Owen, Oklahoma University's renowned football coach of the early twentieth century, was one of the young boys who eagerly followed the fortunes of the Browns. "He used to go early in the afternoon to old Sportsman's Park on the days the Browns played. There, pockets empty, he would patiently stand in the long queue of spectators before the admission window, sell his place in line for fifty cents to some impatient late arrival, buy a seat in the bleachers and with a silver quarter profit left in his jeans, see the game in style with the exhilarating sense of having made it pay him for the pleasure. Or if he arrived late, he knew how to climb a telephone post overlooking the park, and placing a small board across the iron spikes protruding from the pole, watch the game from a crow's nest view." (Harold Keith, *Oklahoma Kickoff*, 1978 ed. 104-105). Since the park was located near Paule's school at Grand Avenue and Dodier Street, students were allowed to watch the players go past. Paule vividly recalled the excitement associated with standing on Grand Avenue waiting for his heroes (Arlie Latham file, NBL).

Mike Kelly could well understand such a feeling because he knew that baseball's appeal was, to a great extent, based on the excitement that the game engendered. The King also knew the mind of small boys since, as he wrote in 1888, "I'll remain a boy as long as I live. My boyhood days were a hard struggle for existence, but they were nevertheless, the happiest and best days of my life." He dedicated his book, *Play Ball*, to the people who supported baseball, the players, and "to the small boy who does so much to uphold the game." Kelly praised small boys as the most important followers and spectators of baseball. If he had been able, he would have insured that all boys be admitted free to games. The King urged parents to encourage their boys to play baseball if they wished and all outdoor sports. They were a "tower of strength to the game of baseball." As Dizzy Dean would do sixty years later, Kelly advised boys to study hard in school and only play baseball afterwards. Avoid fighting, slide if necessary, and be able to tell your mother whatever you had done. Soporific? Perhaps, but Mike Kelly truly loved the urchins who flocked to the parks. They worshipped him.

At the end of his book, Kelly spoke to his "best friend, the small boy of America." To him, the King simply said, "God bless you, my boy. Play ball." The book was ghostwritten and for promotional purposes, but Kelly most likely believed that boys were at the heart of baseball. So you see, to fully appreciate the amazingly contentious 1889 season, when baseball truly became the national game, you need to approach it from the perspective of a young boy. America and baseball were growing up together.

Chapter Two
Rivalry and the Heat of Battle

If you were a young Brooklyn boy in the spring of 1889, you would look forward to the coming baseball season with unusual anticipation. Brooklyn President Charles H. Byrne had built his team from scratch since 1883 and by 1889, was ready to challenge the great St. Louis Browns for the American Association pennant.

Born in New York, in 1843, and graduated from St. Francis Xavier's College, Byrne became involved in a variety of occupations before deciding on baseball in 1883. He worked first as a journalist, studying law at the same time. After migrating to Omaha to work for a railroad and spending some years in western mining regions, Byrne concentrated on New York City real estate. Among his properties was a gambling house on Ann Street in Manhattan, operated with his brother-in-law Joseph J. Doyle. When George J. Taylor, night city editor for *The New York Herald*, was advised by his physician to seek healthier employment, he approached Byrne in 1882 about the possibility of financing and organizing a baseball team. Byrne agreed, recruited Doyle's support, and found a third partner in Ferdinand A. (Gus) Abell. Like Byrne and Doyle, Abell made profits from a gambling establishment (S.L., 8 January 1898).

A bachelor, Byrne threw himself wholeheartedly into the work of constructing Brooklyn's first professional baseball team since the 1870s. Seeking a site for the ball park, Byrne chose the area where the Revolutionary War Battle of Long Island had been fought. Located in the Red Hook section of South Brooklyn, near the Gowanus Canal, the plant was aptly named Washington Park. Converting General Washington's headquarters, known as Gowanus House, into a ladies rest room, Byrne started construction in January, 1883. He then advertised for players (Allen, *Giants and Dodgers* 17- 19).

Forty professional baseball players tried out. Choosing sixteen of these and ill-advisedly outfitting them with polka-dot stockings, Taylor and Byrne embarked on their first professional season in a minor league, the Interstate League. After winning the Interstate pennant in 1883, Byrne,

20 Baseball in 1889

Doyle and Abell acquired Brooklyn's first major league franchise in the American Association for 1884. Byrne became the workhorse as President while Abell supplied most of the capital (Graham 4; S.L., 8 January 1898). Taylor became the secretary and found young, energetic Charles H. Ebbets to sell tickets and help with numberless other tasks. Doyle, Taylor, and Byrne tried managing in the early years but finally saw the need to hire someone with more expertise. William G. McGunnigle had caught Byrne's eye during the 1887 season while the former was managing at Lowell, Massachusetts. "Gunner" had managed four different minor league teams to pennants from 1883-1887, and Byrne knew that he had a first-rate man when he hired him for 1888.

By 1887, the team had acquired the informal name Trolley Dodgers or Dodgers, since Brooklyn and the Washington Park area were crisscrossed by so many horse trolley tracks (Holmes, *The Dodgers* 12; Dan Parker in Fitzgerald, ed. 6; Benson 57). Byrne's team was a pennant contender by 1888 because of his aggressive methods in acquiring players. When the Cleveland National League team disbanded late in 1884, Byrne went to Ohio and signed most of its players. He thereby acquired third baseman George Pinckney and shortstop George Smith. After the 1887 season, Byrne bought the New York Metropolitan franchise from Erastus Wiman for $25,000. He kept the best players, left fielder Darby O'Brien among them, and eventually sold the franchise to Kansas City. Byrne's greatest achievement after the 1887 season was to buy Bob Caruthers, Dave Foutz, and Doc Bushong from St. Louis Browns' owner Chris Von der Ahe for approximately $18,000. During the 1887 season, Von der Ahe and Byrne had discussed the possibility of St. Louis selling some of its star players so that the American Association would have better balance. The two owners thought that more competition would enhance attendance. In the latter half of 1888, Byrne acquired Tom "Reddy" Burns from Baltimore and Pop Corkhill from Cincinnati for his outfield. He also bought Louisville second baseman Hub Collins at the end of 1888. The Bridegrooms, as they became known because seven of them were married before the season, finished a close second to St. Louis in 1888. Strengthened by Burns, Corkhill, and Collins, they eagerly anticipated dethroning the four time champions, the St. Louis Browns managed by Charlie Comiskey (Byrne file, NBL, *The Brooklyn Citizen Almanac*, 1893, 129).

As noted previously, the presence of three ex-Browns on the Bridegrooms enhanced the rivalry between the two teams. Bob Caruthers had irked Browns' owner Chris Von der Ahe by holding out for a higher salary after the 1885 season. He had dramatized his holdout by accompanying catcher Doc Bushong to Paris, France. Acquiring the nickname "Parisian Bob," Caruthers resented Von der Ahe's later accusations about his alleged carousing during the 1887 World Series against Detroit. He enjoyed defeating the Browns as did Dave Foutz and Bushong. Since 1884, Von der Ahe and Byrne had argued about numerous issues relating to American Association policies. Their personal differences were transmitted to their teams, and by 1889, the Bridegrooms and Browns could expect to draw huge crowds in Brooklyn and St. Louis.

While intense rivalries existed then as now, the game that the Bridegrooms and Browns played was different from present-day baseball, although still recognizable. To the great delight of Charlie Comiskey, Darby O'Brien, and King Kelly, one umpire tried to control the game. Home plate was only a twelve inch white rubber square. Visiting teams often batted last because the home team wanted to get "first licks" at a clean ball. This habit began to change in 1890 when more balls were used in games. By 1889, the shoulder to knee strike zone plus four balls and three strikes determined batters' fates. That was the same.

Baseball officials instituted the four ball rule after the 1888 season so that pitching speed would be reduced and accuracy stressed. Five balls and three strikes had made 1888 a poor hitting season. Baseball's hierarchy sought to create a greater number of walks, divide the pitcher's attention, and help the batters. They also thought base stealing would increase though this proved incorrect. Pitchers paid much attention to base runners in 1889 because they also expected more base stealing. In all the discussion about rule changes, Brooklyn President Charles H. Byrne and New York Giant President John B. Day played prominent roles. Byrne received praise for his systematic methods while John B. Day acted the part of reactionary. He wanted the pre-1887 batter's call for a high or low pitch reinstated. Day hoped to aid his veteran pitcher, the great Tim Keefe, and his batters. Other National League owners voted against Day's wish since umpires could determine balls and strikes easier without the high or low call. The National League also discussed whether or not to allow overrunning all bases to prevent serious injury from sliding. Because crowds liked sliding to bases, this idea was vetoed. The new substitution rule definitely made baseball more entertaining. For 1889, a pitcher could be replaced at the end of any inning at the manager's discretion. Actually, the rule provided for one substitute player per game excluding injured players. Pitchers were most often replaced, rescuing crowds from the boredom of drubbings and providing the possibility of a "saved" game. The four ball rule helping batters and the substitution rule greatly enhanced baseball's entertainment value in 1889 (S.L., 28 November 1888).

Pitchers stood on flat ground only 55 and 1/2 feet from the batter. They threw from a box 5 and 1/2 feet long and 4 feet wide and could take one step while delivering the ball. Most threw the ball with some sort of overhand delivery, although Pittsburgh's Pud Galvin and Boston's Hoss Radbourn still threw underhanded. Silver King, great St. Louis Browns pitcher of the late 1880s, provided an excellent description of a pitcher's tribulations long after he had retired. Born Charles Frederick Koenig, King earned his nickname because his hair resembled burnished silver. A big, broad-shouldered youth, King pitched his first full major league season for the Browns in 1887, at age nineteen. A fast ball pitcher with an occasional change of pace, King used no windup but mixed his pitches well. He threw everything with the same motion and possessed remarkable control. Comiskey pitched him in 707 innings, including exhibition games, during 1888. Pitchers obviously needed to have strong constitutions. They also benefited from innovative deliveries, as King did. Silver would start in the back left corner of the pitcher's box and step across to the right side while throwing the ball in a "crossfire" motion over his left shoulder. He stretched the rules since opponents often complained that he was out of the box when he threw the ball (King File, NBL; Tiemann and Rucker 72).

Pitchers not only had to pitch long and often. They were also expected to infuse their team with spirit, to be the team leader. John Montgomery Ward, great New York Giant shortstop in 1889, began his career as a pitcher. He gave an excellent description of the ideal pitcher's role in his 1888 book, *Baseball*.

In short, a pitcher should make himself useful wherever he can, and use his wits in fielding as well as pitching. He should not be disheartened by poor support or unavoidable accidents, but should keep up his courage...there are [pitchers] not so successful in the matter of base hits, who yet win more games, on account of the aggressive spirit they impart to their fellow-players. Let the pitcher be alive, then, and if he has any "heart" let him show it, let him keep up his spirits, have a reason for every ball pitched, and use his brain as well as his muscle; for it is only in this way that he can ever take a place in the front rank. (64)

Hitters could swing at King's deliveries with bats flattened on one side, but the practice became more uncommon by 1890. In 1889, most overhand pitchers concentrated on fast balls or curves. Since pitchers delivered the ball close to the batter, every hitter needed a certain degree of courage. John Montgomery Ward gave a personal example:

> The most important attribute of all in the composition of a good batter is
> *courage*. In this term I include the self-control and the resolution by which a man
> will force himself to stand before the swiftest and wildest pitching without
> flinching...poor batters are so because they are afraid of being hit...It is absolutely
> necessary, then, to first conquer one's self, to fight fear....In my own case I was
> forced to change from right to left-handed hitting. I had been hit so hard several
> times that I grew afraid of the ball and contracted the habit of stepping away from
> the plate. (Ward 126-127)

Then as now, some pitchers deliberately pitched close to hitters or were suspected of doing so. The great Cincinnati pitcher, "Count" Tony Mullane, twice threw close to the head of Cleveland's Bill Gilks during an April 9, 1889 exhibition game. Gilks cursed Mullane violently, causing Mullane to challenge Gilks to a fight. After being soundly beaten, Gilks later vowed that he would kill Mullane (*Times,* 10 April 1889). Such savagery was never far below the surface of baseball since batters greatly feared being hit by swiftly thrown baseballs. Ward stated the fear succinctly in the spring of 1888:

> There are a few moments after a man has been hit during which he wishes he
> had never seen a baseball, and for the next couple of games, at least, he will think
> more of escaping a recurrence of the accident than of hitting the ball. [Paul] Hines
> [Indianapolis outfielder]...has already been hit on the head this season...and the
> result is a long, ragged-looking scar that he will always carry. (Ward 120-121)

The desire to avoid unnecessary pain and injury led players to protect themselves in numerous ways. By 1889, most fielders used rudimentary gloves, but some of the greatest like Cincinnati second baseman Biddy McPhee and Indianapolis third baseman Jerry Denny still played barehanded. Sliding pads came into vogue in the late 1880s. Ward, one of the best base stealers in the game, advised wearing the kind which could be buttoned to a player's athletic supporter. For that matter, Ward highly recommended that all players should wear the strap "which binds tightly the lower portion of the body...not only as a matter of comfort and safety, but also for the sake of decency" (Ward 135). The concern for decency became more pronounced in the late 1880s as more women attended baseball games. Face masks, rubber chest protectors, and padded catchers' gloves made life more bearable behind the plate. Shoes were much improved and spikes came into general use by 1889. Depending on the playing surface, footwear sometimes became optional. Ward once played a game without shoes or socks because of terrible field conditions.

Playing fields varied greatly. In 1889, as will be explained later, the Giants had to play in three different parks. Mud, water, downward sloping outfields, and outfield embankments made life miserable for Giants and visiting players. In St. Louis, Sportsman's Park featured crowds standing behind ropes only a dozen feet from the outfielders (Lowry 39, 63). In all baseball parks, crowd control was a primary concern. Since the 1889 season would feature the closest pennant races in baseball history to that time, owners struggled throughout the year to control rabid supporters.

Brooklyn cranks had already gained a reputation for unruly behavior. In the spring of 1889, they eagerly awaited the arrival of their favorites and the start of the season. It would be a glorious yet tragic year, filled with excitement yet concluding in rancorous debate and the first players' revolt. The American Association almost destroyed itself while National League players formed their own league at the end of the season. The popularity that baseball had acquired during the 1880s would dwindle during 1890 and succeeding years. But 1889 was unique. Brooklyn *Sporting life* correspondent, J. F. Donnolly, might well have applied his description of the riotous September 7 Brooklyn-St. Louis game to the entire season: "a lobster-Frankenstein nightmare" (*S.L.*, 18 September 1889).

Chapter Three
Bridegroom Hopes and Giants' Woes

Brooklyn baseball enthusiasts had never been so interested in the pre-season arrivals of their team. For one thing, Albert G. Spalding's world baseball tour had kept the game in the sporting public's mind throughout the 1888-1889 off-season. Baseball followers were also intrigued by how players would react to the owners' attempt to limit salaries and impose more discipline. However, Brooklyn cranks were primarily interested in their beloved Bridegrooms, touted by many to be the American Association champions in 1889.

The usual rumors about Charles H. Byrne wanting to enter the National League circulated in early February, and the ongoing Byrne-Von der Ahe feud flared again over a player arbitration issue. Byrne, a member of baseball's Board of Arbitration, resisted Von der Ahe's attempts to acquire a minor league player from the east, one Jim Cudworth. On a happier note, second baseman Hub Collins married in February, encouraging the continuation of the team name, Bridegrooms, for yet another year. Doc Bushong and Bill "Adonis" Terry, noted for their good habits and conditioning, had been riding bicycles in Prospect Park for two months. Every morning, they rode for two hours and hoped that they could convince other Bridegrooms to accompany them in March. Bob Caruthers, like some other major leaguers, chose to go to Hot Springs, Arkansas to "boil out" for a few weeks. By the end of February, right fielder Tom Burns had joined Caruthers while other players worked out at their homes.

Caruthers thought that the American Association race would be among St. Louis, Brooklyn, Cincinnati and the Philadelphia Athletics. He believed that the Bridegrooms were the strongest ever because of excellent team work. *The New York Clipper* agreed with Caruthers' assessment but thought that the New York Giants were the best nine in baseball (23 March 1889). The spring series between the two teams caused great anticipation in both cities. As the Bridegrooms began reporting to Washington Park from mid-March, Manager Bill McGunnigle decided to

OLD JUDGE CIGARETTES Goodwin & Co., New York.

Bill McGunnigle—Manager for the Brooklyn Bridegrooms from 1888 through 1890.
Photo credit National Baseball Library, Cooperstown, N.Y.

join the chorus. "Gunner" said that he would "make a head long plunge from the top of one of the towers of the Brooklyn Bridge" should Brooklyn fail to win the pennant (*Clipper*, 6 April 1889). A number of Brooklyn players reciprocated McGunnigle's confidence by praising him as the best manager of their careers. Rather surprisingly, St. Louis' sports weekly, *The Sporting News*, spoke highly of the Bridegrooms, noting that Hub Collins and Pop Corkhill had greatly strengthened their pennant chances (23 March 1889).

With all of the promising predictions, small wonder that Brooklyn cranks paid unusual attention to their team's arrival. Henry Chadwick, columnist for Francis C. Richter's renowned *Sporting Life* and editor of Spalding's Baseball Guide, resided in Brooklyn and openly supported the Bridegrooms. Before the exhibition season began on March 30, Chadwick fretted about whether or not McGunnigle would use Harry Wright's excellent tactic of batting practice before games. Meanwhile, Bridegroom player arrivals elicited public interest which normally attended political conventions. Even the time of team meals became newsworthy.

McGunnigle asked his players to report daily at Washington Park by 10 a.m. for exercise. After the noon meal, the entire team sauntered over to Prospect Park for cycling. Experts like Terry, Bushong, and Caruthers rode bicycles for about five miles, while the less experienced went in tandem on tricycles. Even then, numerous tumbles occurred with accompanying "scraped faces and injured noses." When the roads were good and as inexperienced cyclists gained confidence, the players rode down Ocean Parkway to Coney Island and back. At 2 p.m., they were in Washington Park for 2 and 1/2 more hours of exercise and throwing the ball. By the beginning of April, the Bridegrooms had even acquired a team mascot. A policeman decided that a "puny monkey" would do nicely, presenting it as a gift for the 1889 season. Unfortunately, the monkey had his own discipline problems, eventually inhabiting saloons and becoming a lush (*S.L.*, 19 June 1889). The Brooklyn players received further solicitous attention when they were urged to chew gum on road trips since varieties of drinking water could cause problems.

Despite the preparation and optimism, the Brooklyn exhibition season began inauspiciously on March 30. Mickey Hughes, promising young right hander who had done so well in 1888, pitched the first three innings against Newark and then sat in the cold. He developed a sore arm and never again regained his 1888 form. McGunnigle received some criticism for not letting his pitchers warm up enough in the cool, spring weather. Caruthers also had a sore arm and was ill with a cold. On the bright side, Tom Lovett showed great promise and some experts compared him to the great Giants' pitcher, Tim Keefe.

The Bridegrooms were a basically fraternal team with no discordant elements. McGunnigle's inattention to a lot of rules contributed to such harmony. He assumed that his players were responsible gentlemen. Henry Chadwick admired Gunner's handling of his players but disagreed with his policy of only fifteen minutes pregame practice. McGunnigle did not wish to burden his team with too much practice, and his players respected him. The Brooklyn team was a happy one in the spring of 1889, careening through Prospect Park and dreaming of unseating the champion Browns.

New York Giants' President John B. Day, on the other hand, stewed over a number of problems during February and March. He should have been optimistic about his team's ability to defend their 1888 world championship. However, Day worried about where the Giants would play and also about the status of his star shortstop John Montgomery Ward. A wholesale tobacco merchant, Day absented himself from New York during much of the off-season for business and health reasons. By the early spring of 1889, he was faced with the possibility that the Giants would be unable to play games at the Old Polo Grounds, located at 110th Street and Fifth Avenue. Previous assurances from the New York City Board of Aldermen no longer applied as real estate interests pressured them to use the Polo Grounds for housing development. As early as February 7, 1889, Inspector McGinnis of New York City's Board of Encumbrances had hired a gang of men to tear down the Polo Grounds fence so that 111th Street could be extended into the playing field. Either Day or Giants' Manager Jim Mutrie had enough warning about the fence's destruction to engage another group of men to remove the free seats so that they could be used elsewhere. The effervescent Mutrie oversaw the removal of seats (Henry Chadwick Diaries, Vol. 14). Day did not immediately arrange for playing Giants' home games elsewhere because he still hoped that the old Polo Grounds site would be made available. These hopes were eventually unfulfilled, and Day had to scramble for a playing site as the season opened.

Day also had to deal with the personality conflicts on the Giants. John Montgomery Ward had felt some antagonism toward him during the 1888 championship year. Before he left on Albert G. Spalding's world baseball tour in October, 1888, he had told Day of his desire to be sold to the

Boston Beaneaters. However, when Boston bought four great players from the disbanded Detroit Wolverines, Day reasoned correctly that Ward's sale to Boston would insure the 1889 National League pennant for them. Boston owners Arthur H. Soden, James B. Billings, and William H. Conant had achieved a major coup in acquiring first baseman Dan Brouthers, utility man Hardie Richardson, and catchers Charlie Bennett and Charlie Ganzel. With Ward at shortstop, Boston would have strengthened its weak link. Day then opened negotiations with the Washington Senators owner, Walter Hewett. When Ward learned of this development, he left the Spalding tour early, on March 14, returning to New York for a settlement with Day. On April 1, Day and Ward had a long discussion about the merits of Ward's sale to Washington, where he would be playing manager. However, Ward did not enjoy the prospect of playing or managing for a last place team. Henry Chadwick reported that Ward had lost some of his desire for managing during the world tour, (*S.L.*, 10 April 1889) finding the job of managing the All America team against Cap Anson's Chicago White Stockings to be an exhausting task.

The problem of team strife seemed less important to Ward by early April. He no longer thought that there was antagonism toward him as he had at the end of 1888. Granted, friction still existed among Ward, Ewing and first baseman Roger Connor. Ewing and Ward were natural leaders, and the differences between them were probably inevitable. They respected each other's ability, however, and were ready to put personal problems aside. Tim Keefe and other Giant players hoped that Ward would stay with the Giants. Ward thus decided to block the $12,000 deal that Day had arranged with Washington, and he began negotiating for his 1889 salary. Keefe was holding out for more money himself, presenting yet another problem for John B. Day.

The Bridgegroom-Giants series proved to be the bright spot in a dreary spring for the Giants. Although Giants' Captain Buck Ewing had questioned the value of such a series, by early April, Day needed the attendance revenue. With the Old Polo Grounds unavailable, the Giants played exhibition games in Jersey City before poor crowds. Ten thousand people saw the first inter-city game on April 6. Brooklyn players had bet heavily on themselves, with Dave Foutz and Bob Caruthers leading the way. They and Brooklyn cranks were sorely disappointed by their 11-3 beating, but the game did provide some grand entertainment. Gongs signaled pregame practice for the two teams at 3 p.m. in Washington Park.

At 3:30, just at the time for the game to begin, Spalding's baseball tourists arrived. "Gunner" arranged the players in two lines for a proper greeting while Brooklyn President Charles H. Byrne gave them a special section in the grandstand "amid the greatest enthusiasm ever witnessed on a ball field" (*Clipper*, 13 April 1889). Ed "Cannonball" Crane contributed further drama to the game by pitching for the Giants even though he had just arrived from England.

Brooklyn lost again on April 11, but won the last game on April 13, behind Mickey Hughes. The Brooklyn-New York baseball rivalry had existed since the 1860s, and bitter, partisan feeling was demonstrated by the teams' supporters during the series. The players competed intently, but, since a number were absent or holding out, did not take the outcome too seriously. Many New York observers expected to see a World Series between the Bridegrooms and Giants in the fall.

New York City celebrated the return of Albert G. Spalding's touring baseball teams with a grand banquet at Delmonico's on April 8. Three hundred dined that evening to hear Mark Twain, Theodore Roosevelt, Chauncey Depew, Spalding himself, and other celebrities speak glowingly of baseball's importance for America. Francis C. Richter attended the banquet and had stressed the same theme in a recent editorial. Richter noted that baseball's popularity had grown tremendously in the 1880s. He expected 1889 to witness record-setting attendance because of the interest sparked by the Spalding tour, the player changes in important teams like the Boston Beaneaters, the promise of close pennant races in both major leagues, and the rule changes and discussions which further whetted the sports public's appetite (*S.L.*, 3 April 1889).

Baseball had become very popular and people truly thought of it as the national game. New York newspapers commented often, during the spring of 1889, on baseball's importance for the people's entertainment. They wondered how city officials could possibly ignore the fact that the Giants needed to have adequate grounds for 1889 so that the numerous cranks could fully enjoy the game. *The New York Clipper* opined that "our national game has reached the stage where the public look upon it as an actual necessity. The day has come when the public will not do without their games." (2 March 1889) *The New York Times* editorial writer, Edward Cary, expanded this idea:

It is to be hoped that some arrangement may be arrived at by which the ballplayers will not be forced to leave the limits of the city for their daily expositions of the national game during the coming summer. Last year the average attendance upon the championship games would have sufficed to fill three theatres, while upon specially exciting contests it has risen to 15,000 or more...No reasonable moralist can object to the manifestation of the public interest in the national game except on the ground that to look at a game of baseball is merely amusing to the spectators, or that it is not amusing to the moralist himself. (4 April 1889)

Cary argued further that people could possibly do better than attend a baseball game on a Sunday afternoon but that "very probably they would be doing something worse." National League teams played no baseball on Sunday, but they did on Saturday afternoons. Perhaps Cary was thinking of the American Association allowance for Sunday baseball. Citing the brevity of the game as one of the attractive features but agreeing that the Old Polo Grounds might be put to better use, he thought a baseball park in New York City a necessity. The game had "come to play a prominent part in the summer life of New York" by 1889 and excluding the games from the city "would be a public misfortune" (*Times,* 4 April 1889).

Despite the widespread public concern about where the Giants would play in 1889, New York's Board of Aldermen dithered through the spring. In mid-April, they decided to leave 111th Street ungraded, thereby allowing the New York state legislature to close the street so that the Old Polo Grounds could be used for baseball. This artful passing of the buck clearly demonstrated that the city fathers did not want to alienate either baseball cranks or real estate and business interests. By April 20, The New York legislature had passed a bill which allowed the Giants to use the Old Polo Grounds despite property owners' desires to keep 111th Street open for housing. Governor David Bennett Hill then confounded everyone with his veto of this bill on April 23. Hill insisted, as he did throughout his governorship, that local authorities needed to decide such issues and not the New York legislature. He may also have been influenced by New York Mayor Hugh J. Grant's west side real estate interests and the latter's power position in Tammany Hall (Hammack 117, 164-165). By returning the Polo Grounds question to the New York city officials, Governor Hill insured that the Giants would have to play elsewhere since the aldermen did not want to decide anything. One wit commented that Day had not understood New York's officials. What they wanted was some good reason to allow the Giants to play at the Old Polo Grounds—money (See Breen 726-732 for bitter humor about the Public Parks Commissioners' corruption and self-interest, the location of streets, and the repair, or lack thereof, of city streets). Day could not afford to spend such money when he was still trying to hire two of his stars, Ward and Keefe, for 1889. Because the Board of Aldermen wallowed indecisively, Day would have to play the first two home games of the season at Oakland Park in Jersey City. After that, he would arrange to use Erastus Wiman's St. George Park on Staten Island. Both choices were bad ones.

Complicating Day's difficult negotiations with Ward and Keefe was that they were the President and Secretary of The Brotherhood of Professional Base Ball Players, founded on October 22, 1885. Both players were incensed by the salary limits and disciplinary measures that National League officials had decided to impose during the 1888-1889 off season. Ward had learned of the salary plan and classification system during the Spalding world tour. Under the plan, players were to receive a maximum salary of $2,500 and a minimum of $1,500. They were also to be divided into five groups according to skill and personal habits. That piece of news plus the possibility of his sale to Washington brought Ward home early. Tim Keefe had a sporting goods business and had no interest in playing under the proposed salary restrictions of Indianapolis owner John T. Brush. Many other National League players were equally opposed to the Brush plan, and they looked to Ward and Keefe for leadership against baseball's management. Day needed both players to have any hopes of winning the 1889 pennant. Yet, he also faced financial problems because of poor attendance at spring exhibition games in Jersey City and because he would have to play Giants' home games out of New York City. Day had a reputation for paying his players well, and he was liked by them. Clearly, Ward and Keefe had a bargaining advantage (*New York Tribune*, 20 January 1889 for Keefe's wealth).

As John B. Day thrashed around in his problem thicket during the spring of 1889, Brooklyn prepared for the opening of their season. While many baseball forecasters predicted that the Bridegrooms would win the American Association pennant, the Philadelphia Athletics and St. Louis Browns were expected to present strong challenges. American Association teams were to begin play on April 17, but rain delayed the Brooklyn-Athletic game until April 18. The Bridegrooms' opening games were inauspicious, to say the least.

Chapter Four
Early Problems

As so often happens to a baseball team for which great things are predicted, the Brooklyn Bridegrooms began the 1889 dismally. They lost three out of four to the Philadelphia Athletics, which boasted such stars as Ted Larkin at first base, the young catcher Wilbert Robinson, Louis Bierbauer at second, third baseman Denny Lyons, and speedy outfielder Harry Stovey. Former St. Louis Browns' center fielder Curtis Welch also played for the Athletics, though his skills were diminishing because of alcoholism. His dependency was great enough that, once, to fortify himself for the July 4, 1888 doubleheader in St. Louis, Welch had secreted a keg of beer behind the bulletin board and he became "full as a tick" (S.N., 8 June 1889). However, Welch could still hit and so could the Athletic team. They would lead the American Association in hitting during 1889, and they pounded Brooklyn starters Mickey Hughes, Tom Lovett, and Bob Caruthers for 48 hits in the series. Hughes pitched well in the first game but was hit very hard in his second outing. The Bridegrooms fielded horribly, making 26 errors. This fact was duly noted by sportswriters, since good fielding had become recognized as an important part of a winning combination. Journeying to Baltimore, Brooklyn continued to kick the ball around with 18 errors in three games. Understandably, they lost all three to Baltimore. Lovett and Hughes were again hit hard, while "Adonis" Bill Terry pitched well in a losing cause.

Expecting to leave the starting gate with a rush, the Bridegrooms sulked back to Brooklyn with a 1-6 record. Meanwhile, the St. Louis Browns had begun very well, despite continual bickering during the spring between owner Chris Von der Ahe and most of his players.

Only one week before the exhibition season opened in March, 1889, seven Browns' players were still holding out for more money. Among them were the great right fielder Tom McCarthy, second baseman Yank Robinson, and impressive young pitcher Silver King. Von der Ahe had been wrangling with third baseman Arlie Latham since February over how Latham would pay back advance money during the 1889 season. Despite

The 1889 Bridgegrooms on the field—Opening day in Philadelphia—1889. Left to Right: Top Row—George Pinckney, Mickey Hughes, Tom Burns, Darby O'Brien, Hub Collins. Bottom Row—Pop Corkhill, Tom Lovett, Bob Clark, Bill McGunnigle, Dave Foutz, Joe Visner, George Smith. Missing—Bob Caruthers and Bill Terry were both ill. Photo credit National Baseball Library, Cooperstown, N.Y.

the furor, Browns' Manager Charlie Comiskey expressed guarded optimism about being able to defend their string of four American Association championships. He expected that his team would do very well against poor teams and predicted that they would take twenty games from the new Columbus nine. Commy thought that new players Shorty Fuller at shortstop and center fielder Charlie Duffee would work out well, though he would not be disappointed if the Browns failed to win the pennant. With Latham and McCarthy reporting over a week late and Silver King unsigned into April, Commy probably knew that he would encounter more than the usual problems in 1889. Additionally, for the first time, Commy himself was twenty pounds overweight. Yank Robinson set an example for his teammates by shedding thirty pounds before the season and was in the best condition of his baseball career. However, Robinson, King, pitcher Icebox Chamberlain and McCarthy all argued bitterly with Von der Ahe about salary increases during a "hot scene" in early April. With opening day fast approaching and St. Louis cranks becoming increasingly critical of Von der Ahe, the Browns' stew pot approached the boiling point.

Charlie Comiskey could abide no more after the Browns were defeated by Pittsburgh in an April 8 exhibition game. Asking for and receiving permission from Von der Ahe to approach the disgruntled players, Commy worked out compromise salary agreements with all but King. Ominously warning that it was not always easy to discern "shirking" among dissatisfied players, he made a long public statement about the importance of players being content and wanting to play their best. Von der Ahe resisted player demands in 1889 partly because he was reported to have made little money in 1888 and because he still resented the 1888 World Series loss to the New York Giants. Ever inconsistent, Von der Ahe had spent lavishly to celebrate the 1888 pennant. According to Alfred Henry Spink, Von der Ahe threw away over $20,000 in transporting Browns' players and supporters to the World Series games in New York. With players being treated to free drinks, small wonder that the Browns lost four out of the first five games. Von der Ahe, of course, blamed the players with blind disregard for his own impetuosity. The holdout players may have reasoned that if the Browns' owner could afford to spend so freely, he could then afford to pay them higher salaries. Silver King was certainly convinced of this rationale, but finally did his father's bidding and signed for $3,200 on April 11, just six days before the Browns opened their season in Cincinnati. King had been laying bricks for his father all spring, and the strong right-hander was ready to pitch. Despite the fact that Von der Ahe had lost money on spring exhibition games, he at least had his team intact for the opening.

They began as champions should. With King and Chamberlain alternating in the box, the Browns won six out of their first seven games with the Cincinnati Redlegs and Louisville Colonels. Comiskey must have been incensed by the April 23 loss to Louisville. The famous Louisville slugger, Pete Browning, had imbibed more than usual during the winter months and was in no shape to play baseball. Still, sore-armed Nat Hudson allowed Louisville 17 runs and would not pitch again until June. Commy enjoyed destroying poor teams, and the loss to the lowly Colonels was ill received.

The Browns played their home opener April 26 before 10,000 people, as the proud Comiskey led his team onto the field behind a band playing "The Conquering Heroes Come." Despite injuries to both catchers, the Browns went sailing into May in second place with an 11-2 record.

The National League started its season a week later than the Association, on April 24. John B. Day had one of his problems solved when John Ward signed a contract on opening day for $4,200. Ward had earned the same amount in 1888, and it seemed only a matter of time until Tim Keefe also agreed to terms. Besides, Keefe did not pitch well in cool weather, so Day could afford to negotiate a bit longer. What he could not afford was to continue playing games at Oakland Park in Jersey City. Drawing small crowds of 3,000 and 1,400 against the Boston Beaneaters on April 24 and 25, Day arranged to use Erastus Wiman's St. George grounds on Staten Island for Giants' "home" games. Rightfully displeased with having to play outside of New York City, Day at least had acquired more accessible grounds than those in Jersey City.

The opening series between New York and Boston should have been a classic, but rain washed out the last two games and the poor crowds also disappointed. However, the two teams battled fiercely and gave a clear indication of the great pennant struggle that was to come. John Clarkson beat the Giants' Mickey Welch 8-7 in the opener, but the Giants won 11-10 the next day. Like the New Yorkers, Boston had gone through some minor turmoil during the spring, mainly because Mike Kelly wanted a primary leadership role while many doubted his ability to fulfill it. Kelly expected to be the field leader even though Manager-first baseman John Morrill opposed such a plan. Boston cranks had been critical of Kelly's catching during 1888, and the Boston sportswriters thought that Kelly had contributed to team dissension. Despite the questions about Kelly's leadership qualities, Boston's owners decided to make him captain for 1889. They made this decision even though Kelly continued to publicize his "weakness" by being too drunk to recite "Casey At the Bat" at a Boston Elks benefit. In early April, they sold John Morrill to Washington along with shortstop Sam Wise. Morrill had managed Boston since 1882, dividing the job with Kelly during 1887, and was very popular there. With newly acquired Dan Brouthers occupying first base, Boston owner Arthur Soden thought Morrill dispensable. He also solved the problem of the Kelly-Morrill feud which had dragged on through two seasons. James A. Hart was hired as the new manager, but Kelly was still supposed to be the field leader.

Sporting Life reported that the original arrangement for Manager Hart gave him little authority. Hart himself thought that Kelly should select the lineups, even though Boston reporters had been extremely critical of Kelly's "happy-go- lucky" style during the exhibition season. A fairly objective voice, in the person of the Baltimore American Association correspondent, opined that Kelly was rather "heavy and loaferish" as a coach. The same source also raised the issue of Kelly's drinking.

> Kelly has deteriorated in the last year in play and manner, and people are asking themselves if the saloon business has anything to do with it. Backward, turn backward, oh time, in thy jump—make Kel a kid again 'stead of a chump. (*S.L.*, 24 April, 1889)

One wonders how many fathers were already telling their sons of the old Kelly as the criticism mounted. By May, Hart was given complete control of the team, though Kelly still had the title of captain.

All four pennant contenders had settled down fairly well by the beginning of May. Brooklyn started to win even though Caruthers was still recovering from ill health and a sore arm. John B. Day firmly believed that Tim Keefe would sign his contract soon. Boston was still glorying in having acquired the four stars from Detroit. St. Louis seemed well on the way to dominating the American Association for the fifth consecutive year when Chris Von der Ahe's temper almost caused the entire Browns' team to revolt. The incident was but the tip of the iceberg in a season punctuated by strenuous arguments between players and owners and ultimately, questions of honor within the game itself.

Chapter Five
A Troubled Month Of May

St. Louis continued to feast on the Louisville Colonels at the end of April and the beginning of May. Even lightly regarded pitcher Jim "Deacon" Devlin could beat them, and the Browns swept four from the hapless Kentuckians. On May 2, they won 5-1 before traveling to Kansas City to play the Cowboys. However, a pre-game argument between Von der Ahe and second baseman Bill "Yank" Robinson led to a major explosion among Browns' players.

Robinson came from working class origins in Philadelphia, acquired an early reputation for drinking and disciplinary problems, but was an intelligent, daring player (Tiemann and Rucker 109). He had taken the 1889 pre-season very seriously, shedding extra pounds and not drinking for two months. Like other Browns, he had argued with Von der Ahe about salary for 1889. The May 2 game began innocently enough as Comiskey suggested to Yank that he get a cleaner pair of uniform pants. To satisfy Commy's concern about proper attire for the Ladies' Day crowd, Robinson sent a young boy to fetch a clean pair. Problems developed when the youngster was denied reentry by an elderly gatekeeper. Yank proceeded to denounce the gatekeeper for his stupidity. When the latter worthy protested to Von der Ahe, the Browns' owner took the old man's side and Robinson received a public remonstrance. Yank vehemently argued with Von der Ahe and incurred a $25 fine. Saying he would apologize to the old gentleman if the fine were lifted, Robinson met stubborn resistance from Von der Ahe. The second baseman then refused to travel to Kansas City unless the fine were revoked, and the Browns' players threatened to join their compatriot. Finally induced to leave for Kansas City on a late train, the Browns left Robinson in St. Louis and plotted their revenge on Von der Ahe.

Christian Von der Ahe came to the United States in 1863 at the age of seventeen. (See Richard Egenriether, *Baseball Research Journal*, #18, 1989 27 for varying birth dates.) Born in Westphalia province, Prussia in 1846, Von der Ahe dallied in New York only a short time before migrating to St. Louis. By 1865, he had started his own grocery business and began investing his profits in real estate. His property on the corner of St. Louis and Grand Avenues appreciated rapidly and he became a wealthy man by the end of the 1870s. Becoming active in St. Louis politics, Von der Ahe served for several years as Democratic Chairman of the eighth Congressional District committee. His business activities eventually included the grocery store, a saloon, and a boarding house. During the 1870s, boys played baseball in a vacant lot near his saloon. Spectators at the games were also good customers at Chris's bar, so the son of Prussia soon became interested in the game as a profitable proposition. He had acquired the "refreshment" concession for the St. Louis Baseball Association in 1880 and bought controlling interest in the team by the end of the 1881 season. One of the founders of the American Association in 1882, Von der Ahe made a fortune with his St. Louis Browns team during the years 1882-1889 (*Clipper*, 27 October 1888).

Alternately fining and rewarding his players, Von der Ahe defined inconsistency in the way that he handled his team. As happened to many immigrants who were active in public affairs, he became both a folk hero and the butt of many jokes, with newspaper reporters laughingly recounting his malapropisms. His business methods were lax, to say the least, and he became notorious for spending sprees such as that of the 1888 World Series and for gambling heavily on baseball and horses. Chris Von der Ahe was one of the most controversial and colorful personalities that baseball has ever known. G. W. Axelson, Charles Comiskey's biographer, gave some indication of Von der Ahe's mercurial temperament:

> Fining his players was the great indoor sport of Chris. He fined them individually and in platoons. He would sit on the roof of the stand among his directors, and plaster on fines until the pay roll was exhausted....Arlie Latham...was the clown of the team and was always making life miserable for...'der boss'. As a consequence he was probably fined more often than any other member of the team... An even temperament was not characteristic of Chris. It was either sunshine or darkness, with never a trace of twilight... It was everything or nothing... He was a gambler by instinct... (Axelson 60-62)

Commy usually convinced his boss that fined players did not deserve such treatment, so Von der Ahe's fines were rarely paid. By 1889, however, the stout German had become convinced that he knew a great deal about baseball. He probably compared himself to the millionaire owner of the Chicago White Stockings, Albert G. Spalding, and sought to instill more discipline in his team, as Spalding had attempted to do in Chicago. Like Spalding, Von der Ahe had sold a number of his star players, and the salary arguments plus the outburst against Robinson mirrored somewhat the imperious tactics of the great Spalding during the late 1880's. Pseudo-autocratic Von der Ahe had been threatening to leave the American Association for the National League if he did not get his way in Association policy making. He had talked of the need for one big league with six teams in the east and six in the west. The consolidation idea was opposed by Brooklyn President Charles H. Byrne, and the two owners had also clashed over the best way to divide gate receipts for visiting teams. Von der Ahe still did a slow burn whenever he thought of the 1888 World Series loss to the Giants, and his mood became blacker with the salary disagreements during the spring of 1889. His team's performance in Kansas City from May 3-5 temporarily brought him to his senses.

Though arriving late, all of the Browns except for the rebellious Robinson played against the Kansas City Cowboys on May 3. Kansas City had finished last in 1888, but had acquired a great young shortstop, Herman Long, and featured one of the fastest base runners in the league, outfielder Billy Hamilton. Long got five hits against Chamberlain, one of the early holdouts for St. Louis, as the Cowboys won the first game 16-3. The Browns contributed with eight errors. The next day, King lost a 16-9 game as the Browns made 13 errors. Over 15,000 Kansas Citians went mildly crazy on Sunday, May 5 when their beloved Cowboys scored 11 runs in the 9th inning to trounce the four-time champions 18-12. Devlin hurt his leg, so King was the victim of the late-inning outburst. Rumors circulated wildly about how Browns' players were deliberately throwing the games in defiance of Von der Ahe's fining of Robinson. Tom McCarthy, right fielder, commented obliquely about the wind, sun, and dust in the outfield. Left fielder Tip O'Neill agreed that the dust was extremely bothersome. *The Sporting News* noted the rumors and said that "the Browns like Bre'r Fox said nothing" (11 May 1889). Third baseman Arlie Latham, a spring adversary of Von der Ahe as Chamberlain, King, McCarthy and Robinson had been, could not be silent although he did blandly deny the rumors. Comiskey had had enough. He insisted that Von der Ahe drop the fine on Robinson and let Yank return to the team in Columbus, Ohio. Von der Ahe agreed ands the Browns salvaged the last game with Kansas City on May 6, though Chamberlain still gave up 9 runs. The next day in Columbus, with Robinson once more at second base and King pitching, the Browns annihilated the new team, 21-0.

In the coming weeks, Von der Ahe and the Browns would deny any unusual circumstances surrounding the three losses to the Kansas City Cowboys. Clearly, however, the Browns gave the impression to many sportswriters that they were deliberately not playing their best and that their poor performance was connected to Von der Ahe's mistreatment of Robinson. Despite their disrupted state, the Browns won all their games during the first part of May, excluding a loss to Columbus pitcher Mark Baldwin. Comiskey assured everyone that the Browns were going to win it all again, but he must have known that they could ill afford the three losses to lowly Kansas City. Commy gloried in trouncing the poor teams, not being trounced by them. Of course, excuses were forthcoming about King's sore arm and his malaria. Catchers Jocko Milligan and Jack Boyle were also playing with injuries. Nonetheless, when Brooklyn first visited St. Louis on May 16, the Browns raucously occupied first place with a 20-6 record. It could well have been 23-3 with normal results in Kansas City.

The Bridegrooms began playing well by early May, and Manager Bill McGunnigle was able to work with a four-man rotation as Caruthers' health improved. He was still experimenting with signals, using a hat code of some sort. At times, this unique man would use two hats simultaneously. Since managers were in full view of everyone, the entertainment value must have been of premium quality. Undoubtedly wearing out a few of Gunner's hats, Brooklyn won six out of eight from Baltimore and the Athletics before journeying to Louisville and Cincinnati and taking six in a row. Terry had encountered some problems adjusting to the four ball rule in the early part of the season, but he was settling down. The Brooklyn Sunday crowd at Ridgewood was anything but settled in the May 5 game against the Athletics. Twelve thousand of the faithful attended and approximately 7,000 of those surged onto the field during the sixth inning, causing the game to be forfeited to the Athletics. Philadelphia center fielder Curtis Welch apparently had something to do with the crowd's actions, but nothing was ever proven. Brooklyn President Charles H. Byrne disagreed with the forfeiture decision by the American Association Board of Directors, but he decided to build a barbed wire fence around the outfield at Ridgewood Park to prevent further similar occurrences. Crowd control, especially on Sunday games, was a never-ending problem for American Association owners. Byrne tried to blame Welch for the trouble, but the rules clearly stated that the home team assumed responsibility for keeping the playing field clear.

Still, Byrne was pleased by his team's comeback, after a poor start. Shortstop George Smith had injured his ankle, so Tom Burns switched to shortstop while Joe Visner played right field. Not the best combination for the first visit to St. Louis, but the Bridegrooms occupied second place with a 13-8 record when they arrived on May 16 for a four-game series. The Browns hit Mickey Hughes hard and won the first game 9-7 behind the hurling of Icebox Chamberlain. Tip O'Neill played well in left field for the Browns but would miss the next two games because of being hit on the head by a foul tip at the outset of game two. Brooklyn catcher Doc Bushong suffered a split finger on May 16, so the Bridegrooms had to rely on Joe Visner and Bob Clark. Tom Lovett could do nothing with the Browns on May 17, and St. Louis won handily 11-2. Sticking with his four-man rotation, McGunnigle finally saw Terry defeat Chamberlain the next day 5-3. *The New York Times* called it "one of the greatest games every played in St. Louis," as the Bridegrooms pluckily tied the game in the ninth and won it in the eleventh (19 May 1889). George Smith aided the cause by returning to the lineup.

The Sunday game on May 19 attracted over 14,000 to Sportsman's Park. Silver King, winner of the second game, hooked up with Bob Caruthers' in a classic pitching duel that brought out the biggest crowd in St. Louis since 1883. Umpire Bob Ferguson, a Brooklyn native, "materially assisted" Caruthers 2-1 victory over King with what seemed to be prejudicial decisions against the Browns, said the *Times* (20 May 1889). With the St. Louis crowd two and three deep in the outfield, such an occurrence seems doubtful. Ferguson was a brave man but he was also judicious. He would be careful about making obviously bad calls since he and Comiskey had clashed many times before, and he knew how Commy could work a home crowd to his advantage. Commy had gained a wide reputation for abusing umpires unmercifully, and Ferguson was noted for his courage in a hostile environment. The latter would not yield to Commy's attempts to manipulate umpires' decisions, and the two had developed a mutual dislike for each other. However, Ferguson was not cited for any bad calls by *The Sporting News*, the St. Louis sports weekly, so it seems unlikely that the Bridegrooms won the last game of the series because of biased umpiring. The St. Louis crowd had given Bob Caruthers a warm welcome, and the two rivals could look forward to large crowds in Brooklyn at the end of May.

Disaster had struck at home while the Bridegrooms traveled through the Association's western cities. In the early morning of May 19, the grandstand at Washington Park was almost completely destroyed by fire. The Brooklyn owners' losses were estimated at over $18,000, and they had insurance for only $7,000. Nonetheless, President Charles H. Byrne assured reporters that a new grandstand would quickly be constructed in time for the Browns' visit on Memorial Day.

Byrne's problems paled in comparison with those of Louisville's President Mordecai H. Davidson. By May 15, the Colonels were 5-18 and well on their way to one of the worst records in baseball history. President Davidson responded with fines and suspensions, concentrating his wrath on Pete Browning, previously one of the best hitters in the Association. Browning suffered from chronic mastoiditis and drank heavily to ease the pain (Philip Von Borries, *Baseball Research Journal*, 1983, 147-57). One of the most misunderstood players in baseball history, Browning was still cheered by Louisville fans as they tried to help him out of his hitting slump. The Louisville President could only see Browning as an incorrigible "old soak," and *Sporting Life* concurred in this assessment (*S.L.*, 1 May 1889). The Louisville team became an object of general ridicule.

While the Colonels struggled to maintain their integrity, National League players worked through their Brotherhood representatives to plan some sort of response to the new classification and salary limit system that National League owners had imposed during the 1888-1889 off-season. Meeting at New York's Fifth Avenue Hotel on May 19, player representatives from all eight National League teams undoubtedly had the Louisville situation in their minds. They also received more relevant evidence of how unreasonable baseball owners could be when Indianapolis pitcher Henry Boyle complained of being fined $100 for being sick. Nearly every League player had joined the Brotherhood and was discussing the possibility of a strike during the early days of July. At the May 19 meeting, Brotherhood representatives decided to attempt a peaceful settlement with the owners.

Strike talk persisted nonetheless, but Giants' owner John B. Day thought that such rumors were nonsense. He said that the players and owners could and would come to an understanding before relations worsened irreparably. Recognizing that the players objected strenuously to classification, salary limits, and player sales, Day candidly stated that the first two issues were "dead letters." Having signed Ward for over $4,000 and Tim Keefe for $4,500 on May 9, Day knew that other wealthy owners were breaking their own "rule" and would continue to do so. Noting that the salary limit rule was made on behalf of teams like Indianapolis and Louisville, Day said that "the wrecked condition of [Louisville] shows of what little benefit the law has been. The classification law was wrong in the beginning, has been of no use whatever, and is now, to all purposes, dead" (*Clipper*, 1 June 1889). Day mistakenly thought that the sale of players bothered them the most, overlooking the fact that many were owned by men who did pay attention to the salary limits and classification concept. Day was also overly optimistic about the possibilities for amicable settlement. Owners and players were in a distinctly adversarial relationship, as the beginning of the 1889 season demonstrated.

Another example of players being treated shabbily was offered by Ned Williamson, shortstop for the Chicago White Stockings. Williamson had badly injured a knee on Albert G. Spalding's world tour, paid his own doctor bills in England, and was still not employed for 1889 at the end of May. From Spalding's viewpoint, of course, Williamson was a poor risk, and he had a reputation for drinking too much. Many owners were beset with financial concerns, and disastrous accidents such as that suffered by the Brooklyn club added yet another worry. John B. Day himself struggled with salary problems plus the issue of adequate, affordable home grounds. Giant attendance lagged all during the month of May.

Attendance was not one of Charles H. Byrnes' troubles. After splitting their four-game series in St. Louis, Brooklyn won five out of eight from Kansas City and Columbus before returning to Brooklyn for their Memorial Day doubleheader with the Browns. St. Louis ended their homestand by winning four of seven from the Athletics and Kansas City. Both teams worried about their pitchers as Bob Caruthers was hit on his pitching arm during the May 26 game in Columbus, and Icebox Chamberlain continued to be plagued by a sore arm. Mickey Hughes was being hit hard, and his arm troubles had become a major concern. Brooklyn right fielder Tom Burns suffered a minor injury, and catching was still a problem for the Bridegrooms. But their team had done well in the west, so Brooklyn cranks poured out to welcome them on May 30, setting a major league attendance record during the afternoon game. Eight

Jim O'Rourke—37 years young in 1889, O'Rourke batted .321, scored 89 runs, and knocked in 81. Photo credit National Baseball Library, Cooperstown, N.Y.

thousand people saw St. Louis defeat Brooklyn 8-4 in the morning at magically rebuilt Washington Park. Silver King out-pitched Bill Terry as the Bridegrooms contributed five errors. During the afternoon, the Browns returned the favor with seven errors, and Caruthers held on to defeat the sore-armed Chamberlain 9-7. Twenty-two thousand crowded the new grandstand and free seats to capacity while "in the field, a throng ten deep encircled the players" (*Times*, 31 May 1889). Meanwhile, only 8,000 cranks bothered to make the boat trip to Staten Island to watch the Giants play Indianapolis. Byrne swelled with pride as his newly uniformed, white with red trim, Bridegrooms attracted the sort of homecoming that he had hoped for after Brooklyn's best May road trip ever. After the Memorial Day split with the Browns, the Bridegrooms occupied second place with a 21-14 record. The Browns were 27-12. For John B. Day, the month of May proved that Staten Island was not the place to play Giants' home games.

The Giants had also learned that the Boston Beaneaters would provide a formidable challenge in the 1889 National League pennant race. Behind the superb pitching of John Clarkson and Hoss Radbourn, Boston won eighteen of twenty-two during May and stormed into first place. Plagued by Tim Keefe's holdout and injuries to other pitchers, the Giants won fourteen out of twenty-five and girded themselves for an uphill battle.

John B. Day knew that attendance would be a problem when only 3,000 people came to St. George Park during the George Washington inaugural centennial celebration on April 30. Of course, the Washington Senators did not offer an exciting game, and the weather was cold. The condition of the grounds may have caused some people to regard the games at St. George as undignified. A production of *Nero* had been staged at St. George during 1888, and the area from second base to center field was initially bare and stony. Worse, board scaffolding had not yet been removed from the area surrounding the outfield, and the outfield itself was partially covered with boards to provide fielders with traction in the mud. The field conditions were unimaginably bad, though the word picture provided by *The New York Clipper* aids our musings:

> The ground was hardly in condition for play, as the earth that had been dumped on the field was soft and miry after the recent rains (April 26-28) and the outfield was covered with the vast plank floor that played a conspicuous part in the spectacular play produced there last year. This floor was about forty feet behind second base, and every ball that landed on it bounded away like a shot. (11 May 1889)

The Giants provided all outfielders with special rubber-soled shoes to negotiate the planking, but no one could prepare them adequately for the sharp downward slope in back of third base. As one might imagine, some outfielders used the planks for entertainment. The great Giants' left fielder, Jim O'Rourke, was among them. Some of the warped planks produced noise like cannon shots if leaped upon, and O'Rourke convulsed the sparse crowds with his antics. *The Times*, ever concerned about the proper home for the Giants, noted ruefully that "balls bound by fielders with increased speed after they strike the woodwork, and hits that would ordinarily prove good for two bases will yield home runs" (30 April 1889). John B. Day disgustedly began looking for better grounds early in May, as complaints mounted over the long boat ride to and fro plus the "nine-inning battle with mosquitoes" at St. George (*S.L.*, 15 May 1889).

Worried over finding proper grounds, Day also fretted about injuries early in the season. Ed "Cannonball" Crane was supposed to take Keefe's place until Day could sign the latter, but after two poor starts in Philadelphia, Crane injured a knee while sliding into second base against Boston on May 8. With this development and after having lost four out of five to Philadelphia and Boston, Day succumbed to Tim Keefe's demands for a $4,500 salary. He could do little else, since Mickey Welch had strained his back, and Ledell Titcomb could not regain his impressive pitching form of 1888. In this crisis, the great Buck Ewing rose to the occasion by pitching against the Beaneaters on May 9, defeating Kid Madden 10-9. The Giants' Captain impressed the Boston crowd with his courageous hurling in an emergency, and the New York players joyfully greeted the news that Keefe had signed that day and would pitch the next. Though Keefe put renewed heart in his teammates by defeating Hoss Radbourn, he also developed a sore arm since he had not pitched much during his holdout. Keefe and the Giants looked forward to warmer weather and, hopefully, a better playing field.

President Day was cheered by the hard hitting of left fielder Jim O'Rourke. *Sporting Life* thought that the veteran outfielder was "bathed in the waters of youth" (8 May 1889). *The Sporting News* pragmatically noted that "Orator Jim" ran three or four miles after every game to keep in trim. He neither smoked nor drank and was one of the best conditioned athletes of his era. John Montgomery Ward, advocate of hand-ball for keeping in shape, was also in excellent condition, but his thoughts were increasingly taken up by the ongoing battle between players and baseball owners. Center fielder George Gore and second baseman Danny Richardson were injured for intervals, and Buck Ewing had to pitch utility man Gil Hatfield six times during May because of Welch's and Keefe's ailments. Ewing started and won one more game as the Giants instituted morning practices on May 14 to shake themselves out of their mild slump. Despite the injuries, the Giants won nine of their last thirteen games in May.

Playing on their "home" grounds at St. George during the last half of May, the Giants proved to be good mudders. Heavy rains on May 19 and 20 made the clay soil diamond one of the worst playing fields imaginable. New York players adapted nonetheless, especially enjoying the series with their ancient enemy, the Chicago White Stockings, led by the incomparable Adrian "Cap" Anson. The great first baseman steamed into New York in a foul mood since owner Albert G. Spalding had cut some of his better players from the team just before the season started. In the name of economy and the new disciplinary creed, Spalding had Anson release Mark Baldwin, a strong young pitcher, and Tom Daly, one of the best young catchers in the National League. Anson still had the young Hugh Duffy in the outfield and Bill Hutchinson, an impressive pitcher. But shortstop Ned Williamson was incapacitated from his knee injury, and the whole Chicago team was stirring restlessly under Spalding's disciplinary emphasis. Chicago players believed that Williamson had been treated unfairly by Spalding after injuring himself on the world tour and were unimpressed with the reasoning behind their teammates' releases.

Giants' Manager Jim Mutrie sensed that the moment was at hand when four straight games could be taken from Anson's charges. The Giants particularly enjoyed defeating Chicago, especially center fielder George Gore. Sold by Spalding to New York after the 1886 season for disciplinary reasons, Gore made a brilliant running catch in the first game despite the hideous field conditions.

By May 23, the sun had dried the muddy clay enough to create a rock hard, irregular surface. The result was "a contest that revived memories of games played way back in the sixties." Chicago won 18-17 while the two teams made 34 hits and 19 errors. Old-timers were delighted as they "recalled memories of bygone days when the Eckfords, Mutuals, and Atlantics struggled for diamond-field honors, and the Elysian Fields, the Union and Capitoline Grounds were in their prime" (*Times* 24 May 1889). After serving nostalgia, the best the Giants could do was split the last two games with Chicago.

While the playing field conditions caused John B. Day much concern, sobering indeed were the attendance figures at St. George for May. The average attendance was a pitiful 2,000, and only 10,000 attended the four-game series with arch-rival Chicago. Even the star attractions of shortstop Jack Glasscock and third baseman Jerry Denny failed to draw large crowds for the Memorial Day doubleheader with Indianapolis. Meanwhile, the Boston Beaneaters frolicked through May with more than double the Giants' home attendance. Hoss Radbourn pitched superbly, King Kelly batted, caught and ran bases as well as ever, Billy Nash received praise at third base, and Hardie Richardson impressed everyone with his fielding and hitting.

Albert G. Spalding, Chicago owner, had provided some unintended incentive for Kelly before the season started. Still perturbed at Kelly for not fulfilling obligations on the world tour, Spalding said: "I feel almost ashamed that I sold such bad goods to the Boston club. He isn't the Kel that he used to be when in the Chicago club" (*S.L.*, 24 April 1889). Spalding was certain that the King's drinking habits had finally caught up with him, but Kelly's early season performance seemed to negate that opinion. Responding to his and his mates' play, Boston went baseball crazy as the city demonstrated more enthusiasm for their team than anytime since the pennant winning year of 1883. The Beaneaters swept four from Chicago at the end of May and ended the month in first place with a 20-6 record. The Phillies occupied second with the Giants resting in third at 17-12. All things considered, New York had done well to stay so close to Boston.

After the May 30 Memorial Day doubleheaders in both leagues, all teams rested the next day. On that day, May 31, Johnstown, Pennsylvania was partially destroyed by a great flood. For days and weeks afterwards, newspapers devoted attention to the cataclysm and attendant suffering. Baseball became properly insignificant although the games resumed on June 1. Beginning the month in a piteous fashion, the Giants asserted themselves impressively by the end of June while the Beaneaters reversed that process. Concurrently, the Bridegrooms stubbornly dogged the Browns as the New York metropolitan area began buzzing over the real possibility of a Brooklyn-New York World Series.

Chapter Six
The Idea of Revolt

Although leading the American Association at the beginning of June, Charlie Comiskey stewed over the condition of his pitchers. Icebox Chamberlain's arm was sore as was Nat Hudson's. Silver King's arm did not seem to be as strong as it had been in 1888, although no sportswriter ever suggested that King had been overworked by Commy. Such criticism would not be made in those times when, as the great pitcher "Count" Tony Mullane said, a pitcher "has to go in and pitch whether he feels like it or not" (S.N., 23 February 1889). Mullane also praised Commy for his handling of pitchers, especially young ones like King. So Commy was not faulted, but *Sporting Life* correspondent Joe Pritchard thought that the Browns did need another pitcher to take some of the pressure off of King. On the positive side, Shorty Fuller and Charlie Duffee were playing well at shortstop and center field, two positions that had troubled Commy since Bill Gleason and Curt Welch were sold after the 1887 season. King began the month well by beating Bob Caruthers on June 2, 2-1. Eleven thousand witnessed the pitchers' battle at Ridgewood Park with no reported incidents. J. F. Donnolly, Brooklyn correspondent for *Sporting Life*, thought that the game was one of the best he had ever seen, worth walking twenty miles. The Sunday crowd cheered the Bridegrooms even though they lost. The Brooklyn faithful were further entertained by the enchanting sight of Browns' third baseman Arlie Latham carrying an invading goat from the field. On June 18, the Browns and Bridegrooms played off the June 1 rainout as the flaxen-haired King defeated Bill Terry 5-4. Despite all of his pitching problems, Commy had defeated Brooklyn three out of four and achieved a successful road trip by the time he brought the Browns back to St. Louis on June 25.

The intense competition between New York and Boston partially manifested itself in the play of Buck Ewing at the outset of June. Normally an even-tempered competitor, Ewing was thrown out of the Washington game on June 1 because of abusive language directed against Umpire Wesley Curry. Perhaps Captain Ewing intended to inspire his team, which played listlessly in losing two of three games to the lowly Senators. He was undoubtedly frustrated by the poor pitching of Tim Keefe, still struggling to get into top form after his holdout. Right fielder Mike Tiernan had been ill, and the whole team had not hit as well as it could. Too many errors, poor team play, and reports of team discord led President John B. Day to meet daily with the team to discuss their play. Yet another disruptive element for the team was that John Montgomery Ward, President of the players' Brotherhood, and other Giants were increasingly disturbed by the salary limitation and classification issue. Since Tim Keefe was Secretary of the Brotherhood, the ongoing feud between owners and players was a regular conversational topic among the Giants, though John B. Day paid them exceptionally well and ignored the classification system.

Ward spoke out vehemently against the classification system (*Clipper*, 8 June 1889). He was particularly incensed that the National League owners had reneged on their promise not to reserve players at less than their 1888 salary. The classification system had been ignored by most owners, like Day, but Ward said that a few paid close attention to the $2,500 salary limit, thereby causing their players to be reserved for 1889 at a reduced salary. The Giants' shortstop had developed a closely reasoned attack on the owners' rationale for the salary limit-classification concept. National League owners tried to defend salary limits on the basis of helping weaker, less populous cities like Indianapolis and Washington. Ward fired back by asserting that if those cities could not pay adequate salaries, they should leave the National League. "They have no right to stay in at the expense of their players." If League owners thought their presence necessary, then Ward said that the League should divide the expenses of the weak cities among themselves. "Indianapolis has about as much right in the National League as Oshkosh." But Ward further noted that Boston, New York, Chicago and Philadelphia made large to good profits in 1888. Ward was certain that the eight League teams, with a reported annual combined profit of $200,000 to $300,000, could help weaker cities and not limit players' salaries. He suggested splitting gate receipts 50-50 as one way to help struggling teams. *The Clipper* agreed with Ward's critique and suggested that if Indianapolis and Washington could not afford to pay star players like shortstop Jack Glasscock and third baseman Jerry Denny, they should not be allowed to hold them (Clipper, 15 June 1889).

By mid-June, players' attention in both major leagues was drawn to the bizarre developments on the American Association Louisville team. Louisville owner Mordecai H. Davidson, incensed by the Colonels poor start (8-40), had fined his second baseman for making errors and his catcher for stupid baserunning. When the other Louisville players said that they would not play their June 14 game in Baltimore unless the fines were rescinded, Davidson threatened them with individual $100 fines if they struck and said that he would fine them $25 each if they played and lost. Louisville Captain Chicken Wolf pleaded with Davidson to reconsider his acts and threats, but the latter was intransigent. Six Louisville players refused to play on the 14th and repeated this refusal on the next day. By the time that payday rolled around on June 22, the Louisville players had collected a total of $1,700 in fines, $1,200 of that based on the two days of fines levied against the six striking players. As a result, Davidson subtracted the fines from players' pay. Besides the strike fines, the benighted Davidson had deigned to impose fines for bad language and failing to slide. He had earlier failed to pay salaries promptly. Naturally, the player most fined was Pete Browning, who had also collected a $100 penalty for being drunk in Brooklyn from June 8-11 (*Clipper,* 22 29 June 1889; *Times,* 15 June 1889).

When Louisville pitcher Guy Hecker tried to organize an American Association Brotherhood of players which would be affiliated with the National League Brotherhood, Association officials finally decided to do something on behalf of the Louisville players. Association President Wheeler C. Wikoff had opposed the players' strike of June 15 against Davidson, but the other Association owners finally arranged a fair settlement for the players when Davidson sold his interest in the team to new owners at the beginning of July. The June 15 strike fines were sustained since Wikoff had asked the players to compete on that day, assuring them that their case would be heard. The June 14 strike fines and all of Davidson's arbitrary, capricious fines for "indifferent playing" were cancelled (Orem 393-394; *Clipper,* 13 July 1889). The spectacle of an obstinate owner arbitrarily fining his players for poor play left an indelible impression on players in both leagues, and Ward left on the Giants' western road trip determined to meet with National League owner representatives to mitigate the punitive qualities of the classification system.

Before leaving New York on June 17, Ward told *The Times* (18 June

1889) that he and two other Brotherhood representatives, outfielder Ned Hanlon of Pittsburg and first baseman Dan Brouthers of Boston, would soon try to meet with John B. Day, John I. Rogers of Philadelphia, and Albert G. Spalding of Chicago to determine whether or not the classification/salary limits could be eliminated. Noting that most teams did not pay any attention to the classification system, but paid players what they wanted, one prominent player felt that the reserve system was probably a necessity "but we can and will defeat schemes of the classification order" (*Times,* 18 June 1889). Ward hoped that the player-owner conference could be held in Chicago during the Giants' visit from June 24-27.

After playing the first two games in Cleveland, which the Giants split on June 19 and 20, Ward developed a sore arm that caused him to miss the remaining road games against Cleveland, Chicago, Indianapolis and Pittsburg. Not until the Giants returned to New York on July 8 did Ward play again. During this time, the Giants played creditably and won nine out of fourteen games. For the entire trip, the Giants won ten and lost six, doing that well because Tim Keefe began pitching better and Ed "Cannonball" Crane had recovered from his knee injury. Gil Hatfield filled in adequately for Ward, George Gore played superbly in center field, and Buck Ewing caught at his best. Tim Keefe actually missed much of the trip because of a death in his family, absenting himself from June 24 - 30.

Although it can not be proven, there is a possibility that Ward was not injured so badly as to necessitate missing fourteen games. He could well have been meeting with capitalists in the western cities to determine the possibility of developing a Players' League. Such thinking had been circulating for some time. After they had learned of the owners' classification/salary limitation decision while on their world tour, Ward, Chicago's Fred Pfeffer, Pittsburg's Ned Hanlon and Philadelphia's Jim Fogarty had begun discussing the possibility of getting financial support for a separate Players' League (Allen, *100 Years* 101; *Tribune,* 30 October 1889). Ward definitely spent some time visiting the opposing players of western teams, particularly those in Chicago and Indianapolis where grievances against owners Albert G. Spalding and John T. Brush were well-founded. His discussions with players centered around the advisability of a strike, a course of action which Ward thought inferior to a new Players' League (Henry Chadwick Scrapbooks, Vol. 2, *Cleveland*

54 Baseball in 1889

Press clipping, 14 December 1889; Bass 65). However Ward occupied himself during his absence from the playing field, owner-player relations received a major setback when Spalding decided on June 24 that any discussion about changing the classification/salary limits could wait until the end of the season.

As his team successfully negotiated the western trip, John B. Day received some welcome support regarding proper grounds from *New York Times* editor Edward Cary. Cary had been editorial writer for the *Times* since 1871 and had gained a wide reputation for his calm, succinct, intelligent interpretations of important political, economic, international and social issues. In April, 1889, Cary had expressed concern about the Giants having to play their home games outside New York City and on June 13, he urged action by the Park Commissioners so that the game of baseball could be easily enjoyed by New York's populace.

> ...it is the business of the Park Commissioners to make provision for this as the most extensively popular of any form of outdoor public recreation....It seems to be settled that a ground that must be reached by water [St. George's] is not as attractive as one that can be reached, even in the same space of time, by a land journey. The season has scarcely begun, but it is unlikely that the games of the New York Club will command as large an attendance or as great an interest as they did last year, when they were played upon a ground accessible by both lines of the elevated railway. This is an important public matter. A contest that provides innocent amusement in the summer in New York after the hour of business in the afternoon for a number of people ranging from fifteen hundred to as many as thousands is by no means beneath the care of the proper authorities; only as we have said the proper authorities are neither the Aldermen nor the Commissioner of Works, but the Park Commissioner.

Cary went on to urge the city to open one of its parks for the playing of baseball, profiting thereby since the game would "promote the pleasure of the people." The *Times* editor stressed the growing popularity of baseball and emphasized "that there will be for an indefinite period a requirement for its suitable establishment in the first city of the country and that requirement cannot be met except by some municipal action." Whether or not Cary's calm, rational voice had any influence, by June 22 the *Times* noted that Giants' President John B. Day was working to construct a baseball field and grandstand at 155th Street and Eighth Avenue. James Coogan, wealthy furniture dealer representing the Lynch estate, assured Day that the property was close enough to the west elevated

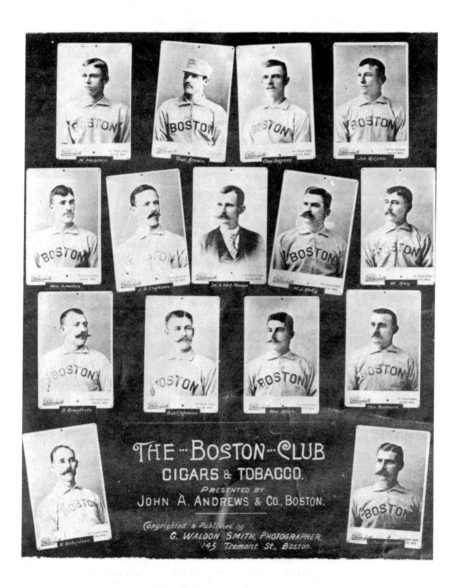

The 1889 Boston Beaneaters—At the season's start. Left to right: Top row—Kid Madden, Tom Brown, Charlie Ganzel, Joe Quinn. Top middle—Bill Sowders, John Clarkson, Jim Hart (Manager), Mike Kelly (Captain), Stubby Ray. Bottom middle— Dan Brouthers, Dick Johnston, Billy Nash, Hoss Radbourn. Bottom—Hardie Richardson and Charlie Bennett. Photo credit National Baseball Library, Cooperstown, N.Y.

railroad for easy access, and Day hoped to finish the grounds and grandstand in time for the Giants' return on July 8. By July 1, a fence had been erected surrounding the New Polo Grounds, and grandstand construction was proceeding rapidly.

In 1889, no better measure of baseball's popularity or importance for urban life exists than the earnest pleadings of *Times* editor Edward Cary. Truly, the necessity for public entertainment made the provisions for baseball "an important public matter", and 1888 United Labor Party mayoral candidate James Coogan (Hammack 177) undoubtedly expected to receive some political as well as economic benefits from his role in returning the Giants to New York City. Whatever Coogan's motivation, New Yorkers of all occupations agreed with Edward Cary that baseball was important enough for city officials to make it easily available for those who, by 1889, identified baseball as a healthy, "innocent amusement."

Even before the exciting news that the Giants would return to New York City, Manhattan cranks had been treated to a marvelous display of baseball between Boston and the Giants. On June 6 and 7, the Beaneaters pounded Keefe and Welch for 10-7 and 9-4 victories in Boston. Clarkson and Radbourn were hit hard by the Giants, but the Giants made more costly errors, especially in the second game. Fully 4,500 Boston cranks cheered their Beaneaters lustily in the June 6 victory, an astounding turnout for a Thursday game. Having lost four out of five to lowly Washington and league-leading Boston, the Giants limped back to New York for a three game series with Boston. The Giants were in bad temper as they returned to New York. They had spent most of the game on June 7 venting their spleen against Umpire George W. Barnum. Fortunately, Tim Keefe returned to his old form on June 10 at St. George. Rain had also provided hideous playing conditions, and the Beaneaters made seven errors as Clarkson suffered only his second loss of the season. Keefe struck out twelve and allowed only three hits in the 5-1 victory. The next day, Mickey Welch pitched his best game of the year in defeating Radbourn 2-1. *The Times* pronounced it "a grand game" as Welch gave Boston only two hits, and the Giants made only two errors. "Smiling Mickey" had been troubled early in the season by the four ball rule but seemed to have adjusted by early June.

One of the many appealing features in the Giants-Beaneater rivalry was the opportunity for cranks to see the two greatest catchers compete.

Cap Anson—A ferocious competitor, Anson knocked in 117 runs in 1889 and brought his relatively young team home in third place. Photo credit National Baseball Library, Cooperstown, N.Y.

Boston catcher Charlie Bennett had earned a reputation as the equal of Buck Ewing behind the plate. He also had gained wide respect for his physical courage, one of the requirements for a catcher in those days. A big, handsome man at 5' 11" and 180 pounds, Bennett disdained the padded catcher's mitt coming into vogue by 1889 and used by catchers like Brooklyn's Doc Bushong. As a catcher for Detroit in the early and mid-80s, Bennett used only an ordinary kid glove minus the fingers and thumb. In one game, his thumb split bone-deep from the hand to the tip. He continued catching regularly, sponging "the gash in his thumb with cotton soaked in antiseptic which he carried with him in his pocket, in order to remove the corruption which was continually flowing from the wound" (Spink 91). Finally, Bennett heeded doctors' advice and stopped playing so that the cut could heal properly.

This sort of action was expected of players in an era when owners did not often pay players if they were disabled from injuries. Curt Welch, great, oft-inebriated center fielder for the Philadelphia Athletics, gave further evidence of expected player behavior during a June, 1889 game in Philadelphia. Sliding into second base, he contacted a hidden piece of glass, running his arm from the wrist to the elbow across the sharp edge. Welch calmly "doctored" the freely bleeding wound with sand and saliva and stayed in the game. Periodically, he would add some more sand for "antiseptic" purposes (Orem 393). Charlie Comiskey, Welch's manager in St. Louis during the mid-80s, would have expected no less of him. In commenting about how players disregarded physical punishment in the 1880s, Commy once reminisced:

> Welch slid into a bag either way as, in fact, did most of the crack runners in my day. We only varied the performance as the bruises on our bodies dictated. It was much like broiling a steak. If rare on one side, turn it over. (Axelson 48)

Aside from his physical courage, Bennett was most respected for his great catching ability. Buck Ewing provided the best testimony. *New York Sun* sportswriter John B. Foster interviewed Ewing after the great Giants' catcher had retired from baseball. Foster told Buck that he considered him the greatest catcher. Ewing replied with honest humility: "I tried to do the best I could and, oh man, but I did love to play with the old Giants. I used to think that if I could catch as well as Charlie Bennett was catching for Boston, we could win the championship" (Ewing File, NBL). Even though the praise came years after the 1889 season, it was meant and gives some idea of the talent and character that both catchers possessed. Granted that Buck Ewing would on occasion throw his mask in the path of runners at home plate, he was basically a good man and an honest competitor. Surely, the cranks in New York and Boston knew that they were watching two of the greats in Buck Ewing and Charlie Bennett. As they competed against each other, they strived to play at their best, thereby enhancing their considerable talents for the admiring multitude.

With Charlie Bennett and Charlie Ganzel sharing catching duties for Boston, King Kelly could play right field regularly. Center fielder Tom Brown was running better than the King and first baseman Dan Brouthers was outhitting him. *Sporting Life* noted that Kelly's special star status no longer obtained in Boston but thought that the Beaneaters were still a harmonious team in mid-June (*S.L.*, 12 June 1889). Manager Jim Hart confidently predicted that Boston would win the National League pennant and could see no reason to worry about the western road trip in late June. *Sporting Life* correspondent Henry Chadwick thought that Boston's success was based on the temperate habits of the team, and he also praised Billy Nash's excellent fielding. Dan Brouthers, great Boston first baseman, affirmed the certainty of a Beaneater pennant by saying that Boston "cannot lose it unless some of us drop dead" (*S.L.*, 19 June 1889). King Kelly, obviously inspired by his teams's play, on one occasion objected to Umpire Wesley Curry's call by balancing on his hands, waving his feet in the air and braying like a mule.

Imbued if not ennobled with this spirit, Boston began their road trip rather ominously as five players became involved in some late-night activity in Pittsburgh, though drinking did not seem to be a problem. After sweeping four from Pittsburg at the beginning of their sojourn, Hart's team appeared to deserve their manager's praise. Even little-used pitchers Kid Madden and Bill Sowders managed to defeat Pittsburgh as Hoss Radbourn rested a bit. Then the Beaneaters lost three out of four to Indianapolis with John Clarkson becoming human by losing two games and being hit hard. In Chicago, Boston dropped three of four again as Clarkson lost one more. They would lose three of four to Cleveland before sneaking back to Boston on July 8.

The Chicago series was especially intense. Boston did not hit and they fielded raggedly. More important, King Kelly finally succumbed to temptations that always attracted him. *The Sporting News* reported that Kelly "went to the races" in Chicago, meaning he went on a drinking-gambling binge (S.N., 6 July 1889). Perhaps Kelly could not resist visiting his old haunts when he thought that Boston was playing well enough to win without him. After all, they had swept four from Chicago at the end of May in Boston. Perhaps Chicago owner Albert G. Spalding hired people to deliberately divert Kelly from baseball while in Chicago. Spalding had been extremely critical of the King since Kelly had backed out of the world tour, and he undoubtedly wanted Kelly to look as bad as he had made him out to be. Most likely, Kelly initiated his spree of his own volition. He simply loved to drink and gamble on horses. Cap Anson said of him in his memoirs that Kelly's only enemy was himself. "Money slipped through Mike's fingers as water slips through the meshes of a fisherman's net....He was a good fielder when not bowled up [drunk]....In such cases he would remark with a comical leer: 'By Gad, I made it hit me gloves, anyhow" ' (Anson 115-116).

Before Spalding sold Kelly to Boston, he had used a private detective to investigate the nocturnal journies of some of his White Stockings, Kelly among them. When confronted with the evidence at a team meeting and having heard the detective's report, Kelly displayed his unfailing humor and frankly admitted his greatest weakness by saying: "I have to offer only one amendment. In that place where the detective reports me as taking a lemonade at 3 a.m., he's off. It was a straight whiskey; I never drank a lemonade at that hour in my life" (Spalding 522 ff). The King could not quit drinking because he enjoyed drinking, and he was an alcoholic. As noted, Spalding had said early in 1889 that he thought that Kelly's drinking was finally catching up with him and that he had sold damaged goods to Boston. Such needling probably made Kelly play harder at the outset of the year, but by June, Kelly may have been bothered somewhat by the fact that he was no longer the one star on the Boston team. He may have decided to prove to his manager and teammates that they needed him to win. No matter what one may surmise, the fact remains that the King indulged in one of his sprees and was useless to his team against Chicago.

Yet another personal conflict that played in Chicago was that between the amazing Boston pitcher John Clarkson and his former manager Cap Anson. Virtually unbeatable before the June road trip, Clarkson's pitching greatness was based on an excellent change of pace, a "drop curve," a rising fast ball and magnificent control. He also threw with an easy, graceful motion. Clarkson studied batters carefully so that he could use his control to maximum advantage. Cy Young said that he, as a young pitcher

OLD JUDGE CIGARETTES Goodwin & Co., New York.

Dave Orr—Pictured here in his 1888 Brooklyn uniform, Big Dave played from 1883 through 1890, primarily in the American Association and Players' League. Never batting below .300, Orr ranked among the top hitters in 1889 during his one year with Columbus. Photo credit National Baseball Library, Cooperstown, N.Y.

with Cleveland, received many helpful "pointers" from the handsome Clarkson. Yet, Anson knew that Clarkson had one weakness. When the latter died in 1909, Anson recalled that "not many know what an amount of encouragement it took to keep him going. Scold him, find fault with him, and he would not pitch at all" (Spink 126). Chicago pounded Clarkson for an 11-3 win in the first game of the series. One can well imagine the critical, verbal barrage that Cap Anson might have hurled against Clarkson to throw him off of his game. Having lost to him twice in Boston, smarting from criticisms of the White Stockings poor showing, Cap was always capable of using any tactic to win a game (Ward, "National Game" 453). He gloried in defeating the League leaders three out of four.

After Clarkson recovered to defeat Chicago on July 1, Boston's lead over second place Cleveland was only 2 1/2 games, while the rain-plagued Giants trailed by 5 1/2. However, the Giants were now hitting hard, playing well and their pitchers were healing. Boston, aside from Clarkson, did not have strong pitching, and they were about to engage Cleveland in eight games.

In the American Association, the pennant race between the Browns and Bridegrooms became more intense toward the end of June. St. Louis returned from its successful eastern road trip to begin a series with Cincinnati on June 25. Comiskey's mood had darkened considerably in the last game at Louisville as the Browns lost to the lowly Colonels, giving Louisville its first win after 26 consecutive losses. Comiskey contributed 4 costly errors, so he could blame few besides himself. The Cincinnati series did not cheer Commy much as the Redlegs won two out of three despite the Browns' acquisition of a new pitcher, Jack Stivetts, from York, Pennsylvania. Icebox Chamberlain still suffered from arm problems, so Stivetts' presence was necessary.

Commy complained that poor umpiring on the eastern sojourn had cost the Browns some crucial games against Baltimore and Philadelphia. Such carping typified Commy's analysis of Browns' losses, and he seldom could speak of defeats without some negative reference about the umpires. *Sporting Life* correspondent Joe Pritchard provided balanced assessment of the Browns' road performance by noting how Silver King pitched well despite some illness. The Browns also displayed good team work, steady fielding and timely hitting before they visited Baltimore and Philadelphia.

Pritchard ruefully noted the poor attendance at Browns' home games.

Even though St. Louis led the league, only 2,000 people attended the June 25 homecoming game with Cincinnati. Pritchard asserted that "the people of St. Louis do not deserve a winning team as they will not support it" and that St. Louis should be ashamed of its poor attendance after the Browns' successful 12-6-1 eastern swing (*S.L.*, 3 July 1889). Earlier, the easy-going Pritchard had excused poor attendance in St. Louis by surmising that the locals were too accustomed to winning teams. Chris Von der Ahe was nearly apoplectic over the poor crowds. After the Cincinnati series, he threatened to move the Browns to another city, observing that his champions drew three times better away from home than in St. Louis. He broodingly opined that St. Louis was a twenty-five cent city, referring to the American Association admission price, but indicating that he would prefer the greater profits from a National League city where admission would be fifty cents. Von der Ahe thus joined two other Association teams in reportedly considering a shift to the National League.

Rumors circulated, as they had for some time, about the possibility of Brooklyn and Cincinnati joining the National League. Some Cincinnati civic leaders severely criticized Sunday baseball, and the Redlegs President Aaron S. Stern did not think that enough profits could accrue from twenty-five cent weekly admission. Brooklyn also faced opposition to Sunday baseball and was being courted by the National League because of its high attendance. Ideally, the Association should have been benefitting from the best pennant race in its history. Sadly, because of problems within the St. Louis organization, and some dissatisfaction with the Association in Brooklyn and Cincinnati, the Association ended the month of June in a rather disrupted condition.

Von der Ahe found some comfort in his team's ability to attract crowds away from St. Louis. Not all of this attendance was attributable to baseball, as one lady in an eastern city said of the Browns: "The Browns are all good-looking but that man O'Neill is the handsomest man on the team, and he is shaped like a Samson" (*S.L.*, 26 June 1889). Aside from his ability to attract women, left-fielder Tip O'Neill fielded and hit well. In right field, Tom McCarthy matched O'Neill's fielding and also ran bases with gusto. Catchers Jack Boyle and Jocko Milligan were playing "the games of their lives" and hitting as was new center fielder Charlie Duffee. Shortstop Shorty Fuller impressed with his fielding. The Browns' pitching received a needed boost at the end of June from hard-throwing Jack Stivetts. Silver King's arm was fine, but he had malaria and had been weakened considerably.

While *Sporting Life's* Henry Chadwick censured Commy for blaming umpires for the Browns' losses in Philadelphia, editor Francis C. Richter quoted Commy's criticisms of the umpires without comment. Richter also praised the Browns' manager for his "wonderful amount of baseball intelligence combined with good hard sense." Referring to Commy's ability to deal with volatile players like third baseman Arlie Latham and second baseman Yank Robinson, Richter complimented further: "He is a strict disciplinarian but never unnecessarily harsh and always sides with the players against club tyranny [Von der Ahe]" (*S.L.*, 26 June 1889). On the surface, the Browns seemed fit for the Bridegrooms' invasion on July 3 and 4.

When Brooklyn left Washington Park after defeating Columbus 10-3 on June 26, they could look back on a 13-8 record at home in June. The most aggravating losses were those to the young Kansas City Cowboys and to the new Columbus team. However, *Sporting Life* Bridegroom correspondent J. F. Donnolly praised the quality of the Cowboys' play in Brooklyn, citing center fielder Jim Burns as a "rare jewel." The Columbus team competed fiercely against Brooklyn since it contained four former Bridegrooms. The most important of these was big, 5' 11", 250 lb., hard-hitting first baseman Dave Orr. Orr did his team a disservice on June 24 by urging Columbus' manager Al Buckenberger to reject substitute umpire William Paasch and to refuse to play the game. Paasch waited the requisite number of minutes and then declared the game a forfeit to Brooklyn. Orr and company were livid but inexplicably agreed to play off the April 25 tie game which they won 13-7. Buckenberger later admitted to *Sporting Life* correspondent F. W. Arnold that he did not understand the rules fully and that he had made a mistake in not playing the regularly scheduled game. Brooklyn President Charles H. Byrne eventually waived the $1,500 fine that was supposed to accompany a team's refusal to play since he did not wish to punish Columbus' owners for Orr's and Buckenberger's stupidity (*S.L.*, 3 July 1889).

This was the second time that Byrne had been magnanimous toward Columbus, the first instance occurring during the May 25 game in Columbus. In that contest, Orr had argued with umpire Fred Goldsmith so heatedly after being ejected that Goldsmith had declared Brooklyn the winner by forfeit. Byrne intervened and requested that the game continue, which Brooklyn won 6-3 (*S.L.*, 5 June 1889). Francis C. Richter complimented Byrne for both actions, although his initial reaction to Columbus' belligerence at Washington Park was to withhold gate receipts and also request the $1,500 fine. Dave Orr denied that he had any grievance against Byrne, but clearly, Columbus played with particular intensity against the Bridegrooms.

Charles H. Byrne could afford to be forgiving toward Columbus' manager and players since the Bridegrooms were playing well despite some injuries. Team Captain Darby O'Brien received accolades for the "genial manner of dealing with his men." He also fielded superbly in left field, though he was so upset by his costly error against St. Louis on June 18 that afterward he became ill for two days. George Pinckney and Dave Foutz were hitting, and George Smith and Foutz fielded their positions exceptionally well. Catching had become something of a problem since Bob Clark had to sit out the entire month of June with a sore hand. Byrne bought Charlie Reynolds from Kansas City to team with the veteran Doc Bushong. Joe Visner was struggling at catcher, and his hitting had fallen off as well. Bob Caruthers pitched magnificently through June while Bill Terry and Tom Lovett worked steadily. Mickey Hughes' arm was very bad, and he was lost to the team until August. Rainy weather had hurt Byrne's profits during the June homestand, but he took heart as his Bridegrooms began their long road trip with two victories against Philadelphia. As they entrained for St. Louis, the Bridegrooms seemed to be in fairly good condition to encounter the champion Browns. On July 1, they trailed by 4 1/2 games but probably thought that they had a pitching advantage since both Icebox Chamberlain and Nat Hudson suffered from sore arms.

Unknown to Brooklyn and to Charlie Comiskey, Browns' third baseman Arlie Latham had been nursing grievances against Chris Von der Ahe since the spring. His actions in the Brooklyn-St. Louis games of July 3-4 would cause a mild explosion on the St. Louis team.

In the National League, Albert G. Spalding had greatly angered Brotherhood President John Montgomery Ward by refusing to meet with him and other player representatives in Chicago on June 25. *The New York Clipper* (6 July 1889) reported that Ward and Spalding had met on June 24, the first day that the Giants played Chicago on their western trip. Spalding listened to Ward's presentation of players' concerns about classification/salary limitation and then informed him that these issues were not of enough importance to require the immediate attention of

National League owners. Spalding led the owners in insisting that player grievances should be dealt with in the November, 1889 National League meetings and not before. Ward, of course, vigorously disagreed with Spalding and began considering how the Brotherhood could retaliate effectively. One of his first problems was how to prevent a players' strike on July 4, which some players were advocating. Giants' *Sporting Life* correspondent William Ingraham Harris condemned Spalding's action as ill-advised. Such cavalier deportment typified Spalding's treatment of players, but Harris thought that the players were entitled to a hearing on the classification/salary limitation issue during the summer (*S.L.*, 3 July 1889).

The millionaire Spalding could casually treat players with little respect since he did not depend on a baseball team for his livelihood. His sporting goods business had made him financially independent by 1889. First selling sporting goods in March, 1876, A. G. Spalding & Bros. Company gained additional capital from Spalding's brother-in-law William T. Brown in 1878 and started manufacturing as well. Despite a destructive fire in the original factory, by 1889, Spalding Bros. sold approximately $1 million of sporting goods and employed five hundred people (*S.L.*, 17 April 1889). However, other owners like John B.Day could ill afford to alienate the players, yet they cooperated with Spalding in resisting player requests for a conference until the fall National League meeting.

During July, the St. Louis team would begin to unravel, and Brooklyn-St. Louis relations worsened as Charlie Comiskey initiated a personal vendetta against Brooklyn President Charles H. Byrne. In the National League, John Montgomery Ward and other player representatives started organizing financial support for a new league, composed of revolting National League players. Both major leagues teetered as players, managers, and owners struggled to deal with the normal stress of close pennant races plus the widening conflict between players and owners. Issues of gambling by players and owners' autocratic abuse of players became prime topics of discussion as the 1889 season heated up considerably.

Chapter Seven
The Context of Revolt

Before discussing the relations between baseball owners and players during July, when National League players decided to seek financial backing for their own league, a socio-economic context provides a worthwhile perspective for the developing conflict.

While no official connection existed between the National League players' Brotherhood and other labor organizations, the players had been organizing during a time of unprecedented labor agitation and organization in the United States. Many players came from working class backgrounds and/or worked in states and cities where American workers, skilled and unskilled, were agitating for their basic economic rights within the restructured post-Civil War industrial-corporate economic system (Gordon, Edwards, and Reich 121).

Regarding professional baseball players' status in 1889, one should keep in mind that they were not truly members of the working class, in a historical or academic sense, since they were not wage earners. Baseball players, in both the National League and American Association, were paid salaries. A few of the best players earned $5,000 in 1889 while approximately a score of National Leaguers made $3,000 or more [See The Appendix]. It is difficult to make straight dollar comparisons between then and now, but one can understand how well some players were paid by considering that 1890 mechanical engineers and Harvard professors earned between $3,000 and $5,000. By virtue of the 1888 National League classification system, the lowest paid League players still made $1,500 in 1889.

Connie Mack was one of the lesser lights as catcher for the Washington Senators but earned $2750. Attesting to low living costs, he recalled in his dotage that "you could get a suit of clothes for ten dollars and a good dinner at a hotel for fifty cents" (Mack 22). Even if tight-fisted owners required players to contribute fifty cents for meals on the road, twice that amount provided room and board for a day. Rarely did players experience the humiliation which the Louisville team endured in late June,

1889. Louisville owner Mordecai H. Davidson only paid railroad fares and hotel bills while his team toured six of the American Association's eight cities during June. By the time the poorly-paid Colonels reached Kansas City and St. Louis, most had to borrow money to defray personal expenses and "some of them got back...with beards of several days growth because they were not able to pay the barber for shaves" (*Herald,* 4 July 1889).

That same year, 1889, common laborers in the United States earned, on the average, $1.39 per day, average manufacturing wages were $1.50 per day, and unskilled factory workers made $1.21 per day (Montgomery 69). At the Cambria Steel Company in Johnstown, Pennsylvania, near John Montgomery Ward's home area, first class blast furnace laborers in 1890 worked twelve hours a day for $1 while blast furnace cinder men earned $1.20. In the same plant, Bessemer, open-hearth, and blooming-mill laborers worked ten-hour days, making $1.10, $1.20, and $1.30 respectively (Brody 44). These were typical daily wages for unskilled steel workers nation-wide in 1890 (Brody 43). Assuming that such unskilled factory workers could be employed for a full year and work the "normal" six-day, ten-hour per day week, (Rodgers 106) which is a false assumption, the most that they could earn in a year was $380.

On that maximum pittance, they struggled to adequately house and feed themselves and their families. Skilled urban workers, such as carpenters, could earn $680 annually, enabling them to afford a four-room house. In 1886, the average wage for a skilled mechanic had been $2.50 per day (McNeill 578). The difference between a comfortable and a squalid existence was seemingly small, but those who lived in 1889 knew it as a chasm. Unskilled workers survived on $6.50 food expenditure per month, but they neither lived well nor long. Life was extremely hard for thousands of Americans, and even the lowest paid baseball players were well-remunerated compared to most of their fellows. Since many of the players came from working class backgrounds, they were well-aware of this fact.

Michael Joseph "King" Kelly had directly experienced the unrelenting toil of factory work by 1878 and quite happily chose to pursue baseball as a career. Orphaned relatively young and playing professional baseball by age fifteen in 1873, Kelly resolved to learn a trade at nineteen and worked in a Paterson, New Jersey silk weaving factory during the winter of 1876-77. The discipline required was too great for Kelly. He returned to baseball with the Columbus, Ohio Buckeyes in 1877 and then landed with

John Montgomery Ward—This famous photograph shows Ward in his 1887 Giants' uniform. During 1889, Ward stole 62 bases. Photo credit National Baseball Library, Cooperstown, N.Y.

the Cincinnati National League team in 1878 (Kelly *passim*). Perhaps Kelly never intended to seriously pursue a trade in the Paterson silk industry, but the opportunity was certainly available to him.

With one of every four silk workers under sixteen years of age, Kelly may have realized that wages would be kept low and opted for the higher, albeit temporarily declining, (Seymour 106) salary that baseball offered even then. He may also have heard talk of the unprecedented general strike that eventually occurred among ribbon weavers in Paterson during the summer of 1877. Women textile workers struck successfully in 1878 (Gutman 239-46). An orphaned son of the working class, Mike Kelly possessed the highly specialized skills to choose baseball over silk factory work, and he did so. He became a hero for urban workers, skilled and unskilled, in every city that he played by 1889.

Strict economic designations concerning baseball players' status are further qualified, however, by considering the economic relationships within the game itself. Professional baseball players thought of themselves as workers, and they and team owners had arrived at that conclusion as early as the late 1860's. By that time, professional baseball was separating into three distinct, highly recognizable classes: directors (owners), managers who were recruited from among players and hired by owners, and the player-workers (Goldstein 100). Baseball had become professionalized and fragmented into economic classes even before the first professional league was formed in the 1870s.

John Montgomery Ward, eventual President of the Brotherhood of Professional Baseball Players from its inception in October, 1885, (*Players' National League Guide* 7) was born in Bellefonte, Pennsylvania in 1860 and began attending nearby Penn State College in 1873, when only 13. While at Penn State, where he impressively played baseball, the Knights of Labor consolidated its original Philadelphia organization and spread to other parts of the East (Grob 35). During the same period, major conflicts over deep, punitive wage cuts flared between coal diggers and coal companies in Johnstown and around Blossburg. Both sites were approximately sixty crow miles from Penn State. The 1870's depression temporarily halted labor organization in both areas (Gutman 321-43).

In spring, 1877, perhaps in response to the deepening 1870's depression and having become an orphan in 1874, Ward left Penn State and struck out on his own. He had dreamed of travel and first tried his hand as a traveling salesman for a nursery. The territory of Northwest

Pennsylvania was rocky ground, and Ward gave it up after two weeks. Hitching a ride in the caboose of a freight train, Ward ended up in Renovo, near his hometown. There he began his career as a professional baseball player for ten dollars a month and board (Penn State University Archives, Bellefonte *Centre Democrat*, 5 October 1961; Ward, "Notes" 212-13).

Intending to play baseball only until he could find other means of support, Ward bounced among six minor league teams before signing with the National League's Providence Grays in July, 1878. During his minor league tenure, he was not paid at times and had to work ten-hour days as a steam engine attendant to exist through the 1877-78 winter (Ward, "Notes" 214-15). Determined to be a "first-class" player, the plucky young Ward became the League's winningest pitcher in 1879 and led his team to the National League pennant.

By the time that he had begun his major league career in 1878, The Knights of Labor had grown enough, even during the trying depression years, that they had held their first General Assembly in Reading, Pennsylvania. In the policy statements which the Knights adopted in January, 1878, the explicit theme throughout was the demand for respect for all working class people, the demand to be treated like human beings (Grob 35-38; Powderly, 240, 243-45, 248).

Through the early years of the 1880s, the Knights' leader, Terence V. Powderly, stressed the importance of establishing producer industrial cooperatives and regarded strikes as an essentially ineffective tool for achieving organized labor's goals (Powderly 5, 453, 460, 463, 507; Ware 379; Grob 37, 48). Nonetheless, hundreds of strikes broke out across the United States in the mid-1880s as labor militancy increased (Grob 36; Gordon, Edwards, and Reich 121).

In 1883, Ward was sold to the New York National League team. By that year, baseball owners were tightening their grip on players by extending the reserve system, and professional players in the two major leagues began to grow concerned over their diminishing freedom (Seymour 142-47). John Ward became interested enough in baseball's legal issues that, after coming to New York, he decided to resume his education at Columbia College. He quickly received a law degree in 1885 and a prize in political science in 1886 (Voigt 156; Ward, "Notes" 220; *Clipper*, 25 August 1888 for a slight variation).

When Ward came to New York City, the garment workers were initiating a series of successful strikes in the clothing and textile industries

(Montgomery 121). On a national level, "in the winter of 1885 and spring of 1886, the Order [of the Knights of Labor] grew with unprecedented rapidity. Never in the history of the world were the workingmen everywhere of all trades and callings, so aroused to the needs of organization" (McNeill 423). As the eight-hour movement of 1884-86 attracted the immediate allegiance of thousands, (Grob 36) not coincidentally then, but as part of the burgeoning labor movement in the United States, nine players on the New York Giants organized the Brotherhood of Professional Baseball Players on October 22, 1885 with John Montgomery Ward as their President. In the following baseball season, while the Knights of Labor membership swelled from over 100,000 to over 700,000, (Powderly 641) over 100 National League players joined their new organization (*Players' National League Guide* 7-8).

Armed with his law degree, Ward was a natural choice to lead the players. Another Giants' star, Tim Keefe, became the Brotherhood's Secretary. As a resident of Massachusetts, Keefe had been exposed to the increasingly militant labor movement. Many Massachusetts textile workers joined the Knights during the mid-1880s, organizing largely unsuccessful strikes in the process (Montgomery 159).

Despite the fact that local and district Knights' assemblies often ignored him, Terence V. Powderly continued to oppose strikes as a primary labor tactic. By 1886, the Knights' overall goal of organizing all workers, regardless of skill, race, or sex, caused increased friction among skilled trade union organizers within the Knights of Labor and its national leadership (Grob 110; Powderly, 640). While the American Federation of Labor, organized on behalf of skilled trades in opposition to the Knights at the end of 1886, eventually publicly supported the Players' League, Powderly ignored it as best he could (Grob 77). Possibly influenced by organized labor's disarray, Ward kept the Brotherhood clear of both houses of labor (Lowenfish and Lupien 30).

Before assessing Ward's dominant role in National League players' actions, a brief look at the Brotherhood's stated goals provides valuable insight. The preamble that the New York players drew up in October, 1885, while brief, reaffirmed the old labor ideal of workers' unity.

We, the undersigned, professional baseball players, recognizing the importance of united effort and impressed with its necessity in our behalf, do form ourselves this day into an organization to be known as the 'Brotherhood of

Professional Baseball Players.' The objects we seek to accomplish are:
>   To protect and benefit ourselves collectively and individually.
>   To promote a high standard of professional conduct.
>   To foster and encourage the interests of the game of Baseball. (*Players'*
> *National League Guide* 7; See Dworkin 5-7 for a comparison with why other
> workers join unions)

The emphasis on professional conduct was intended as a response to owners' growing concern about players' "discipline." Elsewhere, Ward urged fellow players to "keep away from saloons" (Ward 45). He and other temperate individuals associated with professional baseball were well aware that, in the eyes of many, "the whole tone of the game was smelly" (Stagg 105). For that reason, Ward, as Brotherhood President, assured the public that most players were not improvident and dissipated (Ward, "Notes" 216).

Protection for players' rights was at the core of the Giants' players organizational urge in October, 1885, and the reserve clause was probably the initial primary concern. Writing in *The New York Clipper* in February, 1885, Ward demonstrated the practical value of his legal education by questioning the legality of the reserve clause, calling it "an ex post facto law...depending for its binding force upon the players solely on its intimidating effect" (*Clipper*, 14 February 1885). He asserted that the clause did not obligate players legally or morally, though he recognized its protective nature for owners. Two years later, Ward explained further that the original reserve agreement among National League teams made in September, 1879 was made without regard to the fact that no such terms had been included in the 1879 player contracts. From that Ward concluded that the reserve rule was an ex post facto measure (Ward, "Chattel" 310).

The next year, 1886, Ward expanded and qualified his views on the reserve system in an article written for *Lippincott's*. While he thought that the reserve clause in players' contracts should be modified to allow for "gradual change," essentially, he commended it while condemning its abuses in relation to the sale of players. Its primary benefit was that it established professional baseball on "a permanent business arrangement." Capital could safely be "invested in baseball stock without the possibility of seeing it rendered valueless at the end of six months by the defections of a number of the best players" (Ward, "Notes" 215-16). With this combined emphasis on and respect for capital and players' concerns, Ward demonstrated an early desire to balance players' and owners' interests.

This remained a major theme throughout his career (Lowenfish 69).

Ward wrote for *Lippincott's* again in August, 1887. By then, his antagonism toward the reserve system, and its enhancement through the 1883 National Agreement, had increased primarily because of the "present odious system of buying and selling players" (Ward, "Chattel" 315; See Bass, 64-5 for another view; See Ward, *Clipper 1891 Annual* 21 for the special repugnance of player sales). Using moral condemnation effectively, Ward compared players' status under the reserve system and resulting player sales to America's most recent moral dilemma—slavery itself. "There is now no escape for the player....Like a fugitive slave law, the reserve-rule denies him a harbor or a livelihood, and carries him back, bound and shackled, to the club from which he attempted to escape....He goes where he is sent, takes what is given him, and thanks the Lord for life" (Ward, "Chattel" 312, 317). Grudgingly admitting that players had originally accepted reservation because it pragmatically stabilized professional baseball, Ward still indignantly called the reserve rule "a species of serfdom which gave one set of men a life-estate in the labor of another,...no attempt has ever been made to defend it on the grounds of abstract rights" (Ward, "Chattel" 313).

Then Ward pronounced the reserve rule as essentially evil because it was being used "for the manipulation of a traffic in players, a sort of speculation in live stock, by which they are bought, sold, and transferred like so many sheep" (Ward, "Chattel" 313). Noting the strong undercurrent of discontent among players during the 1886-87 off-season, Ward concentrated on the sale of players, particularly criticizing Albert G. Spalding's lucrative sale of King Kelly. Holding that player sales as then arranged denied players money rightfully owed them, Ward found a basic remedy for baseball's player-owner problems. If the reserve/sales system meant basic slavery for players and monopolistic control by the two major leagues, then, Ward asserted, the sound business principles of free enterprise and competition were far superior (Ward, "Chattel" 314-16, 318-19; Bass 65).

At first responding in a compromising manner, National League owners in November, 1887 temporarily agreed to lift salary limits, thereby establishing "a more equitable form of agreement between the clubs and players" in Ward's view (Ward 32). Partially assuaged, Ward cautiously restated some positive elements of the reserve clause in his 1888 book, the year before the National League players' revolt.

To this rule [the reserve clause], more than any other thing, does baseball as a business owe its present substantial standing. By preserving the strength of a team from year to year, it places the business of baseball on a permanent basis and thus offers security to the investment of capital....[managers] are ever ready to benefit themselves, regardless of the cost to an associate club. (Ward 30)

Albert Goodwill Spalding could not have said it better, but, later in 1888, Ward was still concerned about player sales' negative effect on the reserve system:

The reserve rule was made that a club might *retain* its players, not that it might *sell* them. It never contemplated the creation of such a right, and its prostitution to such a vile purpose...has served to bring the rule itself into disrepute....a dishonor to our national sport." (Ward "National Game" 446)

However, in the spring of 1888, the diplomatic Ward was willing to commend some aspects of the reserve rule, with one clear qualification that echoed workers' sentiments from the 1870s on:

The reserve rule itself is a usurpation of the players' rights, but it is, perhaps, made necessary by the peculiar nature of the baseball business, and the player is indirectly compensated by the improved standing of the game....

As long as a player continued valuable he had little difficulty, but when, for any reason, his period of usefulness to a club had passed, he was likely to find, by sad experience, that baseball laws were not construed for his protection;...it is not to be wondered at that he turned to combination as a means of protection. (Ward 31-2)

Finally, in explaining the need for a players' organization, Ward extended the olive branch to the owners at the same time that he asserted the player-workers basic rights. "There was no spirit of antagonism to the capitalists of the game, except in so far as the latter might at any time attempt to disregard the rights of any member [of the Brotherhood]" (Ward 32). Freely admitting the essentially conservative nature of the original Brotherhood goals, Ward did not challenge the National League owners until they imposed the harsh salary-limit, classification system in direct contradiction to their agreement with the Brotherhood representatives in November, 1887 (*Players' National League Guide* 4). Then, he challenged with vengeance.

Basically, Ward, most of the Brotherhood players, and most of the unorganized Association players were conscious or unconscious adherents

Tim Keefe—Even with his late start in 1889, Keefe trailed only John Clarkson in wins and strikeouts. He was among the top five National League pitchers in winning percentage, ERA, and games pitched. Photo credit National Baseball Library, Cooperstown, N.Y.

to what Eric Foner and other labor historians refer to as the free labor ideology of the late nineteenth century United States. These ideals, which most American workingmen clung to, were that individual liberty depended on property ownership, that wage labor was but a stepping stone to true economic independence, that worker-employer relations were not inherently antagonistic, that capitalists and workingmen could cooperate to avoid class conflict, and that workers could achieve economic autonomy through worker-owned cooperatives (Foner 477-78).

Some historians emphasize that while the Knights of Labor revived the free labor ideals during the 1880s, they did so more in the guise of a protest ideal that strongly criticized capitalism and deemphasized the concepts of class harmony and individual social mobility (Foner 514-15). John Montgomery Ward opted for a modified protest ideal since he also eventually sought to achieve the old goal of cooperation between labor (players) and capital (owners), albeit with different owners.

Another factor in Ward's advocacy of the Brotherhood's initial policies and eventual goals was the effect that the May 4, 1886 Haymarket bombing had on the nation's psyche. Even though Terence V. Powderly became a bitter opponent of clemency for the eight Anarchists accused of the bombing, that violent act at a large Chicago workers' demonstration "drove the fear of labor militancy deep into the nation's mentality..." (Avrich 348-50, 401, 429). Faced with the public's antipathy toward labor militancy of any kind and the conflict within organized labor itself, Ward soundly decided to keep the newly forming players' Brotherhood aloof from the Knights or the American Federation of Labor.

Shortly after Haymarket, in mid-May, 1886, when Ward and like-minded Giants players began recruiting other National League teams for the Brotherhood, only three players from the Chicago team joined. Mike Kelly and Jim McCormick, old chums from Paterson, chose to wait until later in the season (*Players' League Guide* 7). The significant lesson of Haymarket must have seemed clear for Ward and Keefe.

As will be described later, John Montgomery Ward urged players to eschew a strike in retaliation against Spalding's and other National League owners' autocratic policies. Instead, he and Brotherhood Secretary Tim Keefe led the players toward consideration of a basic profit-sharing arrangement with financial backers of their proposed new league. In doing so, Ward and the Brotherhood adopted tactics espoused by some Knights leaders such as F.H. Giddings.

Emphasizing the old working class goal of preventing the degradation of labor, Giddings urged profit-sharing cooperation with the capitalist system as a means of securing labor's basic rights (McNeill 522-28). By 1888, nine New England companies had initiated profit-sharing with their workers. Four were in Massachusetts, Tim Keefe's home state. Six new profit-sharing plans were introduced in New York and Pennsylvania after 1886, with Rogers, Peet Clothing Company in New York City probably providing Ward the most inspiration. Nothing could appeal more to the idealistic yet pragmatic Ward than the company spokesman's assertion that profit-sharing was a matter of justice and a practical business measure beneficial to workers and owners (*History of Cooperation In The United States* 82-9, 107-25, 130-32, 156-82).

That players' rights were at the heart of their revolt after June, 1889 was best expressed by Tim Keefe, although he reinterpreted original Brotherhood intentions a bit.

The formation of the Brotherhood of Baseball Players was inspired by the same causes that have doubtless been the corner-stone of other protective brotherhoods. ... the players found that they were being treated and used as so many money-making machines...a ball-player found that he had not even the rights that every laborer in the land is entitled to. Is it to be wondered at that the men rebelled at the thought of being 'goods and chattels' and that some means of self-protection were looked for? (*The Universal Baseball Guide* 38)

In late June, 1889, when National League owners, led by Albert Spalding, refused to meet with Brotherhood representatives to discuss players' grievances until the end of the season, Keefe recalled that "this was the crowning point to the arrogant despotism of these dictators, and the players revolted at this contemptuous disregard of their rights as men and laborers" (See Dworkin 5-7 for a summary of why workers join unions).

Rights as men and laborers. As Tim Keefe said, that was the crux by July, 1889. In the political arena, Henry George had waged a New York City mayoral campaign in the fall of 1886 on behalf of organized labor and won an astounding 31% of the vote. Although defeated, George's candidacy represented labor's "single most effective political initiative" in the city's history. (Hammack 174) His eloquent yet down-to-earth espousal of basic working class rights inspired New York City's heterogeneous working class as never before (Hammack 99-100, 112-15, 172-76, 318). Now, in the summer of 1889, the highly skilled professional baseball player-workers were claiming their rights as men and workers. Many of them were from the working class, and urban workers, skilled and unskilled, in the eastern United States cheered them in saloons, as telegraph reports were posted, (Betts, *Sporting Heritage* 163) or in the ballparks, if they were taking a break or momentarily free from their unrelenting, mind-dulling toil. As workers, they understood the players' complaints concerning salary restrictions and blacklisting (Dworkin 11), but most of them probably would have favored a strike.

Amid the social and economic turmoil of the late 1880s, one subtle and probably unnoticed benefit for skilled and unskilled workers and middle class Americans was the nation-wide concern over the hectic pace of life (Barth 153). The need for more leisure time, a slower pace, was espoused by many, particularly the clergy, as early as the 1870s. Ministerial support for leisure activity was essential, as a Boston editor ruefully noted by describing the grim days when a young New England man "who was fond of rowing or riding, or any other vigorous sport, was considered to be on the high road to ruin" (quoted in Hardy 6). By the 1870s, however, New England's men of the cloth would have firmly agreed with the New Orleans editor who asserted that "no parent will object to his son taking up bat and ball in preference to the dice, the cards or the glass" (quoted in Somers, *The Rise of Sports* 117). Even foreign observers commented on the American proclivity for overwork. The famous English sociologist, Herbert Spencer, while visiting the United States in 1883, warned Americans that they suffered from "excessive toil" (Rodgers 102-14). The New Jersey miner who, in 1881, saw the need to "enjoy the pleasures of the world" by working fewer hours would have firmly agreed (Rodgers 159).

Edward Cary, *New York Times* editorial writer, intelligently advanced baseball as a healthy, necessary leisure time diversion for all urban social classes and wrote in support of adequate, accessible grounds for the Giants during the early months of the 1889 season. Although not concerned only about workers, Cary had observed the growing militancy among urban workers, the large number of strikes in the '80s, and the unprecedented urban growth to that time. In promoting baseball's utility, Cary may have been heeding, not only the increased workers' demands for the eight-hour work day, but also their specific references to "the great uplifting influences of leisure" and their demands that the industrial-corporate system confer "sufficient leisure upon the masses for their development"

(McNeill 482, 486). Despite some concern over misuse of leisure, the average work-week for urban workers declined gradually during the latter nineteenth century (Hardy 54). With growing baseball attendance through the '80s (record setting in 1889), (Riess 196) one can assume that urban Americans were using more of their free time to watch baseball games. Thus, professional baseball player-workers were benefiting as their fellow urbanites began to acquire hard-won leisure time.

As many historians have noted, baseball was popular among all social classes well before the Civil War. After the war, amidst the Cincinnati labor movement of the 1870s, "a number of unions formed baseball teams as a means of promoting fun and camaraderie outside the workplace" (Ross 215). In Worcester, Massachusetts, workers' baseball games on holidays such as July 4 became common after 1870, and while city authorities objected to them playing baseball in the city park, they did not ban the activity. By the 1870's, baseball had become associated with Worcester workers' leisure activities (Rosenzweig 85, 129, 137). New York businesses and unions organized annual public picnics where sports events were featured, and, by the 1880s and 1890s, unions and other labor organizations sponsored baseball teams that played in local amateur leagues (Riess 82-83). Factories in St. Louis were sponsoring teams by the 1870s (Betts, *Sporting Heritage* 96). New Orleans firemen, telegraphers, typographers, railroad workers, factory hands, longshoremen, brewery workers, journalists, Black workers, young women, and federal and state employees organized teams throughout the 1870s and 80s while middle and working class social clubs made Sunday baseball a regular practice (Somers, *The Rise of Sports* 117-21).

Using these cities as urban examples, it appears obvious that baseball had become a popular participant sport for workers by the 1880s. Since most major league players came from working class origins in the 1880s (Riess 87), it becomes equally obvious that workers had been playing the game for some time (Seymour, *The People's Game* 215-20).

The question remains, with low pay and with long work hours, how could urban workers possibly attend many games other than on Saturday in the National League, or on Saturday and Sunday in the American Association? (Hardy, 185-87 for a slight qualification of Riess's findings) A partial answer can be found by ascertaining what other types of leisure activities urban workers could afford in the 1880s. The question of workers' available time, especially during the week, leads one into the realm of informed speculation. In other words, one can be wrong in a big way. (See Guttmann, *Spectators* 111-13 and Sullivan, "Faces," for contradictory conclusions about workers' attendance at baseball games. Sullivan used statistical evidence, but Voigt's cautionary note about baseball attendance/social class assessments is instructive, "Crowds" 102-103).

Again using Worcester as an example, after 1870, the saloon emerged as a major center of working-class social life because of slightly shorter workdays, greater regulation of public recreation, and some increase in workers' incomes (Rosenzweig 36). *Sporting Life's* Joe Pritchard witnessed the same development in St. Louis, and Jacob Riis' statistics for New York's Lower East Side confirm the importance of saloons for that city's workers. In Boston, church leaders and social reformers wrote, spoke and worked vigorously after the Civil War to combat the saloon's influence among workers. Nonetheless, by 1897, daily patronage of the Hub City's saloons nearly equaled half its population (Hardy 54-8).

Yet another reason for saloons' growth was that, by the 1880s, drinking at the workplace was becoming increasingly unacceptable to employers. Saloons came to replace the workplace as the proper social drinking environment. While kitchen grog shops had thrived in Worcester and other cities for a time after the Civil War, by the mid-1880s, urban licensing requirements gave a decided advantage to saloons. The old home-based drinking place had often been operated by married women. In the 1880s, "when leisure was removed from the home or its immediate vicinity, it became predominately a male privilege. While some women continued to patronize saloons, these public leisure spaces increasingly became male preserves....the male saloon became the mirror image of the male factory" (Rosenzweig 37, 43-5). During this decade of saloons' expanded importance, major league baseball was also attracting the attention of more urban males.

Most notably, Chris Von der Ahe effectively combined beer and baseball in St. Louis, profiting impressively throughout the 1880s. Some observant cranks took advantage of the combination, as St. Louis resident L. A. Paule recalled in the mid-twentieth century, by hanging around Vondy's saloon until game time and then sneaking into the grandstand through a side door without paying the twenty-five cent admission (Latham file, NBL). Of course, this happy conjoining of beer and baseball was available to few owners and cranks. Although the American

Association catered to working-class cranks by allowing the sale of alcoholic beverages at ballparks, most ballparks were not located near working class areas, where saloon's concentration was highest (Riess 70; Rosenzweig 51). However, most owners paid careful attention to proximity to urban transport when they built their ballparks, as Charles H. Byrne had in 1883, (Benson 57) as John B. Day did in June, 1889, and as Brotherhood financial backer Al Johnson would in the coming months (See also mass transit lines in relation to ballparks in New York and Chicago in Riess 215, 218). No matter what public transport did or did not avail, (Riess 70) Joe Pritchard reminded every reader that St. Louis saloons lured people away from the ballparks by providing telegraphic reports of games from other cities and a place to gamble on the results. Some urban dwellers, workers included, could enjoy their baseball vicariously without ever going to the ballpark (Somers, "The Leisure Revolution" 138). Doubtless, many of them did.

Saloons in working class areas did well. This is not to say that workers were the only drinkers in the United States. It is to say that "working class dominance of public drinking places" was widely observed and commented upon in late nineteenth century America and "produced a corresponding working-class predominance among those arrested for public drunkenness" (Rosenzweig 51). Obviously, if a poorly paid worker could afford to drink in a saloon, that same person could afford a relatively inexpensive visit to the ballpark. The American Association admission price was only twenty-five cents while the National League's was double that, and the Association also offered the timeless opiate of the masses-booze. So it can be assumed that workers could afford to attend baseball games, even during the weekday, if they could find the time. What would lure them to the ballpark? What was there that would be able to compete with the saloons' environment, which attracted so many of them?

First of all, it should be emphasized that many workers went to saloons for simple companionship, for socializing more than drinking. This said, let Amos Alonzo Stagg, who grew up in a family of eight children and whose father was a cobbler-general laborer, describe his experience from the 1870s in West Orange, New Jersey.

Our neighbors, native and Irish in the main, were as poor as we. They were hat-factory workers, petty craftsmen and laborers. The hat makers were well paid when they worked, but their work was irregular, and whatever they made beyond a bare living they spent at the corner saloons.

...In bad luck, men drowned their sorrows at the bar; in good luck, they celebrated it there. When too warm, they drank; when too cold, they drank. In high spirits, they let off steam at the saloon; when bored, they bought high spirits from the bartender.

...We got our drama at first hand and in the raw from the saloon, and the show was continuous....Beer was the drink of our street, drunk in the hope and expectation of getting drunk, and rarely disappointed. Carrying pails of beer from the saloon was as routine a chore for most of the boys I knew as carrying coal or cordwood. ... The woman in the next house but one to ours got drunk on a schedule of about every third day. In her cups, she scorned any antagonist of her own sex. Her husband had learned discretion, but the man who lived across the street would fight with her hand to hand in the middle of the dirt street. (Stagg 46-47)

Stagg's father, while not a teetotaler, drank temperately during the summer and never sent his children to a saloon for his occasional pint or quart of beer.

Contrary to Stagg's testimony, Boston's Committee of Fifty for the Investigation of the Liquor Problem determined in 1893 that saloons ministered to "nothing less than the satisfaction of the deeper thirst for fellowship and recreation" (Hardy 58). Weary workers enjoyed popular music, baseball scores and stories, pool, and gossip with their beer (*Ibid.*). Story telling and jokes relieved the boredom and ferocity of their work. Favorite targets for their humor were hypocritical temperance advocates, dishonest police, corrupt politicians, clergy, and pompous judges— authority figures all (Rosenzweig 53-4). If a team was coming into a city that was disliked because of its manager and/or owner, and/or if a known enmity existed between an opposing manager and an umpire, it is not too difficult to imagine workers in bars arranging their workweek so that they could attend as many games as possible. What entertainment! It could provide material for weeks and well into the cold winter months (See Hardy 58, for indications of more proper allurements).

Even if the opposition was uninteresting, umpire-baiting was always available for venting pent-up frustrations, (Betts, *Sporting Heritage* 222) and many players and managers could be counted upon to lead the way in this endeavor. John J. McGraw remembered that fans in his day were as rough as the players and that crowds often encouraged umpire-baiting: "An attack on the umpire often was a genuine treat for them" (McGraw 82). Boston cranks in the late 80s sometimes chorused to their heroes: "Hit him and I will pay your fine!" (quoted in Hardy 8).

Popular songs in saloons often addressed the subjects of noble,

organized workers and their ongoing struggle with wealthy employers
(Rosenzweig 55). As the 1889 season provided more evidence of the
conflict between players and owners, working-class cranks could identify
more meaningfully with the players. In New York, for example, they
could shout with greater vigor, "We Are The People," as they cheered on
Ward and the Giants. Since so many workers played baseball themselves,
they also went to ballparks to enjoy the game and to watch their own kind,
such as Mike Kelly, Buck Ewing, Arlie Latham, Darby O'Brien, and
Charlie Comiskey perform skillfully before cheering thousands (Ward,
"National Game" 450). What could be more ennobling for those who often
experienced humiliation, physical suffering or maiming at the workplace,
or successive defeats in their often violent strikes? Vicarious glory, indeed
(See Hardy 17, 192-94, 200 for the association theme). But how could
they find the time to get to the ballpark, other than on weekends?

For one thing, workers' employment in the 1880s, as at many times in
history, was cyclical and irregular, even for skilled workers (Barth 153;
Riess 70; Stagg 45). Walter Wyckoff said in 1892 that spring came "like
the heralding of peace and plenty after war" because work was so plentiful
(quoted in Montgomery 63). Skilled workers often took unskilled jobs
when they were unemployed. Because of the heavy labor associated with
many unskilled jobs, unskilled laborers were irregularly employed by
choice. They simply could not work very many consecutive ten or twelve
hour days and maintain their physical or mental health. So "they took their
own holidays, be they religious festivals or 'Saint Monday', which
foremen punished with dismissal, sometimes simply ignored"
(Montgomery 90). During such time, or when they were temporarily
unemployed or feigning illness, depending on the baseball attraction,
workers could and did go to the ballpark (Ward, "National Game" 450;
Barth 153). More often, they probably went to the saloon, where, as Jack
London once said, "men talked with great voices, laughed great laughs,
and there was an atmosphere of greatness" (Montgomery 90).

If baseball could offer a clear atmosphere of greatness, entertainment,
and conviviality, such as when players like Mike Kelly or Pete Browning
were in town, they who drank steadily and played greatly, workers
attended games in large numbers and not just on weekends. Also,
ballparks offered a welcome change of affordable scenery to workers who
spent so much of their leisure time on what Wallace Stegner once called
workingmen's streets, "mean and cheap, crammed with all the cheap

stores a workingman could patronize and all the cheap amusements a workingman could afford and all the cheap opiates to make a workingman forget who he was and how he created all the wealth in the world for others to enjoy. A sad, gray, unlovely street—but such a street as men could march up thirty abreast" (Stegner, *Joe Hill* 109). These same avenues could lead workers away from valid violent demonstrations and to ballparks (Hardy 14, 17, 198-99). Otherwise, they were often satisfied in saloons where they gambled on the posted reports.

Wherever they enjoyed the game, from July, 1889 on, baseball in both the National League and American Association attracted their attention as it never had before. The baseball player-workers, most of them from the working class, were stirring as they never had before. For a brief moment, they were the people.

Chapter Eight
Players Plan their Own League

July promised to be a warm month in both leagues if only because six teams were competing fiercely for the pennants. At the outset, Boston, the surprising Cleveland Spiders (often referred to as the Infants by the *Times*), and the Giants held the top three spots in the National League while St. Louis, Brooklyn, and the hard hitting and drinking Philadelphia Athletics headed the American Association. Giants' hitters were led by Roger Connor, .342; Buck Ewing, .341; George Gore, .316; and Jim O'Rourke, .307. Mike Tiernan had battled illness but still hit .281, while Ward and second baseman Danny Richardson contributed respectable .268 and .271 averages. Third baseman Arthur Whitney batted a woeful .198, but he was highly valued for his fielding. Boston's Dan Brouthers dominated the Beaneaters' hitting with a league-leading .395 average. King Kelly and Hardie Richardson hit respectably at .287 and .277, but Billy Nash, Dick Johnston, Charlie Ganzel, and Charlie Bennett were all below .230. Joe Quinn was hitting .271 at the outset of July but would miss numerous games because of illness. Boston's pitching also suffered as John Clarkson had become their only dependable starter.

The St. Louis and Brooklyn hitters were more evenly matched. Commy, Tom McCarthy, Jocko Milligan, and Tip O'Neill all hit above .310 with O'Neill's .338 leading all Browns. The rest of the team hit in the .250 range. Tom Burns led Bridegroom batters at .322 as Dave Foutz, .299; Darby O'Brien, .288; and Hub Collins, .264 provided steady support. The others were in the mid-.200s except for the weak hitting catchers, Doc Bushong and Bob Clark. Brooklyn seemed to have a pitching advantage even though St. Louis had been strengthened by Jack Stivetts.

The Giants were in a good position in the National League because they possessed three solid starters, and they led the league in hitting. The Browns and the Bridegrooms were closely matched, as St. Louis hitting balanced Brooklyn pitching. If either team claimed an advantage, it appeared to be the Browns since their two catchers were superior to Brooklyn's. The Bridegroom's Bob Clark had torn two fingers on his

86

The 1889 New York Giants—National League Champions. Left to right: Top row—George Gore, Elmer Foster, Mike Slattery, Buck Ewing (Captain), Big Bill Brown, Bill George, Gil Hatfield, Jim O'Rourke, Mike Tiernan, Ed Crane. Bottom row—Danny Richardson, Ledell Titcomb, Roger Connor, Mickey Welch, Jim Mutrie (Manager), Art Whitney, Tim Keefe, Pat Murphy, John Ward. Missing—Hank O'Day since the photo was taken after the 1888 regular season. By mid-May, 1889 Foster was released for poor hitting, and Titcomb, ill all spring, was released before the end of the month. Sore-armed Bill George was released at the end of June. Photo credit National Baseball Library, Cooperstown, N.Y.

throwing hand on June 26 and would miss much of July.

While the Bridegrooms journeyed from Philadelphia to St. Louis, Commy's Browns completed a three game sweep of the hapless Louisville Colonels, with rookie pitcher Stivetts getting one of the wins. The small crowds for the Louisville series, while predictable, still made Von der Ahe fume. Such paltry attendance did not even pay for the money guaranteed to visiting teams. A certain Frank Hotchkiss of St. Louis wrote *Sporting Life* (10 July 1889) to give some reasons for the public's discontent with Von der Ahe. Hotchkiss said that the Browns' owner had alienated St. Louis cranks by selling five popular, star players (Caruthers, Foutz, Bushong, Welch, and Gleason) after 1887 and then raising the admission price to fifty cents for 1888. Hotchkiss righteously proclaimed that even when the price was reduced he refused to go back to Sportsman's Park. For one thing, the grandstand had been allowed to deteriorate badly and all the beer drinking and smoking provided a distinctly unappealing environment. Von der Ahe condescendingly replied to Hotchkiss (*S.L.*, 17 July 1889) by citing numerous improvements made to Sportsman's Park, including free seat cushions. The stout owner also averred that he had not made much money in baseball, only "some."

Sporting Life's Joe Pritchard noted another factor in low St. Louis attendance when he pointed out that many cranks had become enamored of checking the bulletin boards at "the 1,001 saloons and pool rooms" in the city rather than going to the ballpark. Pritchard urged that bulletin boards be abolished in St. Louis, although he must have been aware that their prominence testified to the close relationship between gambling and baseball (*S.L.*, 10 July 1889). Gambling had become a major element in the national game, and cranks found saloons and pool rooms friendly environments for placing bets on games throughout the country. The bulletin boards kept them informed of scores nationwide. Money was on the land in the 1880s, speculation was widespread, and many Americans were gamblers at heart. Baseball, money, and gambling had remained inextricably intermixed even after the National League had supposedly cleaned up the game after 1877. Players commonly bet on their own teams during the 1880s, and the practice, while criticized somewhat by baseball enthusiasts, was not made illegal by either major league.

The St. Louis public was not alone in its dissatisfaction with Chris Von der Ahe. Pitcher Nat Hudson was suspended for "insubordination" at the beginning of July. Von der Ahe did not lose greatly from this act since

Hudson had not pitched well all year. An even more typical example of Von der Ahe's capriciousness and downright nastiness was his denial of former Browns' outfielder Harry Lyons' $71.40 share of the team's 1888 pennant bonus. Lyons sued in a Philadelphia court, and the judge decided in his favor. Von der Ahe stubbornly refused to let the matter drop and had his attorney appeal the decision, saying that "he never promised to divide with the players the [$1,000] prize money offered by the American Association to the team winning the championship" (*Clipper*, 10 August 1889). Since Von der Ahe had already given shares to other players, his claim rang false. Some St. Louis players testified on behalf of Lyons, adding yet another antagonistic element to their relations with Von der Ahe just before the crucial series with Brooklyn.

Brooklyn won the first game 7-4 on July 3, with Bob Caruthers outpitching Silver King. Both teams fielded superbly as Pop Corkhill in centerfield, shortstops George Smith and Shorty Fuller, and second baseman Yank Robinson shone. The Browns actually outhit the Bridegrooms, but the *Times* reported that umpire John Gaffney seemed to favor Brooklyn in calling balls and strikes, thus forcing King to "split the center of the plate." Naturally, St. Louis cranks hissed Gaffney severely. On Independence Day, 6,000 people watched Chamberlain defeat Bill Terry 4-3 in the morning game. Brooklyn helped with five errors, and catcher Joe Visner made two costly wild throws while the Browns stole bases with ease. St. Louis once more fielded brilliantly. However, during the afternoon contest, Browns' third baseman Arlie Latham made three costly errors, Yank Robinson played stupidly, and Brooklyn hit King hard to win 12-10. Bob Caruthers had to relieve Tom Lovett in the sixth inning to hold off the Browns. Brooklyn was overjoyed to win two out of three, but they lost another catcher when Doc Bushong injured himself in the fourth inning of game three. Visner and the young Charlie Reynolds would have to do at catcher for most of July.

Brooklyn President Charles H. Byrne gloried in Brooklyn's road record through mid July, as the Bridegrooms played well enough behind Bob Caruthers and Bill Terry to win ten and lose only four. Pitcher Tom Lovett did not live up to pre-season expectations, but Pop Corkhill continued to sparkle in center field and Captain Darby O'Brien provided leadership as a hitter, fielder and runner. St. Louis attendance did not excite Byrne in the least. The Browns had gained $2,000 as their visitors' share of Memorial Day receipts in Brooklyn. That record-setting attendance could not be matched in St. Louis, but Byrne undoubtedly regarded the possibility of National League membership even more favorably when he received only $600 after the St. Louis July 4 doubleheader. Joe Pritchard praised St. Louis cranks for comprising the largest crowd in the country on July 4, but it did not translate into enough money for Byrne. Coupled with poor attendance in Philadelphia, Brooklyn's President had yet another financial reason to consider the National League's welcoming pose after July (Orem 397).

After the Brooklyn series, small crowds continued to plague the Browns' home stand. However, they left St. Louis on July 16 having won thirteen of nineteen games. This, despite Arlie Latham's poor hitting and continued bad fielding against Baltimore on July 15. Icebox Chamberlain cheered Commy by returning to his winning form, and the Browns' manager undoubtedly thrilled to the thrashings given Columbus, 14-0, and Baltimore, 25-5.

One of Commy's closest friends, Ted P. Sullivan, reminisced in 1903 that Commy "had a volcano fire burning inside him to make himself famous" (Sullivan 26). Thus driven, Commy competed fiercely and required his team to do the same. He "doted on speed...no pitcher could show enough of it...It was the same on the bases...He was a glutton for totals. Never was the score big enough...players were on the field to run up the score." The combative Commy acquired a reputation for being the hardest loser, and "he never could get it out of his head that Fate had picked out the other side for the doormat" (Axelson 44-5). Small wonder that by 1889, many teams regarded the Browns with a mixture of respect and hatred.

Despite the good homestand, trouble loomed for Commy. As with most great managers, Charlie Comiskey could forgive mechanical errors, but he could not abide shirking. By mid July, he was particularly troubled by the play of third baseman Arlie Latham. Something seemed amiss.

Few things seemed awry in New York as July brought a new home and renewed hope for another pennant to John B. Day's Giants. Unknown to Day and other National League owners, the real action in early July took place on the night of July 3, when League players voted on whether or not to strike the following day. Probably because of Ward's urging, players decided not to strike but instead to begin organizing a separate players' league for the 1890 season (Henry Chadwick Scrapbooks, Vol. II, clipping from *Cleveland Press*, 14 December 1889).

Jim Mutrie—Manager for the New York Giants from 1885 through 1891. Here, Mutrie poses after the 1888 Giants' championship year. Photo credit National Baseball Library, Cooperstown, N.Y.

Tim Keefe, Secretary of the Brotherhood and inspired by the new cause, defeated Pittsburgh on July 4th and again on the 6th. He undoubtedly expressed the feelings of most League players when he commented heatedly on July 5:

> Spalding and a few of the moneyed people may regret their step. I won't say what the Brotherhood will do, but we will move. Spalding says they can't call a meeting in Summer. Why, didn't they hold one at Asbury Park last Summer and consider a trifling matter? There is one thing certain, they won't classify as many men this Fall as they think. Why, this talk about Nick Young [National League President] classifying men is rot. The clubs send in the salaries, and he puts them in classes to correspond. (*Clipper*, 13 July 1889)

When Keefe later wrote his brief history of the Brotherhood, he would point to the National League owners' decision to refuse the players a hearing as "the crowning point to the arrogant despotism of these dictators, and the players revolted at this contemptuous disregard of their rights as men and laborers" (*The Universal Baseball Guide* 40-1).

Precisely because the League owners regarded them as laborers, and because the class conscious sentiments of the times assigned semi-autocratic powers to business owners of any kind, players were bound to be treated as underlings. Albert G. Spalding, leader of National League owners and one of the prime movers behind the classification system, stated the owners' viewpoints about the proper players' role years after the great conflict occurred:

> The inference drawn by the players...was that they ought to manage the game themselves... and reap a much larger portion of the proceeds of their skillful services.

> I did not believe then, nor do I now believe, that their contentions were based upon safe or sane business theory.... like every other form of business enterprise, Baseball depends for results upon two interdependent divisions, the one to have absolute control and direction of the system, and the other to engage —always under the executive branch—in the actual work of production" (Spalding 269-70).

Spalding the absolutist easily convinced other League owners to resist players' requests for a summer conference about classification/salary limitation, and the players called for a meeting in New York City on July 14 to lay plans for their revolt.

John B. Day heard rumors about the proposed players' revolt, but he busied himself with readying the New Polo Grounds at 155th and 8th for his Giants' return on July 8. Bad weather, wretched grounds, and low attendance at St. George had greatly depressed Day and Giants' Manager Jim Mutrie. Day had labored ceaselessly from June 24 to provide a playable surface and grandstand at the New Polo Grounds. About 400' by 460', the new playing field could accommodate 13,000 New York cranks. *The Clipper* initially reported that an elevated railroad station would be located at the main entrance, which must have been music to Day's ears (29 June 1889). The double-decker, oval shaped grandstand was built to seat 6,000 people, while free seats would be distributed along the left and right field lines.

In the past, Mutrie had gained notoriety for avidly promoting his team. He first used the term "giants" in reference to the New York team during an April, 1885 exhibition game and it stuck. The flamboyant manager's promotional style was recalled by his great pitcher, Mickey Welch, in a 1938 interview with New York sportswriter John Kieran:

> He [Mutrie] stirred up interest. He'd stand on the steps at the park with his high hat and fancy Prince Albert coat and as the crowd came in or went out he'd be shaking his cane and shoutin' 'We are The People!' He'd stand up in the hacks in other cities and shout it as we drove to the ball parks with the rooters for the other team hootin' at us. (Mutrie file, NBL)

On July 8, Mutrie satisfied himself by merely smiling at the 10,000 plus patrons as they streamed into the New Polo Grounds to watch the Giants battle Pittsburgh. Standing in the broiling sun and wiping sweat from his corrugated brow with a silk handkerchief, Mutrie could only regret that the new site did not hold more people. Originally, Day had hoped that Ex-President Grover Cleveland would speak and that his wife would formally open the grounds with President and Mrs. Benjamin Harrison, Governor David Bennett Hill, New York Mayor Hugh John Grant, and Brooklyn Mayor Alfred Clark Chapin also in attendance. However, such ambitious arrangements could not be made, and the New Polo Grounds opened with none but the numerous New York sporting public present.

Pittsburgh normally drew small crowds in New York, but cranks were so pleased with the Giants' surge and the Beaneaters' fall that many had to be denied admission when the gates closed. Undismayed, these worthies simply walked across the street to a beer garden and watched the game from the windows. Others clambered up the hill west of the ballpark where they were soon "bunched together as closely as checks in a dude's trousers" (*Times*, 9 July 1889). At least 5,000 people watched the game outside the park, many sipping beer or reclining under shade trees while those inside suffered under the sun in the uncompleted grandstand.

Despite these minor problems, Giants' owner John B. Day undoubtedly believed that his financial problems were largely solved now that he had the team back in New York City. With his minor league team in Jersey City losing money, Day had decided to sell his interest in that team during mid-June. He needed money for constructing the new ball park, and the big turnout on July 8 must have been a great relief.

John Montgomery Ward's return to the lineup also inspired those who predicted a first place finish for New York. But the man who attracted the most attention from cranks upon the Giants' return from the west was the great Buck Ewing. Thousands cheered his appearance on the new field, and Stock Exchange admirers presented him with an inscribed, gold watch when he came to bat in the first inning. Ewing blushed and bowed, Cannonball Crane pitched well, and Pittsburgh's nine errors helped the Giants win the inaugural game 7-5. Pittsburgh's numerous errors may have been partially caused by the hastily prepared playing surface. While the new infield had been sodded, the outfield was loam on ashes with macadamized stone rolled hard (*S.L.*, 10 July 1889).

The next day, Tim Keefe pitched a three-hit shutout, as the Giants waltzed 9-0. Day's great disappointment was the 1,800 paid attendance with double that number watching the game from the beer garden and "Dead Head Hill." *The Times* attributed the renewed low attendance to the uncompleted grandstand roof. "Sensible patrons...see no reason why they should risk being overcome by the heat or having their faces and necks tanned like oarsmen" (10 July 1889).

Henry Chadwick had warned before the opening that the New Polo Grounds would be very hot, since "Coogan's Bluff" on the west blocked cooling breezes. However, he praised Day for superhuman efforts in constructing the new park between June 24 and July 8, noting that a swamp had to be filled for right field to exist (*S.L.*, 10 July 1889). Despite the obvious drainage problem, Day also included steep embankments in center and right fields (Lowry 63). This construction decision would prove especially problematical during the fall rains.

But the Giants kept winning, *The Times* gloried in their championship form, and Cleveland Manager Tom Loftus predicted that New York would win the pennant over Boston since the latter had only one dependable pitcher. By Saturday, July 13, Day had stretched a canvas awning over the grandstand, and a veritable army of cranks swarmed into the new grounds to see Mickey Welch defeat Cleveland 11-6. After Keefe's 7-4 win over Cap Anson's Chicago team on July 15, New York trailed the slumping Bostonians by only one and one-half games.

Two other developments on July 14 would cause John B. Day yet more headaches. On that day in the Fifth Avenue Hotel, player representatives from the National League Brotherhood chapters met to decide a course of action based on the owners' decision not to meet with them until November. As John Montgomery Ward recalled a year later, "each representative was instructed to look up the feasibility of securing capital in his own city, and report at an early date" (*Players' National League Guide* 4). Their intention was to begin organizing on a new basis, that is, outside the National League and with different owners backing their various teams.

While the players deliberations were secret, the fact of their meeting was well known. Perhaps because Albert G. Spalding suspected that the players may be planning to organize a new league, as rumors purported, he chose July 14 as the day to have his detailed plan for baseball's reorganization to be published in *The New York Times*. Presumably, the publicity conscious Spalding also published his views in other major papers. Briefly, Spalding suggested dividing the minor baseball leagues into four classes according to salary limitations. Essentially, the minor leagues were to serve beneath the two major leagues as training areas. He further advocated a modification of the classification system for the National League and American Association. Players who led exemplary lives and had completed three years in either league could escape classification. Trying to present himself in a charitable, conciliatory light for the public, Spalding also urged that player sales provide 1/4 of the price for the player, making the process less odious.

The New York Clipper expressed the feelings of most baseball analysts when it described Spalding's plan as a baseball trust, with the Association and National League in clear control (20 July 1889). Minor leagues would obviously object to becoming "stocking ponds," and players wanted classification eliminated, not merely modified. *The Clipper* concluded that the sporting public would oppose League and Association

control since "public opinion is very decided against the theory of trusts."
Undoubtedly, the player representatives read Spalding's epistle in the
Times and were even less impressed. Enough Chicago players already had
grievances against Spalding, so his plan was one of the last straws in the
process that led to the players' decision to organize their own league, free
of Albert G. Spalding's obduracy (Levine 58).

Of course, had John B. Day known of the players' decision to revolt,
he would have been greatly worried. As it was, he could briefly rejoice
over the Giants' resurgence and Boston's corresponding collapse. The
Beaneaters slunk into Boston on July 7 after losing nine out of twelve to
Indianapolis, Chicago, and Cleveland. Shortstop Joe Quinn's illness
explained Boston's slump to some extent, but *Sporting Life* Boston
correspondent William D. Sullivan directed his attention to other issues.
Writing under the pseudonym of "Mugwump" for Sporting Life, he flatly
stated that the pennant so confidently predicted in June was no longer
certain since Boston needed another good pitcher, "less good times after
the games," and more ginger on the field. Then, Sullivan directed some
fire at the great one, King Kelly. Boston required a "captain who will be a
captain ... and up and hustling and coaching...instead of sitting on the
bench." Sullivan, also assistant city editor of *The Boston Globe,* used
strong journalistic sarcasm to demonstrate Kelly's incompetence as a team
leader (*S.L.,* 17 July 1889).

Although not intended to be a brief on behalf of National League
owners, Sully's diatribe against Kelly must have pleased Albert G.
Spalding. Kelly's example could be used to further strengthen his and
other owners' resolve for the classification system

Despite Boston's slump, Beaneater cranks demonstrated their undying
loyalty as 6,000 of them welcomed the team from the western debacle.
The team responded by winning four of the next five games even though
their infield became rutted from the heavy rains. Still, their lead over the
Giants had shrunk to 1 1/2 games by July 15. Boston papers rode King
Kelly hard for his indifferent leadership, but the journalistic storm on the
east coast over Kelly's drinking habits was mild compared to the news
emanating from St. Louis.

In mid July, *The St. Louis Post-Despatch* reported that Browns' owner
Chris Von der Ahe had reason to suspect pitcher Silver King and third
baseman Arlie Latham of "crooked" playing and that a detective had been
hired to investigate the situation. Even though the St. Louis cranks had

jeered him for his poor play during the July 4 afternoon game, Latham predictably laughed at the charges, citing his illness during July and King's bad arm. According to the irrepressible Latham, Commy had wanted him to play even though he was ill (S.N., 20 July 1889). *The New York Times* indicated that Von der Ahe's investigation was caused by "letters said to have been received from Omaha and Kansas City with regard to peculiar bets offered against the Browns on days when King was in the box and when Latham was doing some of the bad playing which he has exhibited on a number of recent occasions" (19 July 1889). With the *Times* clearly defining the national, inter-city character of baseball gambling, Arlie Latham's laughter would appear to ring a bit hollow. However, Latham had some allies during July, foremost among them *Sporting Life* editor Francis C. Richter.

Richter denounced the *Post-Despatch* for giving credence to the Latham-King story but praised Von der Ahe for investigating the "ignorant" charges. So certain was Richter that the charges were unfounded, that he urged Latham and King to institute libel suits against the *Post-Despatch*. Often a defender of players' interests and one who would avidly support the future players' revolt against the owners, Richter offered only his personal assurance of Arlie Latham's honesty as a rationale for his defense of Latham and King. Another *Sporting Life* correspondent, Oliver Perry Caylor, an articulate baseball reporter-promoter-owner from Cincinnati, chose to draw attention to Browns' owner Chris Von der Ahe by noting his notorious unpopularity with the respectable classes of people. The general tenor of *Sporting Life's* reporting on the Latham-King incident asserted that the St. Louis players had been falsely accused, since more money would have been necessary for Latham or King to risk their careers by deliberately "throwing" games. Second baseman Yank Robinson had also attracted suspicion, and all three were first appraised of the charges in Cincinnati on July 18. Heated denials naturally followed.

St. Louis *Sporting Life* correspondent Joe Pritchard undoubtedly strengthened Richter in his support of Latham and King, referring to the ongoing rumors caused by the troubled St. Louis-Kansas City series during early May. Pritchard rationalized further that King had been plagued with a sore arm and malaria for some time, while Latham and Robinson were bothered by "trouble outside of baseball." Pritchard assured readers that Von der Ahe's investigation had proved the charges groundless, Henry Chadwick denounced the charges, and even Brooklyn President Charles H. Byrne joined the chorus concerning Latham's and King's innocence (*S.L.*, 24 July 1889).

Perhaps one reason for the rallying cries on behalf of Arlie Latham and Silver King, aside from the self-serving need to preserve the good name of baseball, was the unpopularity of Browns' owner Chris Von der Ahe. Besides his arbitrary treatment of Browns' players and alienation of numerous sports' enthusiasts in St. Louis, Von der Ahe had developed a rather seedy public image. Noted baseball historian Frederick G. Lieb said that "Chris seldom passed when drinks were on the house [and] his proboscis usually was lit up like a red bulb on a Christmas tree" (Lieb, *The St. Louis Cardinals* 9). Von der Ahe dressed gaudily, making a display of his wealth by flashing numerous diamonds. He entertained lavishly, partying through most nights. "He loved the ladies, and never was squeamish about their social standards. He had a well-trained horse who knew the way home in the early hours of the morning" (Lieb, *The St. Louis Cardinals* 9).

Speaking with a thick German accent, Von der Ahe provided endless ethnic stories to sportswriters across the nation at a time when ethnic stereotypes informed Americans with positive or negative definitions of each other. Von der Ahe neatly fit many Americans' image of a boorish, drunken, aggressive German immigrant. Display became Von der Ahe's hallmark, as he ostentatiously hauled the take from each home game to the bank in his grocery wagon. Anti-immigrant animosities stirred in the United States throughout the 1880s, and ethnic chauvinism undoubtedly contributed to the sometimes venomous dislike of Von der Ahe which circulated among baseball circles (*Tribune*, 20 January 1889). However, he had helped the American Association prosper, and he had made a fortune in baseball despite his highly questionable personal morals. Chris Von der Ahe could not easily be dismissed as an influential force in baseball since he had economic power. His credibility could be questioned, and both Latham and King benefited for a time by the fact that their owner's public reputation contained some corrosive qualities.

Charles H. Byrne took the side of Browns' players partly because he had developed an antagonistic relationship with Chris Von der Ahe as the two owners sought to gain primary influence within the American Association. Byrne also owned a gambling establishment, and two key Bridegroom players, Dave Foutz and Bob Caruthers, regularly wagered on

Roger Connor—Slugging Giants' first baseman. Connor led the National League in slugging average and RBI's in 1889 and was second in triples and walks, third in total bases, and fourth in homeruns. Photo credit National Baseball Library, Cooperstown, N.Y.

their own team. By July 11, *Sporting Life's* J.F. Donnolly reported heavy betting in the New York-Brooklyn areas on Brooklyn as a pennant winner (*S.L.*, 17 July 1889). Surmising, it seems clear that since Charles H. Byrne was closely involved with gambling, he did not wish to publicize the possibility of two baseball players, from whatever team, deliberately losing games. Such publicity might cause more restrictions on baseball gambling.

By mid July, Brooklyn's owner could be forgiven for wanting to think the best of baseball since his Bridegrooms had played so well in the west. Winning ten of fourteen from the Athletics, Browns, Kansas City Cowboys, Louisville, and Cincinnati, the Bridegrooms could only complain of the weather. As happened often during the 1889 season, nature provided a reminder of human frailty during the Brooklyn game in Cincinnati on Sunday, July 14. Five thousand people were watching an exciting game even though rain threatened. Rather suddenly, cyclonic winds plucked up 150 yards of outfield fence, dashed it on a score of carriages and caused several horses to run madly onto the baseball field. A section of the grandstand roof collapsed amidst terrorized screams "while at the same time the big canvas curtains in front were ripped into shreds with a noise like a thousand rifles" (*Times,* 15 July 1889). Miraculously, no spectators were harmed though many rushed heedlessly for exits. Players were spared as well. Such elemental danger accompanies all human activity through the ages, but the 1889 season contained more than the usual number of violent storms, flooded grounds, and grandstands destroyed by fire.

Brooklyn players and Manager Bill McGunnigle slogged happily homeward on July 17, though they still trailed the Browns by five games. At least two Bridegrooms, Tom Lovett and Joe Visner, looked forward to seeing their small children who attended every game at Washington Park, and catcher Bob Clark welcomed the team with his healing fingers. Hopefully, he would be ready when the Browns visited in early August. Charlie Reynolds was dependable at catcher as he drank nothing stronger than iced tea, but Joe Visner did not throw well. Clark was needed.

Five thousand Brooklyn cranks, 1,000 of those women, welcomed their beloved Bridegrooms at Washington Park for the July 18 game with the hard-hitting Philadelphia Athletics. Despite the presence of such stars as first baseman Ted Larkin, Denny Lyons at third, Harry Stovey in left field, and Curt Welch in center, the Athletics had fallen eight games behind the Browns by mid-July. But the Athletics always competed fiercely against Brooklyn, and the latter counted themselves fortunate to win two of three as Bob Clark returned to the lineup.

With Caruthers and Adonis Terry alternating as pitchers, Brooklyn drew good crowds during rainy weather through the rest of July. A large turnout of women swelled the ladies' day attendance on Thursday, July 25 against Kansas City. On July 27, Byrne was so anxious to take advantage of 5,000 cranks appearing despite the grounds' poor condition that he ordered the game played against Cincinnati. Byrne undoubtedly wanted to play as many home games as possible, rain or shine, since the western trip had been a financial disappointment.

Although Tom Lovett continued to disappoint and Mickey Hughes' arm mended slowly, Byrne took satisfaction in the superb play of center fielder Pop Corkhill, second baseman Hub Collins, and shortstop George Smith. Manager McGunnigle impressed many with his careful attention to game strategy and players. He maintained a harmonious atmosphere, and J.F. Donnolly reported that Bridegroom players admired McGunnigle's ability.

After the August 1 doubleheader victories against the woeful Louisville Colonels, the Bridegrooms had won 9 of 11 at home and looked forward to battle with the Browns. St. Louis, despite rosy predictions about their eastern trip and Commy's confident statements that his Browns were in the best shape ever, lost five out of their eleven games at the end of July and saw their lead shrink to only two games by the time that they rolled into Brooklyn on August 2.

One reason that Commy brimmed with confidence before the Browns embarked for the east on July 17 was that Von der Ahe had bought Toad Ramsey from Louisville. Thomas A. Ramsey was baseball's first great knuckleball pitcher, though "drop curve" was the name given the pitch in the 1880s. Count Mullane described Ramsey's pitch as a "combination down and in ball [that after delivery] seems to be above the batter's head [but takes] a big drop and passes over the plate about waist high" (S.N., 23 February 1889). As a young brick layer's apprentice, Ramsey had cut the tendon in the middle finger of his left hand. He learned to throw what today would be called a knuckleball and had won seventy-five games for Louisville in 1886 and 1887. Then, angered by low pay, the talented young pitcher began to drink steadily (Smith, 1970: 54). A superb pitcher when sober, Ramsey had developed a reputation for heavy drinking from the time that he joined the Louisville Colonel team in the mid-1880s. Purportedly, his favorite drink was a pint of whiskey poured in some beer. This combination he drank regularly and in quantity.

Why then, did Commy think that Ramsey could help his team? For one thing, Toad had always wanted to play for Commy, assuring writers that his drinking reputation was undeserved and that Commy would inspire his best (S.N., 20 July 1889). More to the point, Nat Hudson had not adapted well to the four ball rule. As early as 1887, he had reduced his speed to adjust to the five ball rule, down from six. Though he pitched impressively during 1888, Hudson became relatively ineffective in the early months of 1889.

Ratio Of Strikeouts And Walks 1887-1889

American Association	*National League*
1887 - 3075 (S.O.) 3320 (W)	2837 (S.O.) 2732 (W)
1888 - 4234 (S.O.) 2634 (W)	3998 (S.O.) 2093 (W)
1889 - 4177 (S.O.) 3704 (W)	3492 (S.O.) 3612 (W)

(Source: *The Baseball Encyclopedia*, 1990, pp. 98-108)

He and Von der Ahe quarreled regularly, and trading him for Ramsey must have seemed like a worthwhile venture to the Browns' owner and manager. Hudson terminated his combative relationship with Von der Ahe by simply refusing to report to Louisville and quitting baseball.

Ramsey happily joined the Browns in Cincinnati on July 20 but did not pitch for Commy until late in the season. The Browns' manager saw fit to use his two youthful veterans, Chamberlain and King, for most of the games preceding the Brooklyn series in early August. As Chamberlain lost each one of his three starts, plagued by rain, and insulted by the Athletics' young catcher Lave Cross who threw out four Browns' base runners on July 31, Commy employed one of his favorite tactics on August 1 in Philadelphia. Claiming that the grounds were to wet to allow play, Commy refused to let his team take the field (*Clipper*, 10 August 1889). Philadelphia correctly noted that such refusal should have led to a St. Louis forfeiture according to American Association rules. However, Charlie Comiskey had become accustomed to being a law unto himself and thought that the rules were his to bend. As he had often done, he blamed most of the road losses on poor umpiring.

A new, wholly irrational dimension of his whining was the assertion that umpires disliked the Browns and favored Brooklyn because Brooklyn owner Charles H. Byrne controlled their salaries (S.N., 27 July & 10

August 1889). His mood had lowered noticeably when he brought his Browns into Brooklyn with only two games separating them from the confident, surging Bridegrooms.

The New York Giants' run at the first place Boston Beaneaters slowed considerably during late July, as the Giants lost to Philadelphia and the lowly Washington Senators on the road. John B. Day had watched his team return to reality on July 16, when "Cannonball" Ed Crane lost their first game in the New Polo Grounds to Chicago, 13-10. Welch and Keefe won the next three out of four games, but Crane lost again to Indianapolis. Clearly, he had not recovered fully from his early season knee injury, and he had also encountered another problem unknown to most people. Crane did not have any drinking problems before he went on Albert G. Spalding's world baseball tour during the 1888-1889 off season. During the tour, he began to enjoy drinking and imbibed heavily during the 1889 season. Overweight and having some trouble with the four ball rule, Crane was dropped from the starting rotation for the rest of July, and Day started looking for another pitcher. Fortunately, attendance continued good as women arrived in impressive numbers on weekdays. *The Times* noted that women cranks knew enough about baseball by 1889 to use score cards (*Times,* 18 July 1889). Perhaps because of increased women's attendance, John B. Day outfitted his team in new, loose, white uniforms. They replaced the tight-fitting black ones that had received some tongue-clucking criticism for indecency (*S.L.,* 24 July 1889).

The Giants continued to attract special attention, particularly their captain Buck Ewing who received a fox terrier before a game with Indianapolis. He declared it a mascot and probably envied Roger Connor for receiving a gold medal after hitting the first home run over the new grounds' center field fence. Ewing was playing the best he possibly could, and Jim Mutrie let him run the team. Despite Ewing's superb play, the Giants began to lose and received less favorable publicity.

John Montgomery Ward incurred the wrath of *The Times* when he missed the July 19 game against Indianapolis. Ward's replacement, Gil Hatfield, committed three errors in the 9-8, eleven inning loss. Mike Tiernan drew criticism for a "stupid throw," but the major target was Ward. "In order to win, the Giants must put in their strongest team each day. If a player complains of a pain or an ache he should not be allowed to lie off whenever he feels so disposed....Hatfield is a good man, but he can not be expected to play up to the standard of the regular shortstop. It is not customary to allow a star or a man drawing a star's salary to lie off....Capt. Ewing, Gore, Connor, Richardson and perhaps one or two others are playing in the best possible manner....If the Giants want to win every man in the team must put his shoulder to the wheel" (*Times*, 20 July 1889). Ward responded the next day by contributing to a victory with three stolen bases and good fielding, despite having to play in a small lake after heavy rainfall.

Even though Ward had returned, the Giants fell apart in Philadelphia, losing three straight. Tiernan again played badly because he was very ill. Finally, Mike Slattery substituted in right field against the Senators on July 26. Slattery had been injured most of the year, but with Tiernan's illness he was forced into service. With Keefe and Welch being hit hard, John B. Day took advantage of the Washington Senators' presence in New York by buying their young, hard throwing, right hander Hank O'Day. Day also bought former Browns' outfielder Harry Lyons from the Jersey City team, seeking to shore up the Giants for the stretch drive.

Such purchases demonstrated more than ever Day's determination to win the pennant even as he was experiencing financial problems. Francis C. Richter reported that Day had lost money on his Jersey City team, a newspaper venture, and the St. George fiasco (*S.L.,* 31 July 1889). At least he was making money in the New Polo Grounds before the late July rains. The Giants attracted over 4,000 people per game in July despite problems associated with the rapid construction.

Everyone, even relatively mild-mannered Buck Ewing, felt the strain of the close pennant race as July ended. Ewing was fined $25 and thrown out of the Washington game on July 30 for disrespectful language. O'Day lost that game in his first start for the Giants against his old team, but he pitched impressively. Having lost seven of their last twelve, the Giants hoped that O'Day would be their third dependable starter.

One worry Jim Mutrie did not have was too much carousing among his players. Like Brooklyn manager Bill McGunnigle, Mutrie proudly told reporters that he had no restrictions on drinking and found that his players responded well (*S.N.* 27 July 1889). The Giants were undoubtedly self-regulating, since, with the exception of Crane and center fielder George Gore, all the players were temperate individuals.

In Boston, however, sportswriters rode Mike Kelly hard for his poor play and indifferent leadership. William D. Sullivan disgustedly reported for *Sporting Life* that "Mike Kelly says that the Bostons will not land better than fourth. That is pretty talk for the captain of a team which is thought to be a pennant winner" (*S.L.*, 17 July 1889). In a mere week, Sullivan said that Kelly "came out of his trance" and played very well against Chicago on July 18. Even though Joe Quinn had been ill and was thus not playing well, Boston received a boost when Hoss Radbourn defeated Indianapolis on July 17 in his first start in two weeks. Newly acquired Jersey City pitcher Bill Daley completed the doubleheader sweep on that day, thus allowing Boston to rid themselves of little-used Bill Sowders. Though the Beaneaters lost two of three to Cap Anson's White Stockings, they did have a successful home stand as they won nine out of fourteen at the end of July and increased their lead over the slumping Giants to 4 and 1/2 games.

Kelly and some of his mates still drew caustic criticism from Boston's sportswriters, but the King seemed to be emerging from his pout when he pulled one of his patented "tricks" in the July 29 game against Philadelphia. With John Clarkson pitching, the Phillies threatened in the fifth inning as hard-hitting Sam Thompson batted with two on base. Thompson slugged a long drive to right field, and all present thought that it was going over the picket fence. The two Philly runners assumed the same and started jogging toward home plate. However, right fielder Kelly picked up the ball that he later said had hit the top of the fence and bounced back onto the field. Kelly threw the ball to his catcher and held the lead runner at third. Philly Captain Sid Farrar immediately began to protest furiously to the umpire that the ball had cleared the fence but that the clever Kelly had thrown home a ball concealed on his person and thrown, by him, against the fence as a ruse. Of course, Farrar's protests were unheeded, and Philly Manager Harry Wright later said that he believed that the hit was not a home run.

Lest one think Kelly's stretching of rules somewhat aberrant, Buck Ewing's growing notoriety concerning the use of his catcher's mask acts as a corrective. Buck had developed the habit, along with other catchers, of leaving his mask on the baseline or home plate to cause problems for base runners. Naturally, this dangerous practice infuriated opposing players and Indianapolis' Paul Hines and the Phillies' Sam Thompson had both recently smashed Buck's mask with their bats. Some catchers far exceeded Ewing's ingenuity. Baltimore catcher Pop Tate once threw Brooklyn's Darby O'Brien to the ground so he could be tagged out (*S.L.*, 8 March 1889). To cite one last example of rule-breaking and rough-housing, Cleveland third baseman Patsy Tebeau pushed a Washington player off of third base in a late July game, held him and tagged him until Umpire Wesley Curry called him out. *The New York Clipper* pronounced this action "smart" (3 August 1889). Umpire Curry explained that he had not seen Tebeau push Walt Wilmot off the base, although the following interference presumably was noticed but not considered. Baseball was not warfare in 1889, but it was not polite either.

Compounding the players' proclivity for breaking the rules was the fact that many umpires simply did not understand them. Umpires were also greatly harassed. William Ingraham Harris censured one of the most admired players, Buck Ewing, for "continual chewing and fussing with the umpire" and called for the double umpire system to prevent blatant rule breaking (*S.L.*, 7 August 1889). "Kicking" and rule breaking offered entertainment for the multitudes, but such actions could also arouse crowds to violence against umpires. Few arbiters could match the courage of Bob Ferguson, who, when one day surrounded by an angry mob, seized a bat and shouted: "I'm only one man to your thousand, but if you don't think I can protect myself just pitch in and give it a trial" (Spink 59).

As the rains fell at the end of July, ending the rainiest month in New York City for the year, Charlie Comiskey brought his team into Brooklyn. They were not playing well, and Commy spouted invective against Brooklyn President Charles H. Byrne, the Brooklyn team, and the umpires. Commy, a primary advocate of "tricks" and the Browns, one of baseball's greatest traveling road shows, were coming to Brooklyn. The American Association season was about to unravel.

Chapter Nine
A Question of Dishonor

On August 1, the same day that Charlie Comiskey autocratically refused to play in Philadelphia because of wet grounds, the Brooklyn Bridegrooms floundered in mud mixed with sawdust to defeat the Louisville Colonels in a doubleheader. Charles H. Byrne reportedly had the games played because he did not wish to disappoint the patrons. However, he obviously did not want to miss any opportunity to defeat the hapless Colonels. Dave Foutz pitched the first game and averted defeat only because his mates rallied for five runs in the last two innings to win 8-6. A reinvigorated Pete Browning played for Louisville and collected two hits in each game. Supposedly, Browning had discovered a worthwhile treatment for his ailments in Brown-Sequard's "Elixir of Life" (Orem 398). Possibly the person most closely resembling Yogi Berra in baseball history, Browning provided writers with endless one-liners. When he heard that another player had injured his anterior detroid muscle, Pete sympathized: "You'se had better get it pulled" (Orem 396). Despite Browning's cheery presence, Brooklyn slaughtered Louisville behind Tom Lovett, 14-1, in the second game. The Colonels fielded horrendously with ten errors. Captain Darby O'Brien entertained the Thursday crowd with his antics in the mud, and the entire city of Brooklyn rejoiced that their beloved Bridegrooms trailed the Browns by only two games.

The 1889 St. Louis Browns took on the rough and tumble personality of their manager, Charlie Comiskey, as all of his teams had in the previous four years. Besides Commy's approval of rule-breaking or rule-stretching for winning games and his desire to destroy the opposition, he also harassed opposing players mercilessly. Jim Hart, Boston Beaneater Manager and associate of Albert G. Spalding, described how Commy had been responsible for the 1887 rule that restricted coaches to a prescribed area.

The chalk lines which enclose the coaching boxes were added...after Charles Comiskey had demonstrated their necessity...Comiskey and Bill Gleason used to plant themselves on each side of the visiting catcher and comment on his breeding, personal habits, skill as a receiver, or rather lack of it, until the unlucky backstop was unable to tell whether one or half a dozen balls were coming his way....So for the sake of not unduly increasing the population of the insane asylums or encouraging justifiable homicide, the coach's box was invented. This helped out the catcher, but the pitcher and other players on the opposing team were still at the mercy of Comiskey, and I know of no man who had a sharper tongue, who was in command of more biting sarcasm, or who was quicker at repartee. (Axelson 74)

Other St. Louis players possessed similar ability to arouse the ire of opposing players and managers. Small wonder that the Browns were hated by many opposing teams and their cranks. However, having won four successive pennants, they also attracted a degree of admiration among baseball writers. The respected *New York Clipper* commented early in the 1889 season about the abilities of the Browns and their manager. Praising the Browns as "one of the most remarkable teams on the diamond," the *Clipper* proclaimed Commy as the "great general." "It is the impetuous spirit of the leader that enables the team to do the fine work it accomplishes season after season" (*Clipper,* 23 March 1889). Impetuous Comiskey certainly was, and this characteristic was definitely attributable to his team.

As early as 1887, the Browns had received strong criticism for their rough play. In mid June of that pennant winning year for the Browns, Philadelphia newspapers portrayed Commy's team as unusually "dirty." "They continually override the coaching rules, coach batsmen, address opposing players, interfere with base-runners, and kick at any and every decision in the most persistent and aggravating manner" (Von der Ahe file, NBL). Spectators' remonstrations had no effect nor did the threat of fines. Granted they played to win, but the Philadelphia reporter thought that they played "the sort of ball that injures the game and deters the better class of patrons from attendance" (Von der Ahe file). Commy was singled out for his unnecessary harassment and intimidation of the umpire. Curt Welch, without provocation, struck Philadelphia pitcher August Weyhing in one game, nearly starting a riot. Commy was also censured for using profane language within the hearing of ladies. Welch was sold after the 1887 season, but the Browns retained their rollicking, belligerent character. Their individual and collective characteristics had gained them a notoriety that would be unmatched until the Baltimore Orioles made life miserable for umpires and opposing players in the mid-1890s.

The 1889 St. Louis Browns could point to only three positions where relatively normal, unremarkable players performed. The two catchers, Jack Boyle and Jocko Milligan, hit well, and some commentators regarded Boyle as one of the best catchers in the country. Possessing unusually long arms, Boyle attracted attention with his strong throws although Milligan was a steadier backstop. Young, twenty-one year old shortstop Shorty Fuller had been bought from Washington after the 1888 season and fielded well in 1889. A weak hitter, Fuller attracted the most attention of his career when he became fearful of contracting tuberculosis in the mid-1890s, quit baseball, and awaited his death which occurred in April, 1904 (*Cincinnati Enquirer,* 13 April 1904). Twenty-three year old rookie Charlie Duffee fielded well in center field, and, despite his small size, hit fifteen home runs in 1889. At every other position, the Browns attracted large crowds because of their skills and their behavior.

At first base, Charlie Comiskey led, inspired, cajoled, and drove his team. A lasting impression of Commy is that of him standing, hands on hips, spewing insults at the umpire or sardonically questioning the ancestry of opposing players. Whether signaling his infielders and outfielders how to play for a particular batter or fielding ground balls and throwing to his pitcher covering first, Commy offered cranks throughout the American Association exciting, highly mobile baseball. As a base runner, he was one of the most daring and did not hesitate to slide head first when necessary. Commy urged his players to be equally aggressive on the bases and in the field, to take chances. He cared not about errors if his fielders tried hard to make difficult plays. As noted earlier, he also encouraged them to break or stretch the rules, to "turn a trick" (Comiskey file, NBL).

As a small boy in Chicago, Commy had rebelled against his father's wishes for him not to play baseball. He flaunted authority all his life and had some problems disciplining his players because he must have empathized with the boy-men on the Browns, especially third baseman Arlie Latham and second baseman Yank Robinson. Commy was only thirty years old in 1889 and enjoyed, to some extent, the childish pranks of his puckish charges. He liked Latham's humor and at one time had urged Browns' players to encourage Arlie's clowning. Latham needed precious little encouragement. With Latham, Robinson, McCarthy, Ramsey, King, and Chamberlain cavorting from game to game, Commy had to use all of his leadership skills to keep his players focused on the task of winning baseball games.

Bill "Yank" Robinson ably supported Commy with his versatility, wit, and aggressive play. A creative, wholly undisciplined individual, Yank played without a glove and could throw with either hand. Beginning as a utility man for the Browns in 1885, he settled at second in 1886 because of his agility and quickness. Particularly proficient at shagging short pop-ups in the outfield, Yank further delighted cranks with his contortions while turning double plays. He made numerous errors playing barehanded, but he had good range and threw quickly and accurately. Yank hit poorly in 1889 but walked frequently and ran the bases daringly (Tiemann and Rucker 109). He was an intelligent player, and Commy liked the tough Philadelphian even though he had to fine him often for drunkenness. Former Browns' shortstop Bill Gleason recalled that "Comiskey was particular about the boys being in bed early but occasionally they played hooky. Robinson...would ostentatiously take his key from the rack and retire only to slide down the fire escape" (Axelson 105). A more endearing trait was Robinson's aversion to sleeping in a railroad Pullman car because he feared train wrecks. Often, Yank would stay up all night in the smoking car, incurring at least one fine from Von der Ahe for failing to retire with the team (Palmer, *Stories* 73-6).

Despite his ongoing battle with Yank, Commy made him one of his lieutenants because Robinson was able to settle team squabbles. In 1890, Yank no longer had Commy to gently rein him. He drank steadily during his tenure on the Pittsburgh Players' League team, contracted tuberculosis, and died in August, 1894. Notwithstanding all of his skills as a manipulative disciplinarian, even Commy shook his head when he looked across the diamond at his third baseman, Walter "Arlie" Latham.

To say that Arlie Latham played third base is wholly inaccurate. He performed there. From the time that he began playing with the Browns in 1883, Latham developed a reputation that caused cranks throughout the American Association to want to see and hear him in action. He attracted crowds with the stunts that he performed while running the bases and playing third. Sometimes, he would cart-wheel home from third on a home run, probably overjoyed because he only hit twenty-seven during thirteen full seasons. He once embarrassed Cap Anson by leaping over the Chicago first baseman, avoiding his clumsy tag, and landing safely on first with a bright "How do, Anse?" (Latham file, NBL). Arlie would even, occasionally, sing during a game at third base. When teammates made good plays, he would frequently do a flip to celebrate. If umpires made

Tip O'Neill—The power in the St. Louis Browns' lineup. O'Neill ranked among the American Association's top five in seven hitting categories during 1889. Photo credit National Baseball Library, Cooperstown, N.Y.

objectionable calls, Arlie would feign a fainting spell, collapsing at third. During one game when Commy raged at him for not trying hard enough, Arlie responded by blowing up the third base bag with a fire cracker to awaken himself. He entertained crowds endlessly with continual chatter during a game. Latham tried to rattle opposing players and umpires with his banter and antics and even his own mates, if he did not like them. Ted Sullivan thought that Latham was unexcelled as a third base coach (Sullivan 34). Spectators throughout the Association would crowd the bleachers around third base just to hear all of Arlie's witticisms as a coach and player.

Assuredly, Arlie Latham loved entertaining the crowds. Young boys thought his faints immensely humorous, and, in many respects, Arlie himself was but a child. The same could be said of most of his teammates. One can only imagine what an umpire would have to cope with during a Browns' game: Latham "fainting" at third, Commy screaming continual objections from first, Browns' players earnestly running over with support when Commy would complain, Silver King making the umpire wonder if he were in the pitcher's box, Yank giving base runners the hip and leg at second, and eagerly joining Arlie and Commy in the din directed against the umpire. But what a show for the cranks in every city, even if the Browns were hated by many.

Cranks also enjoyed watching Arlie Latham because of his playing skills. A speedy, brainy base runner, Arlie was an intelligent, effective batter and good fielder. Despite these obvious skills and his hilarious mannerisms, Arlie evidenced many unsavory characteristics in his private life. Although Ted Sullivan once described him as a "kindly, genial spirit" off the field, Arlie attracted unwanted attention with his matrimonial problems during the 1880s and 1890s. In September, 1887, Arlie's second wife, Ella, sued for divorce after being severely abused during the year of their marriage. According to Ella Latham, Arlie beat her on five different occasions and continued to visit houses of prostitution. These actions may actually have endeared him to some male cranks in a time when many men thought that women should be subservient and when domestic violence was rather casually reported in daily newspapers. However, such physical abuse raises some serious questions about Arlie's emotional stability. He could not manage finances at all and even tried to avoid paying the St. Louis lawyer, D. Castleman Webb, who represented him in his numerous divorce suits. He had, in the parlance of the time, always been a "sport" and gambled, though he never drank much (Latham file, NBL).

In August, 1889, Arlie Latham would be severely challenged and questioned by his manager and teammates over the issue of throwing games. The clown of baseball possessed some decidedly nonhumorous characteristics which began to cause him serious problems during August.

If Latham and Robinson were not problems enough, Commy's pitching staff would have kept any manager busy. Silver King, Icebox Chamberlain, and rookie Jack Stivetts were all twenty-one, handsome, and unmarried. Newly acquired Toad Ramsey was only twenty-four and, though he had vowed not to drink, was now in the company of three compatriots who saw no need to follow his example. King, like Latham, had sown what then would be called wild oats. He had fathered a child by Emma Goldenlogen in 1885 but had not married despite living with her while playing minor league baseball in St. Joseph, Missouri. By 1887, Emma had become pregnant again and filed a seduction suit against King (King file, NBL). Chamberlain frequented pool rooms during the off season and had gained a reputation for being a "sport" by 1889. Stivetts, known as Happy Jack, liked to drink but never had the problems with alcohol that beset Toad Ramsey. Both Stivetts and Ramsey were acquired in mid-season, so this sociable group was just getting acquainted by the time that they visited Brooklyn in early August.

Commy probably gave thanks daily that his outfield contained two great players who helped stabilize his team. In left field for the Browns performed one of the great sluggers of the 1880s, James Edward "Tip" O'Neill. Brooklyn's Charles H. Byrne had tried to buy his release after 1887 and former Browns' catcher Doc Bushong had told Tip that if he "would play for his release" (play poorly), Byrne would subsequently hire him and pay him handsomely (O'Neill file, NBL). To his lasting credit, O'Neill remained loyal to the Browns and was remembered by Commy as "one of the greatest sluggers in the history of the game" (Axelson 100). A true gentleman despite the examples set by his manager and teammates, Tip had become one of the most popular players in the Association by 1889. He had a strong arm and saved some games with great catches, but his forte was his power hitting. Using a tiny bat, O'Neill became the idol of adoring boys who scrambled for the honor of carrying his bag from the hotel to the ballpark. Tom McCarthy performed artistically in right field, though ironically enough it was not until after he had left Commy's tutelage that he would develop the tricks that caused rulemakers to devise the infield fly rule. Still, McCarthy gladdened Commy's heart with his running, hitting, and fielding.

Such were the Browns who stormed into Brooklyn on August 2 to do battle with the Bridegrooms. Typically, Commy had fumed noisily about poor umpiring after leaving St. Louis in mid-July. A new twist developed when the acerbic Browns' manager whined that umpires were favoring Brooklyn because Charles H. Byrne controlled their salaries (S.N., 10 August 1889). The only possible basis for such an amazing charge was the fact that Byrne had been on the committee that revised the American Association Constitution for 1889. The inadequate Association President, Wheeler C. Wikoff, later felt it necessary to meet with umpires in Byrne's office so that the new rules could be explained properly (*S.L.*, 20 February & 6 March 1889). Charles H. Byrne possessed a lawyer's precise understanding of baseball rules and only meant to improve the Association's umpiring system by aiding Wikoff. However, by August, the Bridegrooms were seriously threatening the Browns for first place, Chamberlain supposedly still had arm trouble, the Browns had just lost five out of eleven, and Comiskey needed to strike out at someone in his fury. While he spoke calmly about not expecting a fifth pennant early in the season, Commy dearly wanted to win again. He hated to lose anytime and to lose to Brooklyn was virtually unthinkable. Someone must be cheating in Commy's view, since, as he knew from his own experience, "tricks" had become very much a part of the national game.

Despite slippery grounds, 8,000 watched dejectedly as Icebox Chamberlain won his first game since July 16 by defeating Bob Caruthers 6-2, August 2 at Washington Park. The treacherous footing allowed the Browns to score four runs in the first, and the Bridegrooms could not catch them. The next day, twenty-one Brooklyn businessmen ennobled the proceedings by presenting President Byrne and his team with two heavy crimson silk foul flags. Perhaps intending to outdo the gaudy displays of Von der Ahe, the Brooklyn merchants had embroidered "Brooklyn" in gold raised letters on the flags and mounted them on ebony poles topped by gold-plated eagles. Undoubtedly inspired, the Bridegrooms pounded Toad Ramsey and Jack Stivetts for fifteen hits and defeated the Browns 13-6 behind Bill Terry. The rains had made the grounds' condition frightful, but both teams fielded brilliantly at times. On Sunday, August 4, 17,000 rabid cranks poured into Ridgewood Park to madly cheer Bob Caruthers 7-2 victory over Silver King. The Browns' six errors hurt them, although Commy could not complain that the record-setting crowd interfered in any way. Byrne had wisely put the overflow spectators behind barbed wire in the outfield. Commy could, however rant against the Bridegrooms, and proclaim that Brooklyn did not bat, field, or run bases very well. Charging that Byrne influenced umpires by manipulating their salaries, Commy rationalized the losses even further by carping about King's and Chamberlain's sore arms (*S.N.*, 10 August 1889). Joe Pritchard disagreed with Commy on both counts, noting the pitchers' good shape and simply saying that the charges against Byrne were untrue (*S.L.*, 7 August 1889).

Pritchard's major concern in early August was all of the gambling in pool rooms that reduced attendance at games, especially in St. Louis. He knew that one worthy named Lynch, a pool room keeper from Washington D.C., had lost $3,000 betting against the Browns in various games. As the Browns headed back to St. Louis to host the Grooms, Pritchard still thought that they would win the pennant again, even though their lead had shrunk to only one-half game on August 9. While St. Louis took two of three in Kansas City, Brooklyn won three of four from the Athletics and Columbus before they journeyed to St. Louis. Brooklyn's *Sporting Life* correspondent, J. F. Donnolly, thought that Commy's team had played raggedly and listlessly in Brooklyn, citing Arlie Latham's unusually quiet performances in the last two games. However, he believed that the July rumors about Latham throwing games were just silly (*S.L.*, 14 August 1889).

Donnolly felt confident as the Bridegrooms entrained for St. Louis. Dave Foutz and Bob Caruthers hoped for a financial windfall if they could continue their success against the Browns. Both players bet heavily on Brooklyn in every game and had won a lot of money during 1889. George Pinckney and Captain Darby O'Brien simply looked forward to seeing friends from Peoria, Illinois in St. Louis. The entire team would be given special cigars if they defeated St. Louis, a practice that President Charles H. Byrne had instituted to reward Brooklyn victories. With Caruthers pitching well and having recently mastered a new pitch that he called "the glide," Byrne hoped to win at least two of three. St. Louis cranks had worked themselves into a minor frenzy as they awaited the charging Bridegrooms, and even Arlie Latham felt moved to proclaim that he was anxious to win the pennant. Silver King tucked another pretzel in his pocket for luck (*S.L.*, 14 August 1889).

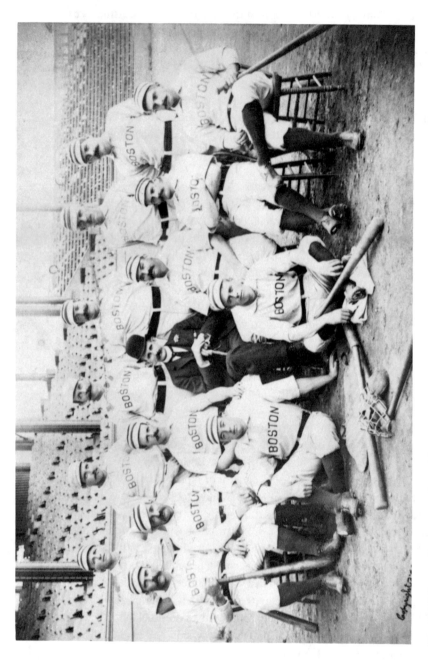

The 1889 Boston Beaneaters—Down the stretch. Left to right: Top row—Joe Quinn, Tom Brown, Pop Smith, Dan Brouthers, Charlie Ganzel, Charlie Bennett. Bottom row—Hardie Richardson, Hoss Radbourn, John Clarkson, Jim Hart, Mike Kelly, Dick Johnston, Billy Nash. Seated in front—Bill Daley and Kid Madden. Note the bats and catcher's equipment. Photo credit National Baseball Library, Cooperstown, NY.

Whether it was the pretzel or Chamberlain's superb pitching, the Browns rewarded 7,000 screaming spectators with a 4-2 win at Sportsman's Park on August 10. Charlie Duffee, Tom McCarthy, and Tip O'Neill all made phenomenal catches, as St. Louis scored two in the tenth inning to defeat Caruthers. George Smith and Pop Corkhill fielded magnificently for Brooklyn, but they fell short with the tying runs on second and third. *The Times* judged the game one of the finest of the season, although Arlie Latham had "played very indifferently." Commy played at his best, receiving hearty applause on several occasions (*Times,* 11 August 1889).

Fifteen thousand cranks, the largest home crowd of the year, swelled Sportsman's Park to the breaking point on Sunday, August 11, cheering the total collapse of Brooklyn's defense in a 14-4 Browns' romp. George Pinckney, Hub Collins, and Bob Clark all fielded badly while St. Louis again only made one error. The Browns battered Bill Terry and Dave Foutz for eighteen hits, and Commy rubbed salt in Brooklyn's wounds by not allowing Clark to leave the game because of an injury. Claiming that Clark could play, Commy summoned three doctors who concurred with the Browns' manager. The overflow crowd swarmed the field during the controversy, and the game required three hours to complete. Both teams wrangled so much throughout the game that many cranks left early in disgust. The ill-will engendered by Commy's act did not bode well for the future relations between the two teams and their proud owners. A further complication arose even before the second game when Arlie Latham was suspended by Commy for "recent poor work" (*S.L.,* 21 August 1889).

Pete Sweeney, acquired the previous week by the Browns from Ted Sullivan's Troy, New York team, played third base in Latham's absence. *The Times* reported that Arlie had been "suspended indefinitely for bad ball playing and for conduct prejudicial to the club's interest" (13 August 1889). *The Sporting News* eventually divulged the full story with a long article on Latham's poor play dating back to the July 4 game in Brooklyn. Commy had charged Arlie with disobedience in the August 10 game and demanded that Browns' owner Chris Von der Ahe suspend him. The enraged Browns' manager claimed that Arlie was responsible for sixteen of St. Louis' thirty-one losses, eleven of which had occurred since July 4. Commy said that all Browns' players favored the suspension, so Von der Ahe could not be criticized for unduly harassing Latham. Obviously, Commy and the Browns were convinced that Arlie Latham was throwing games (*S.N.*, 17 August 1889).

Purged of Latham's supposed detrimental presence, the Browns annihilated Brooklyn on August 12, 11-0. Icebox Chamberlain allowed the Grooms only two singles while St. Louis smashed Bob Caruthers' offerings for seventeen hits. Sweeney fielded brilliantly and hit well. Joe Pritchard divulged that Commy had demanded Arlie's suspension because of his "ungentlemanly conduct" and for associating with gamblers. Von der Ahe and the Browns' Board of Directors had decided on indefinite suspension, though Pritchard did not think that Arlie was a crook. However, the rotund correspondent did admit that valid questions could be raised about Latham's associations with gamblers who purportedly bet $500 to $3,000 per game on the Browns to lose. Von der Ahe confirmed that Commy and his players had demanded Arlie's suspension. Even St. Louis cranks had turned against the once popular clown. Arlie Latham, meanwhile, denied all charges against him except his poor playing (*S.L.*, 21 August 1889).

Naturally, Latham's suspension disturbed the Browns' following, but the sound defeats administered the Bridegrooms caused general rejoicing. Bill McGunnigle had actually wept in frustration after Caruther's second loss, and Charles Byrne struggled heroically to accept defeat gracefully amidst Chris Von der Ahe's beer-swilling celebration. The 24,500 in attendance at the three games could find no fault with Bob Ferguson's and John A Kerins' umpiring, but Byrne did not think that either umpire handled the crowd delay of August 11 very well (*S.L.*, 21 August, & 4 September 1889). While angered by Commy's bulldozing and kicking, Byrne sensibly agreed with Henry Chadwick that Brooklyn needed to hit better if they were to win the pennant.

Still unable to hit against sixth place Kansas City, the Bridegrooms rallied behind pitching from Terry, Caruthers, and Mickey Hughes to sweep three games while the Browns lost one of three to seventh place Columbus. With the remaining schedule favoring Brooklyn, Tom Lovett shedding excess weight, and Mickey Hughes pitching again, Commy and the Browns knew that their two and one-half game lead of August 15 was unsafe. They still had to play three games in Brooklyn early in September, and the relations between the two teams were at an all time low. Brooklyn cranks undoubtedly felt that they had some scores to settle with Commy, considering the extensive wrangling and harassment of Bob Clark during the August 11 game. The question of Arlie Latham's honesty also obstructed Commy's plans for a fifth consecutive pennant.

As the American Association battle between St. Louis and Brooklyn became entwined in questions over personal honor, National League players acted on their July 14 decision to seek financial backing for their proposed new league. The most dramatic development occurred during Pittsburgh's July 22-24 visit to Cleveland when Pittsburgh manager Ned Hanlon approached streetcar magnate Albert L. Johnson. Johnson became an avid supporter of the players' league and organized meetings with Indianapolis, Philadelphia, New York, and Boston players as they came to Cleveland in succeeding weeks (Henry Chadwick Scrapbooks, Vol. 2, NBL; Seymour 226-27). All of these proceedings were accomplished without any National League owners learning of them, including Giants' owner John B. Day. For a time, Day gloried in the Giants winning streak during early August, blissfully unaware of the coming storm.

By the time that the Giants came into Cleveland on August 12, they had won seven of their last eight games and were about to overtake the slumping Beaneaters, losers in five of their last eight. Despite severe drainage problems in the New Polo Grounds, George Gore's nagging leg injury, and Mike Tiernan's illness, Day found consolation in the Giants' heavy hitting. Cannonball Crane began pitching well again, and New York took three games from Cleveland as they swept into first place on August 13. The next day, Buck Ewing caused a near riot as he convinced umpire Philip J. Powers to call Cleveland center fielder Jimmy McAleer out for cutting first base as he headed for second. The game was close, and Buck intended to do all he could to keep possession of first. After Powers decided to agree with Ewing's assessment of McAleer's actions, five hundred Cleveland cranks ran onto the field, threatening Powers with physical harm. Three policemen and the Cleveland players managed to restore order so that Powers could return from his place of refuge underneath the grandstand. As the season neared its end, players and cranks responded with what was even then uncommon emotion to the unusually tight race between New York and Boston. Umpires became most convenient targets.

Boston tri-owner James B. "Josh" Billings definitely felt some pressure after Boston began the month of August with four losses in six games to lowly Washington and Indianapolis. John Clarkson lost twice, and Hoss Radbourn was soundly thumped by the Hoosiers. Before the team left for Chicago, Billings unburdened himself in a telegram to Boston

Manager Jim Hart: "What is the matter with this team? You are disgracing the Boston public...What is the matter with Radbourn?" (*Times*, 9 August 1889). Possibly recalling Dan Brouthers' earlier comment about Boston winning the pennant unless the Beaneaters dropped dead, Billings thought that Kid Madden, Dick Johnston, Tom Brown, Radbourn, and newly acquired shortstop Pop Smith should be put in cotton. Hart, understandably livid, fired off a six-page letter of protest to President Arthur H. Soden. Soden and William H. Conant averted Hart's resignation by telegraphing their support, although Soden wished that Hart had not made the telegram public. Kid Madden and Dick Johnston were having poor years, but public humiliation only added to the Boston players' determination to support the Brotherhood revolt. Billings unknowingly recruited many Beaneaters for the Brotherhood cause as the Boston team traveled to Cleveland in mid-August and their meeting with Al Johnson.

Manager Hart contributed somewhat to the demoralized state of his players by calling young pitcher Bill Daley a quitter. Daley and Madden purportedly drank too much, King Kelly was in a hitting slump, and star pitcher John Clarkson was overworked. With his entire outfield hitting poorly, Hart decided to put Hardie Richardson in left field and Joe Quinn at second. Trying to instill new life in the Beaneaters, Hart anxiously looked for a winning combination before the Giants came to Boston on August 19. Conversely, John B. Day hoped that spending still more money on the New Polo Grounds to solve the drainage problem would be his major concern. The Giants had taken to two-feet deep outfield water like spaniels, but Day needed to eliminate such embarrassments (*Times*, 2 August 1889; *Tribune*, 18 August 1889 called left field "Lake Mutrie"). Even though Tim Keefe lost to Pittsburgh on August 15, the Giants still led Boston by one-half game.

Day's hopes were unfulfilled as the Giants, plagued by George Gore's sore leg, Danny Richardson's sore hand, hideous fielding, and bad pitching from veterans Mickey Welch and Tim Keefe, lost five straight to Pittsburgh and Boston before returning to their water-logged park. Buck Ewing drew unusual censure from all quarters of the baseball world because he caused Pittsburgh catcher/outfielder George "Foghorn" Miller to injure himself during the August 17 game. As he and other catchers had done so often, Ewing placed his mask on the plate to hinder Miller as he scored. Miller angrily kicked the mask and cut his foot in the process. Ewing could accept the chorus of boos from the Pittsburgh cranks, but

when both major baseball weeklies severely criticized him, he knew that
he had extended trickery to unacceptable limits (*S.N.*, 31 August 1889;
S.L., 28 August 1889). After tying Boston on August 19, the Giants were
whipped badly, 12-2 and 10-4 by Radbourn and Clarkson. Besides Gore's
lameness, Ewing made two bad throws in each of the three games while
Welch and Keefe suffered from sore pitching hands. Welch had rubbed the
skin from his pitching thumb almost to the bone, and Keefe struggled with
a rheumatic pitching hand. One Giant player mournfully noted "unless we
get new pitchers or Keefe and Welch brace up we might as well give up
the ship" (*Times*, 21 August 1889).

Brace up they did, as the Giants won four of five from the Phillies
after returning to the Polo Grounds, playing two doubleheaders in two
days. Keefe's initial victory on August 22 did not impress the *Times*,
which raked the team unmercifully:

> With the exception of Captain Ewing and perhaps one or two others...the boys
> seemed to play without life or energy. Five straight defeats have apparently taken
> the sand out of them, and they disported themselves in a dull and lifeless
> manner....A 'chicken hearted' baseball team will never win a championship, and
> the sooner the Giants realize that the quicker they will be on the road to first
> place....nothing is so obnoxious as a nine of 'quitters.' If New York had a team of
> Ewings it is safe to say that it would be in the lead today.... (*Times*, 23 August
> 1889)

Ignoring the train ride from Boston to New York as a factor in the
Giants' listless play, the *Times*' praise of Ewing at the expense of the other
players demonstrated appalling tactlessness. Even Tim Keefe's marriage
while the team was in Boston received cursory mention, although he was
criticized for too many walks and hit batsmen in the Phillies game.

Overlooking the journalistic bias and diatribes, the Giants began
playing like champions. Although only 3,500 welcomed them home on
August 22, compared to the swarm of 13,000 plus Bostonians that cheered
the Beaneaters on Monday, August 19, the Giants ripped through
Philadelphia and Washington for seven wins in the nine games prior to
Boston's visit at the end of the month. George Gore's return to center field
and Hank O'Day's pitching helped immensely. The one bad game against
Washington, a 13-3 loss, resulted from eleven errors and brought another
denunciation from the *Times*:

> The Giants played like so many schoolboys...Keefe was ineffective....the

work of the champions was of a disgusting character, and would reflect discredit on a second-rate team of amateurs....Ewing laid off to take a well-earned rest to get in condition for the Boston games...[but] the Giants without Ewing are like a ship without a rudder, and, while it is unfair to ask him to play every day, it must be done if New York wants to win the pennant. Ewing is the best captain in the profession, and his value can only be appreciated when somebody else attempts to fill his position. (*Times*, 28 August 1889)

The Giants responded to the insults by pounding the Senators in a doubleheader victory on August 28, with Crane and O'Day getting the wins. Welch and Keefe were fairly well rested for Boston, although Keefe's arm was still not completely sound.

The Beaneaters won four of six from Washington and Philadelphia before their last series with the Giants, so their lead over the Giants decreased to two games. The intensity of the pennant race manifested itself in a unique manner on August 26, as Boston defeated the Phillies 5-4 in twelve innings. On a play that foretold the infamous oversight of Fred Merkle in 1908, Boston center fielder Dick Johnston singled in King Kelly with the winning run and then, instead of touching first base, ran toward the dressing room. Phillies' first baseman Sid Farrar hustled to retrieve the ball so that he could tag first and declare Johnston out, negating the run. Naturally, none other than King Kelly got to the ball first and fought Farrar to maintain possession. The struggle must have been impressive, with the agile, strong Kelly well-matched against the big, muscular Farrar. Philadelphia cranks nearly mobbed Kelly and a riot was barely averted. Neither of the two umpires had bothered to watch Johnston's progress, so the Phillies' protests were ultimately disallowed (Orem 415; *S.L.*, 4 September 1889; *Clipper*, 31 August, & 7 September 1889). The fight signaled that Kelly's blood was up again even if he was at least twenty pounds overweight. Hardie Richardson was playing the game of his life for Boston, and John Clarkson, while overworked, still pitched effectively. Thousands of New York cranks awaited their arrival, hoping to win back some of the money that they had lost gambling on the Giants in Boston.

Ten thousand men and women packed the New Polo Grounds for a Thursday game, overtaxing the new grandstand. When the crowd began to stamp and cheer as the game began, the upper part of the grandstand settled, causing some spectators to make a rush for the stairway. Luckily, Building Inspector Conlin led several policemen to the endangered area and managed to quiet the crowd and avert a disaster. In most cases, women were calmer than their escorts. A loose bolt on one of the large cross beams had caused it to slip, and Inspector Conlin thought that upper level crowds should be limited until the wood had seasoned properly.

Once the crowd became relatively calm, Clarkson defeated Welch 6-4 because of "Smiling Mickey's" throwing error in the eighth inning. Captain Kelly demonstrated true leadership by inspiring his mates and contributing a key sacrifice during the inning, redeeming himself for an earlier base-running error. Kelly led his men with the rallying cry: "Now every man to his post and show what you're made of. Come, boys, up and at 'em" (*Times*, 30 August 1889). Hardie Richardson served notice of the game's seriousness by smashing Buck Ewing's mask even though it was not on the base line (*Clipper*, 7 September 1889). Several hundred Boston cranks had journeyed to New York for the three game series, led by General Arthur Dixwell. Yelling loud enough to be heard blocks away, the Bostonians' shrill "Hi, Hi, Hi" cheer brought a resounding "Hey, Hey, Hey" from New York rooters.

Trailing by three games, the Giants rebounded behind superb pitching from Tim Keefe as they defeated Hoss Radbourn 7-2. Eight thousand people watched the Giants nervously commit nine errors, two by the great Ewing, but Radbourn gave up fourteen hits while Boston garnered only three. King Kelly entertained the crowd greatly with his remarks from the coaching box. He further delighted them by pretending that he had caught Mike Tiernan's seventh inning home run by running toward the latter as if he had possession of the ball. Unamused, "Silent Mike" eventually made his way home.

Before the last game of the year between the two great rivals, a building inspector ordered that iron caps be fastened to the New Polo Ground grandstand rafters. Since the caps prevented further settling, this allowed John B. Day to open the upper portion to what would be a huge crowd for the Saturday game. Typically, for such an important weekend game, Captain Buck Ewing was presented with a floral baseball of red and white immortelles. Clarkson started for Boston and was staked to a 6-0 lead after two innings, but King Kelly misplayed a single in the third to give the Giants a big inning. Approximately 15,000 cranks alternately cheered and hissed one of the best games of the year as the Giants rallied to batter Clarkson for thirteen hits and tie the game before darkness brought a halt. William Ingraham Harris pronounced the game one of the most exciting that he had ever seen. New Yorkers had never been so excited over a pennant race, and the continual kicking by Mike Kelly and Buck Ewing served to make the game even more interesting (S.N., 7 September 1889).

The entire series, plus the one in Boston, was fondly recalled by Boston cranks as late as 1897 (Tuohey, *passim*). William D. Sullivan accurately predicted that the rest of the season would be "a tussle" between the two great teams, one which both cities would relish (*S.L.*, 11 September 1889). Harris confidently believed that the Giants would win out, and the Giants did have advantages in both pitching and hitting. On Sunday, September 1, as the Beaneaters and Giants prepared for their Labor Day doubleheaders, Boston led by two games. However, they were overly dependent on Clarkson and they had only two hitters above .300 while the Giants boasted of five such stalwarts. They were about to begin one of baseball's great stretch drives.

As the National League leaders readied themselves for the final push, the Browns and Bridegrooms fumed and sputtered toward their rendezvous with chaos in early September. One of baseball's major explosions was about to occur.

Chapter Ten
A Lobster-Frankenstein Nightmare

Before their last eastern road trip, Commy's Browns closed out their home stand with five out of six wins over two tough teams, the Baltimore Orioles and Philadelphia Athletics, while splitting two with Kansas City. Chamberlain and King alternated in the box, pitching particularly well against the hard-hitting Athletics. The big news, though, was the return of partially penitent Arlie Latham for the Baltimore series.

After the Brooklyn series from August 10-12, Arlie had sulked off to Louisville. Chris Von der Ahe suspected that Brooklyn President Charles H. Byrne had made some arrangement to help the new Louisville owners buy Latham from Von der Ahe. Whether or not Byrne had any hand in it, an inquiry was made, but Von der Ahe asserted that he would not release Latham for $100,000 (*Clipper*, 24 August 1889). Encouraged to discover the meaning behind this statement, Arlie met with Commy and Von der Ahe on August 15 to discuss his suspension and the highly questionable circumstances surrounding it. Latham told his manager and owner that while he had been keeping company with a gambler named Lynch, he had thrown no games. Because Pete Sweeney had not played very well after his first two games against Brooklyn, Commy decided to approve Arlie's reinstatement if he played hard and avoided further associations with gamblers. Latham contritely admitted his poor play, so Von der Ahe agreed to reinstate him. Although nothing had been proven against Latham, St. Louis players still insisted that "he tried to throw us down" (S.N., 24 August 1889). With such suspicions spurring him, Arlie fielded well in his first five games against Baltimore and Kansas City.

The troubled condition of the Browns' team became more evident when Silver King and Icebox Chamberlain complained on August 22, the day of Latham's return, about pitching every second day since August 10. Chamberlain correctly deduced that such a rotation was too hard on his arm and must have wondered why strong-armed rookie Jack Stivetts was being ignored by Commy. About this same time, Nat Hudson left the St. Louis area and major league baseball. Before he journeyed to

125

Minneapolis, Hudson advised Latham to initiate a lawsuit against Von der Ahe. Arlie wisely ignored such advice since he had encountered enough difficulty in his marital legal maneuverings. He only wished to show people that he wanted to win, and even though he fielded badly in a tie with Kansas City on August 28, the Browns felt confident as they left for the east the next day.

Sporting Life's Henry Chadwick regretted Toad Ramsey's drinking habits and the wasting of so much talent, but other baseball observers thought that the Browns could hold off the Bridegroom's renewed challenge even without Ramsey. Otto Steifel of Steifel Brewing Company and J.W. Peckington of The Golden Lion, both of St. Louis, felt certain enough of a fifth straight pennant to initiate a benefit fund for the "coming champions." Commy predicted a successful eastern trip, and Joe Pritchard thought that the pennant would be within relatively easy grasp when the Browns returned on September 21. As they left for Columbus, Commy's men still led the Bridegrooms by three games.

Brooklyn hitters had regained their batting eyes against the woeful Louisville Colonels in mid August. Pounding Louisville pitchers Guy Hecker and Red Ehret for 49 hits in three of the four games, the Bridegrooms swept the Colonels by scoring 43 total runs. Bob Caruthers pitched one shutout and saved another game for the ineffective Tom Lovett. Even Mickey Hughes managed a win, though he was hit hard by Louisville. Cincinnati found Caruthers to be no mystery, and Redlegs' rookie pitcher "Cyclone Jim" Duryea added injury to insult by knocking the slightly built Grooms' pitcher insensible at first base. The Bridegrooms responded to the 18-5 trouncing administered to their star pitcher by rallying behind Bill Terry and the seemingly rejuvenated Hughes to take two from Cincinnati before ending their road trip in Baltimore.

They may have won three from the Redlegs except for the growing opposition to Sunday baseball in the Cincinnati area. After the August 11 Sunday game with Baltimore, Cincinnati's Superintendent of Police had said that there would be no more Sunday baseball, and Mayor John Mosby affirmed the decision (*Herald,* 15 August 1889). Prevented from playing in Cincinnati on Sunday, August 25, Redlegs' President Aaron Stern still tried to gain the benefits of a large Sunday crowd by switching the game to Hamilton, Ohio. Unfortunately, Stern could only attract 1,500 spectators. Worse, after three and one-half innings, police arrested the players on both teams and fined them $159.30. Stern angrily paid the fines and began seriously considering switching his franchise to the National League (Orem 398; *Clipper,* 31 August 1889).

Brooklyn benefited greatly from the absence of Cincinnati's great rookie center fielder, Bug Holliday, while their own Pop Corkhill continued to amaze with his marvelous fielding. In the first game of the series, he "ran from deep center to within a short distance back of second base, and made a one-handed catch while lying on his stomach" (*Clipper,* 31 August 1889). Even Corkhill's brilliant play could not save Terry and Caruthers from two defeats in Baltimore, Caruthers presumably still feeling the effects of his encounter with the big, strong Duryea. When Terry lost 8-7 on Tommy Tucker's home run in the ninth, the telegraphed news to St. Louis made the cranks there "howl themselves hoarse" as they watched their heroes humiliate Kansas City 19-1 (*Times,* 28 August 1889). Terry recovered to shutout the Orioles 4-0 on August 29 as St. Louis journeyed to Columbus.

Even with their three losses in St. Louis, the Bridegrooms had managed a 13-7 road record and still trailed the Browns by only two and one-half games as they headed home to Washington Park. They were hitting again and, except for Lovett, their pitchers seemed ready for the incoming Browns.

To Commy's consternation and Brooklyn's amazement and delight, seventh place Columbus humiliated the Browns by sweeping their three game series. Mark Baldwin, sold by Albert G. Spalding because of alleged poor discipline before the 1889 season, won two games by defeating King and Chamberlain. Columbus skulled King 13-4 on August 30 and collected fourteen hits to defeat Jack Stivetts the next day. Losing to a lowly team like Columbus incensed Commy since he had predicted that the Browns would win every game from the new team. With three earlier losses, the two at the end of August meant five wholly invalid defeats.

Desperately hoping for a win on September 1, Commy was on first base with the score tied in the sixth inning. Fiercely proud of his base running ability, Commy undoubtedly was planning to steal second. To his amazement, the twenty year old Columbus catcher, Jack "Peach Pie" O'Connor, picked him off of first by three feet. The Browns' old nemesis, Umpire Bob Ferguson, called Commy out. The combination of a young catcher and a Brooklyn native exposing him to such public humiliation sent Commy over the edge. Columbus sportswriter F.W. Arnold provided the ensuing dialogue between umpire and shamed manager.

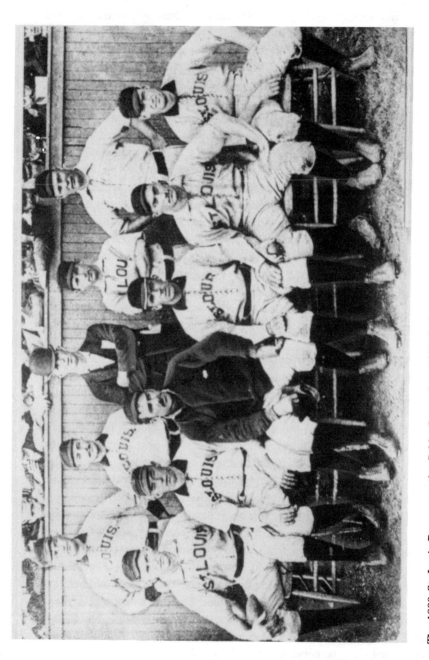

The 1889 St. Louis Browns on the field—September, 1889. Left to right: Top row—Silver King, Tom McCarthy, Charlie Comiskey (Manager), Yank Robinson, Jocko Milligan. Bottom row—Jack Boyle, Charlie Duffee, Arlie Latham, Shorty Fuller, Jack Stivetts, Tip O'Neill. Missing—Icebox Chamberlain and Toad Ramsey. Photo credit National Baseball Library, Cooperstown NY.

Well, well; then began a circus as was a circus. Commy stood still as a rock glaring at where Ferguson was standing.

...Fergy beckoned for him to come in.

...Says Commy: 'What's that?'

Says Fergy: 'You're out; come in.'

Commy slowly followed the white line with his pigeon toes...until His Imperial Highness was right under Fergy's front door. [Ferguson, the only umpire, was behind home plate. To reach him, Commy stalked down the first base line.]

'What's that you said, Mr. Ferguson?'

'You're out, Mr. Comiskey. Just please get off the line and let the game go on.'

'I'm out?'

'Yes, you're out; now get away.'

'...Why, you poor, blind chucklehead, alleged umpire. You have a mission, haven't you, since your second trip on earth?'

'What do you mean?'

'...You are here for a purpose, and your purpose seems to be to rob the St. Louis team....You are in combination to assist Brooklyn to take the pennant, and you can't deny it.'

'I do deny it, and I warn you now to shut up. I've had quite enough of your uncalled-for abuse. Now go and sit down, or I'll give this game to Columbus 9 to 0.'

'Oh, you will, will you?...'

'Now Comiskey, I'll tell you for the last time. If you say one word more, I will order you off the field and give you a $100 slice.' (*S.L.*, 11 September 1889)

Commy stalked back to the bench and it is doubtful if even Arlie Latham had anything to say. Dave Orr ended the debacle by hitting a home run in the tenth inning to defeat Chamberlain 6-5. For the first time, Brooklyn now led the Browns as they had swept three from Kansas City.

Losing control of first place was bad enough, but the scathing criticism from respected baseball authorities must have hurt the proud Charlie Comiskey even more. Francis C. Richter was particularly impatient with Commy's wailing against umpires. "No man knows how to work them better, either by palaver or browbeating and no club gets more close decisions...than the Browns..." Brooklyn correspondent J.F. Donnolly supported Richter by quoting Commy himself: "I do not protest an umpire's decision [to reverse it]...but simply for the effect it will have on him in succeeding games" (*S.L.*, 11 September 1889). Holding up Bob Ferguson as a shining example of honesty as a player, manager, and umpire, Richter denounced Comiskey's charges against him and thought that the latter deserved a public apology. Donnolly predictably derided Commy's assertions as "nauseating trash" and called for a retraction. Clearly, Commy's outburst against Ferguson was caused primarily by his embarrassment over being picked off by a young catcher-and one from St. Louis at that. Having acquired a reputation for excellent base running when a game was close, Commy's pride, not to say personal honor, was at stake. An apology in such circumstances was highly unlikely. Furthermore, Commy and Von der Ahe thought that they had even more proof of Byrne's collusion with umpires because of what happened in the Brooklyn-Kansas City series at the end of August.

Bob Caruthers defeated Kansas City 14-4 on August 30 at Washington Park, ably supported by the hitting of Captain Darby O'Brien and good fielding. The next day, Brooklyn tied the Browns for first by sweeping a doubleheader from Kansas City behind Adonis Terry and Mickey Hughes. When the large crowd heard the announcement of St. Louis' defeat by Columbus, a mighty cheer went up. The Cowboys contributed twenty-two errors to the Bridegroom victories, but what angered Chris Von der Ahe and Charlie Comiskey was that Brooklyn catcher Doc Bushong umpired all three games. Neither the regular umpire nor the substitute were available, so Kansas City had agreed to Bushong's umpiring. Naturally, St. Louis raised some questions about this arrangement, wondering if Charles H. Byrne had some improper influence over Kansas City President William Henry Watkins and again charging that Byrne had control of Association umpires. Von der Ahe lodged a formal protest to the American Association (*S.N.*, 7 September 1889).

Charles H. Byrne was greatly insulted by Commy's and Von der Ahe's tirade and planned to meet with both of them when they came to Brooklyn on September 7. Meanwhile, his league-leading team took four of five from Cincinnati. Twenty-one thousand people attended the Labor Day doubleheader at Washington Park. Brooklyn fielded brilliantly and hit well throughout the series, and Tom Lovett and Mickey Hughes contributed wins so that Caruthers and Terry would be well rested for the Browns. The ever inventive McGunnigle helped Bridegroom hitters by sitting in the grandstand to steal Redleg catcher Jim Keenan's signs. St. Louis continued to struggle in Baltimore as Silver King lost twice. Although Icebox Chamberlain salvaged one game, Commy was enraged when Arlie Latham allowed Baltimore to tie the September 5 game by not attempting to field a grounder, thinking that it was going foul. It stayed fair, and Baltimore tied the game in the ninth inning. Rain the next day prevented a playoff, and the Browns entered Brooklyn trailing by the same margin with which they had led when they left St. Louis, two and one-half games.

What happened between Brooklyn and St. Louis on September 7 in Washington Park was one of the most dramatic and most unfortunate developments in baseball history. It would lead to bitter recriminations between Brooklyn and St. Louis owners and the former's eventual departure from the American Association at the end of the year. Part of the background for the game was that Commy, the sorest loser of his era, had just experienced one of his worst weeks in baseball. His Browns had lost five out of six and possession of first place. He had been humiliated in Columbus, received wide-spread criticism for his actions there, and then had to slog through more frustration in Baltimore. Not a happy camper he. In Brooklyn, Byrne and the thousands of loyal cranks were furious because of St. Louis' accusations about Byrne's control of umpires. Umpire Fred Goldsmith undoubtedly remembered the July 29 game in Baltimore, when he disallowed an Oriole run against St. Louis. The ensuing riot was quelled by the police, but the game ended in a tie, and Goldsmith felt as if he had been manipulated by Commy. With a capacity crowd at Washington Park, he could not let it happen again.

Bob Caruthers started for Brooklyn with three days rest while Icebox Chamberlain got the call for St. Louis. Chamberlain pitched after two days rest. Over 15,000 people crowded Washington Park to witness the battle royal. Continuous wrangling with Umpire Goldsmith and among the players entertained the crowd for a time. Brooklyn scored two runs in the first inning which brought Von der Ahe to the St. Louis bench, field glasses in hand. Commy began railing at Goldsmith who became "a shuttlecock in a cyclone" (S.L., 18 September 1889). Brooklyn used stalling tactics during the fifth inning, but when St. Louis scored once in that frame and twice in the sixth, the Browns demonstrated to what depths that strategy could sink. St. Louis players began talking to Chamberlain in turns, including outfielders Tip O'Neill and Tom McCarthy. Commy insisted that the game be called because of darkness after the sixth inning. He made this claim between every pitched ball, wasting even more time. The Browns also stalled at bat. Goldsmith, with his defenses up against Commy's bulldozing, refused to call the game and fined the stalling players repeatedly. To dramatize the extent of the darkness, Von der Ahe sent for candles and lit them in front of the Browns' bench. Some spectators were amused but others hurled beer glasses at the candles, nearly starting a fire in the grandstand. As the test of wills between Commy and Goldsmith continued, the crowd became angrier. McCarthy infuriated them when he dropped the ball in a bucket of water after the 8th inning so that it would be harder to hit. Even Charlie Comiskey thought that Mac pushed the limits of harassment too far with this act and by exchanging insults with the bleacher cranks in the outfield.

Despite the stalling and McCarthy's dousing of the ball, Brooklyn batted in the ninth. By then it was so dark that Browns' catcher Jocko Milligan could not see the ball and was hit on the arm with one of Chamberlain's pitches. When Bob Clark was declared safe on a close play at second, the apoplectic Commy led his men from the field in objection to Goldsmith's continued refusal to call the game. Goldsmith had warned him that he would forfeit the game to Brooklyn if Commy left the field. The crowd immediately swarmed the field, although Brooklyn players held them at bay long enough for Goldsmith to declare the forfeit. Then the crowd went berserk.

When the St. Louis players left the field they were mobbed, and Comiskey, Robinson, and McCarthy were roughly handled and in imminent danger. All the windows of the dressing room were broken by beer glasses and stones which were hurled at the Browns, and it required a large detachment of police to get them safely away from the grounds." (*S.L.,* 18 September 1889)

J.F. Donnolly aptly termed the game a "lobster-Frankenstein nightmare" and expressed wonder that Goldsmith maintained his sanity (*S.L.,* 18 September 1889). That night at the Grand Central Hotel, Von der Ahe made the corridors echo with anathemas against Brooklyn and Umpire Goldsmith. In his rage, he telegraphed Byrne that he would not allow his team to play at Ridgewood Park on Sunday. He feared that the players' lives would be threatened since only a few police would be at the park. Byrne immediately wired President Wikoff of Von der Ahe's refusal to play a scheduled game and that such action made St. Louis subject to expulsion from the Association. The Browns purportedly said that they would not go to Ridgewood even if they were paid $1,000 apiece. Some may have been that fearful, however, at least two Brownies added a light touch to this sad affair. During the scuffle at game's end, someone grabbed Jocko Milligan's cheek. "Take it along," he said, "but don't hit me" (S.L., 18 September 1889). Arlie Latham told Joe Pritchard that he continued to be treated with consideration at Brooklyn. Other players were targets of empty beer glasses while he was hit in the neck with something in it.

A large crowd, between 15,000 and 20,000, collected at Ridgewood on Sunday, but when the Browns failed to appear, Goldsmith awarded the game to Brooklyn. Byrne, even though he had gained two forfeitures, was so angry that he intended to insist that St. Louis be expelled from the Association, as specified in Section 9 of the Association constitution. "I want to say that I shall never rest until the American Association metes out to this man Von der Ahe the punishment provided by the constitution for his insolent defiance of its provisions....The Association must either expel the St. Louis club or go out of business....I mean to push this matter to the end, because the integrity of our national game demands it" (*Herald*, 10 September 1889).

Opinions varied about who was most to blame for this fiasco. *The Sporting News* predictably ranted against "the Blacklegs and gamblers from Brooklyn," again charged that Byrne had control of the umpires, and even suggested that Byrne accomplished this through American Association President Wheeler C. Wikoff (14 September 1889). *The New York Clipper* sided with the Browns, condemning the hoodlums that assaulted the Browns' players and urging the American Association to overturn Goldsmith's decision. Noting that the Giants-Indianapolis game at the Polo Grounds had been called forty minutes before St. Louis left the field and that both teams had stalled, *The Clipper* thought it too risky to continue the game (14 September 1889). Henry Chadwick strongly criticized Von der Ahe and referred to Commy as an over-rated captain guilty of dirty playing. Concentrating his wrath on the Browns' owner, Chadwick cited Von der Ahe's inconsistent, intemperate, injudicious, reckless acts and charges in relation to Bob Ferguson and Charles H. Byrne as bringing discredit on himself and the Browns. The veteran sportswriter believed that expulsion of the Browns from the Association should be considered.

Between these extremes, William Ingraham Harris and Francis C. Richter provided the most judicious appraisals. Harris puzzled over Commy's action of taking his men from the field since it seemed certain that St. Louis would win anyway. Why leave the field and risk losing the game and a $1,500 fine? Harris thought that Von der Ahe should pay the fine for the Saturday game but had doubts about the validity of the Sunday fine. He did not think that the Browns' actions warranted expulsion, however, Harris said that Von der Ahe's wild charges against Byrne, Ferguson, and Darby O'Brien should be curbed in some fashion. O'Brien, Brooklyn's fun-loving left fielder, had been added to Von der Ahe's enemies list because he jokingly told Umpire Jack Kerins that he would give $100 if the Grooms won the pennant. Von der Ahe tried, unsuccessfully, to show that O'Brien had tried to bribe Kerins (*S.N.*, 14 September 1889). Furthermore, Harris recalled the earlier charges against King and Latham and challenged the Association to make a full investigation of that issue, even though Latham had been reinstated. Noting that St. Louis players still suspected Arlie, Harris urged the Association's thorough, serious consideration of the Latham-King affair because "not since 1877, have we had anything of a dishonest nature to spot the purity of the sport" (*S.L.*, 18 September 1889). Richter blamed Fred Goldsmith for letting the game get out of control although he recognized that the strained relations between Byrne and Von der Ahe, and many previous quarrels, provided a volatile precondition. While Richter believed that St. Louis should have appeared at Ridgewood on Sunday, he said that expulsion was nonsense. Brooklyn had stalled during the Saturday game, and other teams had strolled righteously from playing fields, Brooklyn included. Richter counseled compromise before the Association was harmed irreparably but like Harris, thought a thorough investigation warranted-this time into the issue of unfair umpiring.

Perhaps the most objective opinion came from Joe Pritchard. Some St. Louis cranks were disgusted with the Browns' recent actions, and Pritchard thought that most Mound City people supported Commy's action on September 7 but not the refusal to play on the next day. Pritchard saw great harm to the game in all of these events.

A special meeting of the American Association was to decide the validity of the two forfeitures, the fines, and the issue of expulsion on September 23 in Cincinnati. Meanwhile, heavy rains mercifully canceled the last scheduled meeting between the Grooms and Browns on September 10. With Von der Ahe suggesting that the Browns might not appear unless adequate police protection was provided and Byrne angrily replying that such protection had always existed, some sort of divine providence intervened to wash away the tiresome bickering.

The heavens opened for four straight days as St. Louis made their way to Philadelphia. When the sun finally shone on the 14th, Byrne eagerly welcomed the cellar-dwelling Louisville Colonels. While only three games were scheduled, Byrne wanted to make up an earlier postponed game, so two doubleheaders were played in two days. The Grooms swept both as they fielded brilliantly despite the hideous field conditions. Germany Smith received plaudits for his work at shortstop as he had throughout the year. Virtually forgotten after the great shortstops of the 1890s such as Bill Dahlen, Honus Wagner, and Herman Long received acclaim, Smith was a highly regarded fielder of the late 1880s and early 1890s.

In Philadelphia, sawdust was thrown on the field to allow games to be played, much to the detriment of the Browns. The Phillies hit Chamberlain hard for two wins, and only Silver King saved the Browns from three losses. Misfortune visited St. Louis in another guise when Tip O'Neill had to leave the team because of a death in the family. As the woeful Browns headed toward Kansas City before returning to St. Louis, they found themselves trailing Brooklyn by the astounding margin of seven games. This after leading by two and one-half games as late as August 28.

Chapter Eleven
Revolution

In the National League, the Giants and Beaneaters competed fiercely but in an acceptable manner during the first half of September. From the Labor Day doubleheaders of September 2 through the fifteenth, New York's proud Giants won eight and lost only two to the pesky Indianapolis Hoosiers. Hank O'Day became a major contributor to the Giants' cause by defeating Pittsburgh twice and the hard-hitting Hoosiers once. O'Day replaced Cannonball Ed Crane in the rotation since Crane had injured himself while sliding on August 31. Tim Keefe's arm still was sub-par, but he managed to pitch impressively nonetheless. Buck Ewing missed six of those ten games because of a sore leg and hand, yet Big Bill Brown played magnificently, except for one game, in his place. Significantly, Mike Tiernan hit very well. Boston played creditably but could only manage eight wins out of thirteen games. While Hardie Richardson and Bill Nash performed marvelously, big Dan Brouthers was a bit ill and not hitting his best. Still, Boston clung to a mere one-half game lead as they and the Giants went on the road for the last weeks of the season.

The big news in the National League was the publicizing of the proposed Players' League for the 1890 season. From St. Louis came reports that Will Johnson, owner of the South St. Louis Railway and brother of Cleveland's Albert L. Johnson, would help finance the players' revolt (*S.N.*, 14 September & 21 September 1889). *Sporting Life* had published a story about the proposed new league before Johnson blabbed, so his account seemed credible (*S.L.*, 11 September 1889). Most owners and managers paid little heed; they regarded the rumors as just another ploy for higher salaries (*Times*, 14 September 1889). Giants' owner John B. Day did not think that the reports were accurate, and he busied himself with the serious task of solving the drainage problem at the New Polo Grounds.

The rain and wind storms of September 10-13 had caused the Harlem River to flood the Giants' new park and cancellation of four games. With the high hill on the west, the New Polo Grounds became an enormous bath tub. Having lost thousands in revenue, on the 14th, Day was so anxious to play Chicago before embarking on the last road trip that a doubleheader was scheduled. The Giants responded by defeating the White Stockings twice as Cap Anson's only reward was his home run resulting from the ball sticking in the muddy center field embankment. Giants' center fielder George Gore floundered comically in pursuit of the ball, delighting the crowd and bolstering his reputation as one of the great grandstand players.

Day's confidence in his team and in the future of the National League was such that he reportedly declined an offer from James J. Coogan to sell the Giants' franchise for $200,000. Supposedly, Day informed Coogan that his offer was not enough to buy controlling interest in the Metropolitan Exhibition Company, the corporate entity which owned the Giants (*Times,* 6 September 1889). The ever optimistic Day looked ahead to the 1890 season with a new ballpark and, hopefully, another championship. He was certain that the financial difficulties of 1889 could not repeat themselves, but he was soon to be brought face to face with the reality of the players' revolt.

Undoubtedly, the tremendous interest in the National League pennant race encouraged Day to believe that somehow, harmony would prevail among owners and players. How could rebellion follow such a wondrous season? On September 9, large groups of cranks hovered around tickers in New York's saloons or thronged streets which contained bulletin boards so that they could learn of the Boston-Chicago score after the Giants had beaten Cleveland. Cheered by the tie score, New York's spirits plummeted as the rains canceled the next four games. Even the effervescent Jim Mutrie muttered "Just our luck. Somehow or another the weather has been against us all season" (*Times,* 11 September 1889).

Although Charlie Comiskey could not see how the Giants could lose to the pitching poor Beaneaters, John Clarkson astounded everyone by winning both games of a doubleheader against Cleveland on September 12. Probably depending on his change of pace which was "as big as an ice wagon coming up to the plate," (*Herald,* 2 September 1889) the great Boston pitcher challenged Old Hoss Radbourn to attempt the same feat the next day. Radbourn lost one and tied the other despite the fact that he pitched well. Amazingly, Boston and Cleveland played a third consecutive doubleheader on the 14th with Clarkson winning one and the disheartened Kid Madden losing the other. Three doubleheaders in three days. Obviously, the Beaneaters wanted to get in as many home games as possible before their last road swing.

The Browns just wanted to get home. Even with the absence of Tip O'Neill, they whipped the Kansas City Cowboys in three games before returning to St. Louis on September 21. Commy was in a wholly irrational state by that time. Accusing Charles H. Byrne of trying to buy him and other Browns' from Von der Ahe, he said that "Byrne is a shoe-string gambler, a con man and ought to be thrown out of baseball" (*S.N.*, 21 September 1889). Such an astounding charge was accompanied by complaints about the poor play of Arlie Latham, Silver King as a "dead weight," sub-standard pitching by Icebox Chamberlain for two months, and, of course, poor umpiring on the road. Commy spouted all of this even though he had pitched his two stars on an alternate basis throughout August except for three games. Is it any wonder that the Browns lost two of three to Cincinnati or that Chamberlain's lobs were hissed by St. Louis cranks in his 17-6 drubbing? O'Neill's absence hurt the Browns on September 21 because nineteen year old rookie Tom Gettinger made an error in the ninth inning that defeated Silver King. Happy Jack Stivetts, the only pitcher currently in favor with Commy, managed to defeat the Redlegs on the day that the American Association Board of Directors met in Cincinnati to decide on the disputed games between St. Louis and Brooklyn.

Understandably, rumors had been circulating about the possibility of Brooklyn seeking membership in the National League ever since the September 7 blowup with St. Louis. Charles H. Byrne denied the story, as he had done so often in the past, but he added vaguely that "If we were invited I don't know what we might do. That is another question" (S.L., 25 September 1889). Byrne admitted that he had been hurt by the slanderous remarks about his supposed influence over Association umpires. He intended to come to some sort of understanding about all of the charges at the September 23 meeting in Cincinnati, and he insisted that Von der Ahe's Browns should be expelled because of their refusal to play the scheduled game on September 8. His minimum demands were that St. Louis be fined $3,000 and both forfeits to Brooklyn should stand. Numerous baseball commentators, excepting Henry Chadwick, thought that expulsion was too harsh a penalty, so Byrne appeared to be demanding severe punishments as a rationale for deciding to leave the Association if they were not imposed. Francis C. Richter correctly judged the Cincinnati meeting to be extremely important for the American

Association's future.

Besides the Brooklyn-St. Louis fracas, the Association was threatened by the possibility of Cincinnati going into the National League. Like Byrne, Cincinnati President Aaron Stern denied that the Redlegs were seeking admission to the rival league but said that he would accept a good offer to join it (Orem 400). After Sunday baseball was banned in Cincinnati, Stern thought that the fifty cent admission in the National League was even more attractive. Even Von der Ahe was supposed to be considering buying the Indianapolis National League franchise and leaving the Association. This rumor seemed most unlikely since Von der Ahe had often insisted that Sunday baseball and twenty-five cent admission were necessary in St. Louis. Nonetheless, the American Association was in one of its most unsettled states by mid-September. While the early season problems in Louisville and St. Louis were caused primarily by differences between owners and players, the major conflicts within the Association were among rival owners, especially Byrne and Von der Ahe. By the time that they met in Cincinnati, natural rivalries had become inextricably entwined with questions of personal honor. Charges and countercharges had crowded the sports pages for weeks, and an amicable settlement between Brooklyn and St. Louis seemed impossible.

Needing support from other Association members, the Bridegrooms were hampered in developing good relations with other teams by their cranks' actions. After splitting a pair with the Athletics in Philadelphia, McGunnigle brought his team back to Brooklyn for a four game series with Columbus. Bob Caruthers won the first game 9-4 as Columbus helped immeasurably with eleven errors. Columbus defeated Adonis Terry on Sunday and eked out a 3-2 win the next day. Brooklyn cranks nearly mobbed Umpire Ed Hengle for calling the game because of darkness in the ninth inning. Hengle made his decision after Brooklyn had tied the score, causing the score to revert to the previous inning. Even though rightfully angered, Brooklyn spectators seemed particularly unruly, thus giving some credence to Von der Ahe's and Commy's fears for their players' safety.

Whether the crowd's actions in Brooklyn had any effect on the Association's deliberations is doubtful, however, since the game was played during the meeting in Cincinnati. At the meeting, Association Directors decided that St. Louis should be given the victory on September 7 since they thought that Umpire Fred Goldsmith should have called the

Bob Caruthers—A good hitter, "Parisian Bob" only pitched in 1889 and led the American Association in winning percentage, wins, and shutouts. Photo credit National Baseball Library, Cooperstown, N.Y.

game because of darkness. However, Brooklyn was re-awarded the forfeit of September 8 and the $1,500 fine. This supposed compromise made Commy and Von der Ahe jubilant. They had previously been denied both games, and the fine had been halved. President Wheeler C. Wikoff had said even before the Directors met that expulsion was not an option. They also decided not to consider other matters such as Commy's abuse of Umpire Bob Ferguson or his rantings against Charles H. Byrne. Indeed, Commy used the occasion of the Cincinnati meeting to repeat his previous charges that Byrne was "a dark lantern robber" (*S.L.,* 2 October 1889). All of this, of course, made Byrne livid.

J.F. Donnolly reported that indignation ran deep in Brooklyn and that there was a "keen edge on the desire for jumping out of the American Association and...a new zest to the discussion of the possibility of Brooklyn entering the League" (*S.L.,* 2 October 1889). Since both Commy and Von der Ahe continued to say that Byrne had deliberately turned the Brooklyn public against St. Louis by charging the Browns with unfair treatment in August, Commy was denounced as "an ass." Ren Mulford, Cincinnati correspondent, tried to interject a modicum of reason into the feud by asking that if Byrne was a Blackleg, if he did own Wheeler C. Wikoff, and if he truly controlled the umpires, why couldn't St. Louis prove it? Mulford had no great love for either Brooklyn or St. Louis, but he pleaded for common sense. He thought the Browns' charges against Byrne preposterous.

Amidst the obvious disintegration of the Association, Francis C. Richter denounced the compromise by the Association Directors. He thought that both games should have been given to Brooklyn and that the umpire's decision should have been supported. Henry Chadwick, ever the defender of the rules, echoed Richter. But only Baltimore had supported Brooklyn at the Cincinnati meeting, and the Association's attempt to mediate the warfare between Brooklyn and St. Louis through compromise had clearly failed.

Perhaps angered by the news from Cincinnati, Bob Caruthers, after a number of rocky outings, pitched a three-hit shut out against Columbus on September 24 as his outfielders battled mosquitoes in Washington Park. Well rested after rain and Terry's tie game with Columbus, Caruthers threw another shutout against Baltimore on the 27th and then closed out September with a victory over the Orioles two days later. Brooklyn cranks were overjoyed by Caruthers' return to form, and they undoubtedly

Mike Tiernan—Great Giants' right fielder in the uniform of the 1887 Giants. Third in National League in batting average, fourth in slugging average, and triples during 1889. He led in runs scored and walks. Photo credit National Baseball Library, Cooperstown, N.Y.

expected the Browns to quietly fold their tents after the St. Louis Board of Directors' action of September 25.

Early in September, Chris Von der Ahe had publicized his dissatisfaction with his team by suggesting a trade of Charlie Duffee and Arlie Latham for the Athletics' Denny Lyons and Curt Welch. He also tried to buy pitcher Sadie McMahon from the Athletics but failed in these endeavors to strengthen the Browns, since the Athletics demanded too much money (*Clipper*, 14 September 1889; *Herald*, 6 September 1889). Still frustrated after the Cincinnati meeting, Von der Ahe decided to take even more drastic action concerning the disastrous eastern trip. He called a meeting of his Board of Directors on September 25 and, after deciding that some Browns had "played not to win", fined Latham $200 and suspended him indefinitely. Silver King was also suspended but fined only $100, as was Icebox Chamberlain. Yank Robinson was merely reprimanded for "trying to swallow a brewery" in Kansas City. Both Chamberlain and Latham had gone on a "toot" in Kansas City, but they were also charged with "a general all around inclination to let the other fellows win" (*S.N.*, 28 September 1889).

Although Latham had few supporters among the St. Louis sporting public or his teammates, the disciplining of King and Chamberlain was very unpopular. Von der Ahe had typically overreacted to the Browns' recent losses. *The Chicago Tribune*'s earlier condemnation could be reaffirmed by many of his critics: "Baseball always will remember him [Von der Ahe] as one of the greatest flukes and turbulent spirits ever injected into the game...the game will be well rid of him" (*Herald*, 11 September 1889). Henry Chadwick's reference to him ("Whom the gods would destroy they first make mad." [*S.L.*, 18 September 1889]) seemed even more applicable as St. Louis tried to catch the Bridegrooms without their best pitchers (*S.L.*, 2 October 1889).

Browns' players strongly opposed the penalties imposed on their two best pitchers, yet they managed to win their last two games in September. It helped that Louisville was their opponent. The Colonels had become the first professional baseball team to lose 100 games when Jack Stivetts beat them on September 26. With Pete Browning experiencing his worst season and being laid off for the season after September 1, the Colonels were simply going through the motions (*Herald*, 2 September 1889). Since they played Louisville, Kansas City, and Cincinnati to end the season while Brooklyn tussled with Baltimore, Philadelphia, and Columbus, Commy's grousers still had a chance for the pennant even though they trailed the Grooms by four and one-half games at the start of October.

While the American Association seemed intent on displaying professional baseball's most shameful characteristics, the National League's top two teams embarked on a dazzling race to the wire on September 16. A summary account of Boston's and New York's games gives some idea of the excitement that baseball could engender in two major cities, although it is difficult to recapture the personal involvement that thousands of cranks experienced as their beloved Giants and Beaneaters battled for the championship.

After sweeping their doubleheader with Chicago on September 14, the Giants entrained for their last road trip which would conclude in Cleveland on October 5. Hank O'Day defeated Washington 12-4 on the 16th as New York hitters were aided by Washington errors. In Boston, John Clarkson lost to the Phillies' Charlie Buffinton, 3-2. Charlie Bennett made one of the costliest mistakes of his career when he was picked off second in the 9th inning with the clutch-hitting Hardie Richardson at bat. Clarkson had shutout the Phillies until the eighth when they scored three runs, one unearned. Morose Boston cranks brightened the next day as Hoss Radbourn won, putting the Beaneaters only percentage points behind the Giants. The latter's avid followers, meanwhile, showered telegrams on the team in Washington, e.g. "Hosanna, Hosanna, Hosanna in the highest, is the joyful refrain of the Exposition City tonight. God bless the Giants and good-bye to the Beaneaters" (*Times,* 18 September 1889). As Clarkson began the first of five consecutive starts in six days by defeating Philadelphia, Mutrie's charges rewarded their faithful with a doubleheader victory over Washington on the 18th. Buck Ewing caught Tim Keefe in game one while Cannonball Crane pitched the second game. Crane had not pitched since August 31 but won despite eight Giant errors. Mike Tiernan continued to hit at a torrid pace by winning the first game with his tenth inning home run.

After Boston and New York switched opponents, O'Day, Keefe, and Welch defeated the Phillies in three out of four games. Keefe would have won both games of his doubleheader on the 20th had it not been for Ewing's throwing error which caused a tie. Tiernan led the hitters with two home runs as the Giants were aided by the absence of the great Phillies' pitcher Charlie Buffinton. Many New Yorkers traveled to Philadelphia on the 21st to cheer the Giants. Urged on by *The Boston*

Globe's offer of $1,000 to the team if Boston won the pennant, the amazing Clarkson defeated Washington twice during this same period but was tied on the 21st in twelve innings, thus giving the Giants a full game lead. Then, as Clarkson and Keefe deservedly rested on Sunday, September 22, the full story of the Brotherhood revolt broke in Chicago. Al Spalding read it with some unbelief and much anger.

Frank H. Brunell, Sporting Editor for *The Chicago Tribune*, had written of The Players League concept as early as September 7 (*Universal Baseball Guide* 32). On the same day, reports emanated from Indianapolis about Albert L. Johnson working with Brotherhood leaders on a new league for 1890 (*Herald*, 8 September 1889). Will Johnson also talked freely in St. Louis, so National League owners had ample forewarning about the Brotherhood's highly developed plans for a new league that hit the newsstands on September 22-23. Still, the magnitude of the scheme was a bit shocking. Although mistakes were made in the original report, the major elements of The Players League were outlined accurately enough to cause owners great concern.

The new league would take most of the current players out of the National League and operate in eight major cities. The only city in which it would not compete directly with the National League was Buffalo. Albert L. Johnson, described as a missionary for the Brotherhood cause, had helped convince other owners to adopt a profit sharing plan with the players. The first $10,000 profits would go to the players on the top four teams while the next $80,000 would be divided among the owners. Players would divide the next $80,000, and any further profits would be split among owners and players. Governance of the new league was also to be shared among owners and players while, surprisingly, classification and reserve rules for 1889 were supposed to apply for 1890. Both rules were later modified (Seymour 229).

Some players had already bought stock in their new teams, among them Tim Keefe, Monte Ward, Dan Brouthers, John Clarkson, and Ned Hanlon. It was estimated that less than ten National League players would stay with it. Brotherhood members had considered a strike on July 4 but had instead voted in favor of this total reorganization, and Albert L. Johnson had been the moving force behind lining up capitalists willing to support the new league. Will Johnson expressed the general feeling of the players and new owners when he said "...the players will have the sympathy of the people with them. No man living that I know of feels friendly to the League bosses. This selling and trading of players, as though they were so many cattle, is all wrong, and the time has come when the players must take the bull by the horns and do something for themselves" (*Times*, 23 September 1889).

Despite all of the evidence to the contrary, Giants' President John B. Day simply could not believe that the players would actually leave their teams and form their own league. "I do not think there is anything in it, as I am in a position to know that there is no syndicate, that there is no idea of forming one, and that no man in this city knows anything of such a scheme. I have talked to the New York players and each man has told me that he did not know anything about it..." (*Clipper*, 28 September 1889). Ward and Keefe did at first deny the veracity of the Chicago report, but they were bluffing. Of course, they could rationalize denying its truth since it contained many factual errors about what actually was planned (See Seymour 228-29 and Voigt 160 for the final organizational setup). They also possibly did not want to hurt Day since they liked him, and he had treated them and all Giants players well. So, for awhile longer, Day and his players could devote most of their attention to winning baseball games.

Since losing to Indianapolis on September 6, New York had strung together ten straight wins, but now they were headed into Indianapolis where the formidable Jack Glasscock, Jerry Denny, and Amos Rusie awaited them. The young rookie Rusie had pitched well against the Giants all year with his good fast ball, drop ball, and curve. Monte Ward tried to inject some levity into the concluding games by analyzing how the Giants generally did better than the Beaneaters in the west: "...the Beaneaters drink water. We don't drink water" (*Herald*, 16 September 1889). If anything, the reverse was true, but Keefe managed to eke out an 11-9 win on the 23rd while Clarkson kept pace by defeating Chicago. Glasscock chose to start mediocre Lev Shreve, who had pitched well against the Giants, the next day and relieved with rookie Jack Fee as the Giants pounded out a 16-12 victory behind Cannonball Crane. New York won despite five errors and Welch's inability to get past the third inning. Two Boston cranks, Arthur Dixwell and George Floyd, thought the Hoosiers' pitching choices highly questionable. They telegraphed Player-Manager Glasscock and asked if he was really trying to defeat the Giants. Glasscock fired back a telegram demanding an apology, which Dixwell sent, abruptly concluding this little side show (Orem 417). Meanwhile, Radbourn finally spelled Clarkson and defeated Chicago. Both Keefe and Clarkson lost the next day, so the Giants still led by one game as they exchanged cities. Rusie had mown the Giants down, holding them to six hits.

When the Beaneaters had left Boston for their final road swing on September 19th, the Boston Music Hall opened its doors each afternoon so that faithful Beantown cranks could watch Boston's games be replayed from telegraphic reports (Kaese 53). Dixwell led cheers with his piercing "Hi, Hi," and when Clarkson beat the Hoosiers 12-6 while Bill Hutchinson outpitched Mickey Welch 4-3 in Chicago, the Music Hall rocked. Twenty-three year old Hugh Duffy contributed three key hits for Chicago while, as so often happened after a train ride, the Giants committed a number of errors. Worse, Buck Ewing lacerated his right thumb in the third inning and was replaced by Bill Brown. Pat Murphy caught Keefe the next day as the Giants continued to field badly in the cold weather, but they got twenty hits to beat Chicago 18-6. Clarkson defeated Indianapolis 15-8 as the teams combined for fourteen errors. With the pressure mounting, Buck Ewing returned to the lineup on the 28th while Mickey Welch dueled Bill Hutchinson. The game ended in a 2-2 tie because the usually dependable Giants' third baseman Art Whitney muffed a groundball. Most of the 5,000 Chicago spectators cheered for the Giants, hoping that New York could beat out their former heroes, Clarkson and Kelly. When the bulletin board posted Clarkson's 10-3 defeat by Rusie, the Chicago assemblage cut loose a boisterous whoop that carried for blocks. The Giants now led by a half game.

Such news pleased John B. Day, but he was still shocked by pro-labor James J. Coogan's announcement that he had granted a ten-year lease to the players' Brotherhood for a two-block plot of ground adjacent to the New Polo Grounds. More ominously, Coogan said that the Brotherhood had arranged to lease the Giants' new home after the latter's two-year lease expired. When some newsmen suggested to Day that he might have been wise to accept Coogan's $200,000 offer, Day exploded angrily that he had never received any such proposal and that the whole idea was "an advertising dodge of Coogan, of Coogan's Bluff" (Orem 417).

The validity of Coogan's earlier offer was the least concern for Day. With reports from Boston about Albert L. Johnson trying to buy grounds there for the Brotherhood, Day could no longer discount the seriousness of the players' revolt. Al Spalding definitely thought that the players intentions posed a great challenge to the owners. On Sunday, September

29, Spalding publicized a letter that he had written the previous day to John Montgomery Ward. In it, Spalding offered to meet the Brotherhood's grievance committee which he had summarily dismissed in late June. Ward, Brotherhood President, coyly replied to Spalding that he would have to consult the entire Brotherhood membership about any meeting with the owners. Recalling Spalding's condescending delaying tactics in June, the Giants' shortstop immensely enjoyed turning the tables on the autocratic Spalding and postponing any meetings until later. Assessing the successful recruitment of financiers for the Players League, Ward undoubtedly felt that the players now held the upper hand. Unquestionably, Spalding was worried or he would not have suggested a meeting that he had previously deemed unnecessary until November (*Times,* 30 September 1889). John B. Day worried too.

With the mounting furor over the National League players' intentions for 1890, the Giants and Beaneaters continued their inspiring run for the wire. Disheartened over their tie on the 28th, the Giants had to play Pittsburgh in drizzling rain, sawdust, and mud on the 30th. The great Pud Galvin, even though he looked "fat and forty" (*Herald,* 3 September 1889), battled Tim Keefe to a 3-3 tie. After five innings, the Giants had led 3-1, but Umpire Tom Lynch refused to call the game even though the ball could barely be seen. Despite the horrendous playing conditions and the preceding long train ride, the Giants made only two errors. Pittsburgh's veteran team, (which included first baseman Jake Beckley, second baseman Fred Dunlap, forty-two year old rheumatic third baseman Deacon White, shortstop Jack Rowe, and centerfielder Ned Hanlon), made only one error and caught New York with two runs in the sixth inning.

In Cleveland, John Clarkson watched his mates score four runs in the seventh inning to win 6-3. Even though Dan Brouthers was still not hitting well, Billy Nash was, and Clarkson had won an astounding seven games out of nine decisions since September 18. Ironically, only Hoss Radbourn had interrupted Clarkson's workhorse performance except for Kid Madden's brief mopup stint in the Indianapolis loss. The great Radbourn had set a pitching endurance record in 1884 when he twirled all but two of Providence's last thirty-two games. A major difference between Clarkson and Radbourn was that the latter pitched underhanded. Pitching Clarkson so often was an act of desperation on Manager Jim Hart's part, but Boston's owners concurred in this strategy. They also sought to insure proper discipline on the Boston team by having Director William H.

Conant travel with the Beaneaters. Obviously, King Kelly's activities were the major concern. As the two teams girded themselves for the last five games, the Giants led by mere percentage points.

Chapter Twelve
The Giants Triumphant

Heavy rain and cold weather had hurt attendance in both major leagues during September, cutting into owners' profits at a time when the exciting pennant races should have provided a bonanza. As if the elements were not bad enough, the consuming enmity between Brooklyn and St. Louis had made every Association team edgy about their future. National League owners also looked uneasily ahead after the astounding news of the extensive player disaffection became public in late September.

Boston owners demonstrated the pragmatic skills that would enable the National League to eventually triumph by seeking a new manager, Frank Selee from Omaha, and planning to employ a number of young Omaha players, among them pitcher Charles "Kid" Nichols. Of course, the Boston triumvirate, Arthur H. Soden, William H. Conant, and James B. Billings, could afford such expenditures since they had made approximately $100,000 profit in 1889. Total Boston home attendance was 295,377 for 1889 with over 70,000 cranks coming out for the Giants' games (*S.L.*, 25 September 1889). On the other hand, John B. Day had lost money in 1889 because of the problems with finding proper grounds, the holdouts of Tim Keefe and John Ward, the construction costs of St. George's and the New Polo Grounds, and the revenues lost from bad weather. Decidedly, Day was in an unenviable position as his great team began the final stretch drive. He knew that many of them would be going to the new league, and he had little capital with which to hire new talent. Nonetheless, John B. Day reveled in the moment, the drive for the pennant.

The news from Pittsburgh continued bad for Day. Young Harry Staley out-pitched Mickey Welch, and Billy Sunday brought the 3,500 spectators to their feet with a brilliant catch. Pittsburgh's winning rally was based primarily on four scratch hits plus Buck Ewing's error. After the 7-2 loss, Ewing gave his dejected team a typically sensible assessment. "Well, boys, we've got everything to win and nothing to lose now. Take all chances hereafter, and if we fall let it be after a hard fight. Boston has got plenty of luck, but let us try and stand off that advantage with gameness" (*Times*, 2 October 1889). Boston had captured a one game lead by virtue of Clarkson's 8-5 victory over Cleveland. One ominous sign for the Beaneaters, however, was King Kelly's three errors in right field. Could he hold up under the pressure without going on one of his famous binges?

During the night of October 1, the great King celebrated the victory by attending a party at Albert L. Johnson's. Probably intending to discuss some details about the Players League, Kelly imbibed freely into the early morning hours. In no condition to play on the 2nd, he nevertheless sat bundled in an overcoat on the Boston bench. Severely hung over, Kelly derided his team when they fell three runs behind. "You never win when I don't play. Kelly is king. I am a king" (*Times*, 3 October 1889). Captain Kelly continued to demoralize the Beaneaters by muttering and shouting similar pleasantries as the game progressed. In Boston's sixth inning, Hardie Richardson was called out at the plate by Umpire John McQuaid. Kelly decided to act. When the inning ended, Kelly "strolled toward McQuaid with blazing eye and inflamed face. He told the umpire that he had come west to rob Boston of the pennant and at the same time drew back his fist to strike McQuaid" (*Times*, 3 October 1889). Two policemen grappled with Kelly, eventually using a choke-hold to subdue him. Unceremoniously banished from the park, the disheveled and dishonored king spent the remainder of the game nervously smoking and unsuccessfully attempting to reenter. Cleveland cranks, including the small boys that usually admired Kelly, ridiculed the pathetic Beaneater captain as Boston lost 7-1. The Music Hall crowd was unusually quiet on October 2 (Kaese 53).

Although *The Times* worked overtime to maintain Kelly's image by calling attention to his great abilities, his actions unquestionably demoralized his teammates, especially pitcher John Clarkson. Charlie Bennett and Clarkson had tried to prevent Kelly from threatening McQuaid, and Manager Jim Hart attempted to quiet him, prompting Kelly's ridicule for his pains. Even with Kelly in the lineup, Boston would probably have lost to the great pitching of Ed Beatin. Also, Clarkson could not pitch with any speed, it being his seventh consecutive start. Essentially, Boston was paying the price for depending on one great pitcher after September 17. Nonetheless, the Beaneaters could ill afford the King's jollification in Cleveland.

The Giants rebounded into first by beating Pittsburgh 6-3 behind

Cannonball Crane. Leading Boston again by percentage points, the players could barely restrain themselves from painting the town. Buck Ewing got some key hits, and Crane pitched well with men on base, striking out eight to balance his seven walks. Tim Keefe had asked for another day's rest before the concluding Cleveland series, and Ewing wisely concurred since Keefe had pitched especially well against the Spiders throughout the year. The great Giants' hurler impressed everyone on October 3 by throwing a two-hitter at Cleveland, winning 9-0 as New York collected eleven hits. Boston kept pace when Clarkson beat Pud Galvin 7-2, but the Giants were brimming with confidence that they could hold on to first place.

John B. Day had been traveling with the Giants during the run to the wire, and he and Jim Mutrie decided to leave nothing to chance at this juncture. Mutrie was despatched to Pittsburgh before Mickey Welch defeated Cleveland 6-1 on October 4. In Pittsburgh, John Clarkson had developed a chest cold, but Kid Madden managed to win 4-3 in very cold weather, so the Giants still led by a slim margin. The occasion for Mutrie's departure was the rumor that Boston would try to play a doubleheader in Pittsburgh on the last day, October 5. If both teams won their single games, New York would still win the pennant, but if Boston won two games to the Giants' one, the Beaneaters would be triumphant. Mutrie was assigned to telegraph Day if a doubleheader was being played, in which case, Day had made "arrangements to play two or more games...if necessary" (*Times*, 5 October 1889). Such suspicions now seem ludicrous, but scheduling changes could be made rapidly at that time, and Boston's owners were known for their ability to make last-minute alterations to suit their needs. As if the question of how many games would actually end the final day of the season was not irregular enough, the issue of premium offers by the Beaneaters and Giants to their rival's opponents also intruded.

To obtain a proper perspective, the practice of offering incentives to opponents of rival teams needs to be correlated with the gambling habits of players during 1889. Despite all of the standard comments about the purity and honesty of baseball, gambling was a common feature of the game all through the 1880s. In the famous 1886 World Series between the Browns and White Stockings, both teams wagered $500 on themselves to win. Players also placed personal bets, and when the Browns won the series, Chris Von der Ahe demonstrated his generous nature by helping "quite a few of the Chicago players who went broke backing the White

Stockings with side bets" (Lieb, *Cardinals* 10-11; see also Kelly, *Play Ball, passim*). Gambling was particularly prevalent in 1889 with two close pennant races extending to the last days of the season. Such activity was by no means limited to the thousands of pool room inhabitants in the urban centers.

As noted previously, Brooklyn's Bob Caruthers and Dave Foutz bet heavily and regularly on their team's ability to win and their own. Another reason that Arlie Latham's questionable relationship with a gambler did not cause more of a stir was that Charlie Comiskey himself bet heavily on his team. Reminiscing in May, 1950, Arlie told sportswriter Jimmy Powers that Commy was a Jekyll-Hyde manager "according to how his daily heavy bets on the game came out" (Latham File, NBL). Granted the players were betting for their teams, and Latham's activities were questioned in relation to his poor play, but the fact remains that gambling was endemic to baseball in 1889. The sort of gambling that was prohibited and censured was betting against one's own team, thereby causing suspicions about throwing games. As sports commentators never failed to point out, the national game had supposedly been free of this curse since four Louisville players had thrown away the pennant in 1877 and suffered banishment for life. Gambling for one's team was still condoned.

In this context of open gambling, the issue of financial incentives for rivals' opponents, while reprehensible, can be best understood. Before the final games on October 5, Manager Jim Hart and John Clarkson offered the Cleveland battery, pitcher Henry Gruber and catcher Sy Sutcliffe, $500 apiece if they defeated the Giants. Presumably, this "premium" would cost Boston nothing should they win over Pittsburgh because of *The Boston Globe's* proposal to reward the Beaneaters with $1,000 if they won the pennant. Learning of Boston's shenanigans, Jim Mutrie responded by offering a new suit of clothes to Pittsburgh players should they beat Boston. Some reports had Mutrie waving a $100 bonus in front of pitcher Pud Galvin. The first sportswriter to object to this procedure in 1889 was Henry Chadwick. He correctly labeled Boston's action "open bribery" and thought that all "premium offers" were objectionable, including those of the Giants. Before the American Association season ended on October 15, other sportswriters would join Chadwick in questioning this rather common practice in baseball (*S.L.*, 16 October 1889; Orem 419).

Such financial and scheduling maneuvers were another indication of New York's and Boston's emotional, pell-mell race to win the National

League pennant. As in the highly competitive, unregulated business world, most people did not question these procedures because they agreed that everything should be done to win short of blatant wrongdoing.

In New York, people's concern over the Giants' fate was so great on October 5 that large crowds gathered in Park Row to watch the newspaper bulletin boards. Street cars and trucks negotiated the streets with difficulty, and pedestrians found it virtually impossible to use the walks (Orem 418). Such fascination over the outcome of a baseball game would lead The New York Baseball Bulletin Company, incorporated in January, 1890, to manufacture a machine that could mechanically reproduce games in progress (*Clipper 1891 Annual* 30). It was the television of the late nineteenth century.

All afternoon and well into the evening, baseball dominated conversations at the hotels, clubs, and cafes. The contagious excitement made all social classes kin for a few hours (*Herald,* 6 October 1889).

> There was plenty of excitement around the bulletin boards yesterday. Small boys, beardless youths, middle-aged men, and men past the prime of life crowded each other in their efforts to get close enough to distinguish the figures...Around the tickers in the various hotels and saloons standing room was at a premium. Everybody appeared anxious to get the first news. (*Times,* 6 October 1889)

Tim Keefe did not disappoint these loyal followers as he pitched a six-hitter and defeated Cleveland 5-3. Mike Tiernan continued the clutch hitting that had typified his play down the stretch by belting a two-run home run in the first inning. Jim O'Rourke made a good catch in the 9th, and the Giants fielded flawlessly for most of the game. Cleveland cranks pulled for the Giants, who were recognized as one of the great teams to that time, and gave a loud cheer at game's end. To the great disappointment of 6,000 Bostonians in The Music Hall, Pud Galvin out-pitched John Clarkson 6-1 in Pittsburgh. King Kelly collected three hits, but Clarkson was still suffering from a cold, and his team played listlessly when they learned that the Giants were leading Cleveland. The Beaneaters' five errors included two costly ones by shortstop Pop Smith. Some of the poor play could be attributed to the fact that the Giants had to lose in order for Boston to have any chance for the pennant.

Despite the great rivalry between the Giants and Beaneaters, the entire Boston team and General Arthur Dixwell wired congratulations to the Giants in Cleveland. *The Boston Globe* demonstrated true sportsmanship by offering their $1,000 bonus to the Giants, but Beantowners bemoaned their team's performance on the road and speculated on who most to blame. Of course, John Clarkson and Hardie Richardson received widespread praise for their phenomenal work, but the team's batting had declined noticeably in the second half of the season.

William H. Conant thought the players were indifferent toward the end, looking forward to the new Brotherhood league. Henry Chadwick commended Manager Jim Hart although many thought that he had no control over the players' drinking on western trips. While John Clarkson, Charlie Bennett, Charlie Ganzel, Pop Smith, and Hardie Richardson were exonerated, Mike Kelly, Kid Madden, Dick Johnston, Bill Daley, and Hoss Radbourn were accused of "more or less lushing." Billy Nash and Dan Brouthers slipped only once, but some charged that away from home, Boston players were frequently in no condition to play ball (*S.L.,* 16 October 1889). William D. Sullivan opined that Hart may have given his men a little too much rein, but Francis C. Richter thought that Hart had done his best under the circumstances. Sullivan praised Kelly's play in the last six weeks, except for the one day in Cleveland, and indicated that one other key player had hurt Boston's chances by drinking too much. That player was probably Hoss Radbourn since John Clarkson literally pitched himself out after mid-September. The dependence on one pitcher and the weakness at shortstop eventually spelled defeat for Boston. The Giants were the better team but barely so.

And how they did celebrate their hard-won pennant. The night of October 5, John B. Day, referring to Jim Mutrie's widely known phrase "We Are The People," wired *The New York Sporting Times* that "The People will arrive at the Chambers Street Depot tomorrow afternoon at 4 o'clock via the Erie Road" (Orem 418). By the time that Day sent his telegram, most of the Giants were painting the town. The usually sober second baseman Danny Richardson rejoiced so strenuously that he missed the train that night. All was excused since most of the Giants were normally temperate in their consumption of alcohol, if they drank at all. The players had felt so much pressure in their last series with Cleveland that they had slept little, so their ensuing three day spree seemed a normal reaction.

John Montgomery Ward went to Pittsburgh, undoubtedly to confer with Ned Hanlon about Players League business, but the remaining players, excluding Richardson, poured themselves onto the train car with the words "We Are The People" emblazoned upon it. Between seven

hundred and one thousand baseball enthusiasts lustily cheered the Giants'
arrival in Jersey City on October 6, among them, ex-assemblyman Joseph
Gordon, and part owners William Primrose, Walter Appleton, Charles
Dillingham, Edward Dillingham, and William Quinn. Some renowned
New York cranks had accompanied the Giants on the last leg of their trip,
including bar-restaurant owner Nick Engel, Dolly Merrill, and Cy
Goodfriend. Manager Jim Mutrie was moved to speak:

> It was a hard struggle, and I'm mighty glad it's over. For weeks I have passed
> sleepless nights...We played ball that surpassed anything that I have ever
> witnessed....Those tie games in Chicago and Pittsburgh came at a very bad
> stage....At that juncture the boys showed their sand. They never quit for an
> instant...That last game...they went to do or die, and they would have risked a limb
> to score a run....The Bostons are good players, but we are the people. (*Times,* 7
> October 1889)

Whereupon, the assemblage sang and hollered the Giants' battle cry,
"We Are The People," as the players made their way into the city. The
Giants' popular Captain, Buck Ewing, was recognized by many cranks,
but Giants' owner John B. Day ambled through the crowds virtually
unnoticed.

Edward Cary, *The Times* editorial writer, took time out from his usual
attention to political, economic, and international issues to laud the Giants,
particularly noting that "the managers and players of the League are to be
congratulated that no suspicion of dishonorable practices has marred the
record of the year's play" (*Times,* 6 October 1889). Since Cary had
previously emphasized the importance of a proper playing field for the
Giants on Manhattan and the great value of baseball for New York City, it
is understandable that he would promote the honor of the game as did so
many sportswriters and owners. As stories of urban violence continued to
crowd news columns, Cary wished to champion a game which, he
believed, offered needed wholesome entertainment for thousands. On the
very next page after his editorial comments appeared a horrifying story of
a young girl beaten to death by other young girls. The next day, the paper
reported that a gang of young boys from the slaughterhouse area was
accosting other youths in the Bryant Park area. Surveying such appalling
violence, Cary can be forgiven for overlooking some of baseball's failings,
proclaiming its honorable qualities, and hoping that such a spectator sport
could bring some necessary diversions to all classes of people in New

York City, young and old. The United States needed an honest, upright sport for the growing cities, and baseball was the best choice (See Barth 183 for further commentary on baseball's image).

As they had done all year, *Times* sportswriters chose to heap praise on Buck Ewing, and Ewing did deserve special mention for his great play plus catching more games than any other National League catcher. However, four other Giants, Mike Tiernan, Jim O'Rourke, Roger Connor, and George Gore, joined Ewing in batting over .300 with the quiet Tiernan third best in the League. Johnny Ward came close at .299. Tim Keefe and Mickey Welch had their last great years and ranked near the top among National League pitchers. Yet without fast-ball pitchers Cannonball Crane and Hank O'Day, the Giants would not have won the pennant. Granted, Buck Ewing demonstrated great courage in often catching with sore hands, but the Giants won the pennant because of a great team effort as Henry Chadwick pointed out. Chadwick thought that the Giants excelled in what he termed teamwork as well as hard hitting, and modern statistics bear him out. They used the hit and run on occasion in 1889 although they did not develop this tactic to the extent that later teams did. Chadwick also noted that the Giants were blessed with two skilled strategists on the field, Buck Ewing and Monte Ward (*S.L.*, 23 October 1889).

Perhaps the reason that Buck Ewing was so often singled out by *The Times* was his ability to get the best out of his players even if it meant antagonizing them momentarily. One example of this quality occurred while the Giants were playing Chicago early in the season at St. George's. Ewing motioned center fielder George Gore to play a batter differently. Gore playfully faked a move but stayed put. Ewing then took off his mask, walked toward center field, and told Gore "If you don't want to do what I tell you, you can get out of the game" (Palmer, *Stories* 38). The stunned crowd hissed Ewing vigorously at first but eventually cheered him for his firm leadership. Buck never carried a grudge, and his players respected him for his playing ability and keeping them alert in the field. They also enjoyed his continual chatter directed towards cranks and umpires during a game. He was an excellent captain on a superb team.

John B. Day gloried in his champions, but his losses during 1889 necessitated a profitable World Series. Twenty-five games in Jersey City and St. George's had lured only 57,260 cranks whereas thirty-nine games at the New Polo Grounds attracted 144,402. In contrast, Boston had drawn over 295,000, and in the American Association, Charlie Byrne's

Bridegrooms had set an attendance record with 353,690.

National League Attendance: 1889

Team	Games	Attendance
Boston	67	283,257
Philadelphia	68	282,957
New York	63	201,989
Chicago	69	151,000
Cleveland	68	144,425
Pittsburgh	70	117,338
Indianapolis	69	105,850
Washington	56	68,652
	530	1,355,468

(Source: *Reach's Official American Association Baseball Guide, 1891*, 26. Reach's 1890 Guide provided different attendance figures for Boston (295,000) and New York (201,662), 4; S.L., 25 September 1889 gives Boston attendance as 295,377.)

American Association Attendance: 1889*

Team	Games	Attendance
Brooklyn	69	353,690
St. Louis-1	69 (69)	236,228
Cincinnati-2	73 (73)	233,833
Philadelphia-3	66 (68)	203,103
Kansas City-4	71 (70)	195,926
Columbus-5	71 (69)	134,414
Baltimore-6	64 (64)	128,056
Louisville-7	64 (65)	91,004
	547	1,576,254

* - Unofficial except for Brooklyn.
1 - Includes estimates for 8 games.
2 - Includes estimates for 5 games.
3 - Includes estimates for 4 games.
4 - Includes estimates for 8 games.
5 - Includes estimates for 9 games.
6 - Includes estimates for 4 games.
7 - Includes estimates for 5 games.

(Sources: *Reach's Official American Association Guide, 1890*, 4; *The New York*

Herald, 18 April 1889-16 October 1889; *Spalding's Baseball Guide...1890*, 78 for home games; *Total Baseball*, 2171 for home games, in parentheses, without ties counted; Robert L. Tiemann, *Through The Years In Sportsman's Park*, 1991, gives lower estimates for St. Louis attendance-ca. 200,000.)

Obviously, Brooklyn would provide New York a perfect opponent since the keen rivalry between the two cities would enhance attendance and bring the revenues which Day sorely needed. Buck Ewing began the pre-series psychological warfare and promotional verbiage by asserting that only an accident would allow an American Association club to defeat a League team. Brooklyn's reply was not immediately forthcoming because the supposedly defeated Browns were mounting a serious challenge. The American Association pennant race was heating up again.

Chapter Thirteen
Brooklyn's First Pennant

Despite Chris Von der Ahe's suspension and fining of Silver King and Icebox Chamberlain, despite Charlie Comiskey's batting slump, despite the demoralized condition of the Browns, they won all of their eleven games from September 26 through October 10 excluding one tie with Louisville. Granted, they were playing the bottom two teams during this period, but they held true to Commy's maxim of never giving up until the very last and began gaining ground on the Bridegrooms. Brooklyn had stiffer competition as they had to entertain the hard-hitting Philadelphia Athletics before their last road trip which began in Baltimore and ended in Columbus. All three teams played well against Brooklyn, and the Browns had an advantage down the stretch.

Fortunately for the Bridegrooms, Bob Caruthers continued to pitch brilliantly, shutting out the Athletics on October 3 and 6, 17-0 and 9-0. In a two-week period, Caruthers threw four shutouts in five decisions with three coming against Baltimore and Philadelphia. Excluding the September 7 game against St. Louis, he had not lost since August 28 and seemed primed to carry the load to season's end. Charlie Byrne and Bill McGunnigle exulted over the Grooms' twenty-two hit rampage against Sadie McMahon on October 3, but they were just as pleased that McMahon walked twelve to give Brooklyn another win three days later. McMahon blamed his poor control on the slippery baseball resulting from muddy grounds, but Caruthers walked no one during the game. With the Browns only two and one-half games behind, a large crowd of Brooklyn cranks came out to Ridgewood to cheer Caruthers on despite threatening weather. On Saturday the day before, Tom Lovett had disappointed the faithful by losing 10-2. Lovett's two bad outings within one week made McGunnigle decide that he would have to depend on his two aces, Caruthers and Terry, for the remaining games.

Since becoming ill in early September, "Adonis" Bill Terry had pitched sparingly, splitting two decisions and tying Columbus. Well-rested, Terry pitched magnificently on October 7 despite the cold, raw

160

Icebox Chamberlain—Despite his ongoing battle with Chris Von der Ahe during 1889, Chamberlain was third in winning percentage and wins, struck out over 200, and had an ERA of 2.97. Photo credit National Baseball Library, Cooperstown, N.Y.

weather in Baltimore. However, his mates made seven errors and could only manage five hits against Frank "Monkey" Foreman, as the Grooms lost 3-2 and saw their lead shrink to two games. Undoubtedly feeling the pressure despite stated confidence, Brooklyn almost threw the game away the next day by making seven more errors. Providentially, Baltimore's young shortstop, Dusty Miller, and right fielder, Stubby Ray, made five errors, and Brooklyn scored five runs in the last of the seventh to win for Caruthers, 12-9. Not one of their runs was earned.

The game was called because of darkness after the Groom's rally, demonstrating the importance of the then traditional practice of allowing the visiting team to bat last. Since so few balls were used in a game, home teams wanted to bat first to get "first licks" at a clean ball. However, if a game needed to be called because of darkness or rain, a winning rally in the first half of an inning was canceled, and the score reverted to the last complete inning. Had Brooklyn been playing at home, they would have lost because Baltimore would probably have stalled interminably.

Although Caruthers had been hit hard, he started again the next day and won 17-9 despite giving up fourteen hits. The Orioles contributed an astounding twelve errors, while the Grooms fielded well and pounded Monkey Foreman for twenty hits. With Caruthers having problems in the cold weather, Terry pitched the last game against Baltimore and won 7-2. Catcher Bob Clark responded to recent criticism by playing a fine game and collecting four hits. Entraining for Columbus, Byrne and McGunnigle felt more confident since St. Louis now had to play Cincinnati. Their two game lead seemed secure.

Commy had alternated Jack Stivetts and Toad Ramsey successfully against Louisville, completing a three-game sweep on October 1. The next day he decided to use the recalcitrant Icebox Chamberlain against Kansas City. Chamberlain had not pitched since September 22 and complained of a sore arm. He did so poorly that Von der Ahe reportedly ordered Commy to put Ramsey in his place. This sort of interference enraged Commy even though the Browns won the game. His boss had been intruding all through the season, coming down to the bench to criticize the players and blame him for assorted mistakes (See Ted Sullivan's testimony, Comiskey file, NBL).

Constantly interfering with the make-up of the team, Von der Ahe succeeded in alienating his great manager to the extent that Commy was considering jumping to the new Players League. Of course, Commy denied that he would ever leave the Browns, ("So much moonshine") but he did say that he had had a long talk with John Ward during the four day rain in September (*S.N.,* 5 October 1889). Both men were in New York, and lots of rain enabled them to discuss many issues. Von der Ahe realized that Commy was considering some sort of move and loudly proclaimed that he would not let him go for less than $20,000. It had not yet sunk in to owners like Von der Ahe that players would be able to ignore the reserve rule by forming their own league. It soon would.

The primary Browns' malcontent, Arlie Latham, worked in a St. Louis hotel billiard room after his second suspension. He also attended all Browns' games at Sportsman's Park, and St. Louis players said that he never failed to pull for the other team. Yank Robinson still sulked, but he played. He made it clear that he wanted to play elsewhere in 1890 as did Silver King, Jocko Milligan, and Icebox Chamberlain. Joe Pritchard thought that the other players would return in 1890, but only Shorty Fuller, Charlie Duffee, Tom McCarthy, Jack Stivetts, and Toad Ramsey eventually stayed.

Despite all of the discontent on the Browns, they had their dislike of Brooklyn to spur them on. They also had managed to maintain some good humor. Center fielder Charlie Duffee stated that he would rather hoe cotton in Alabama than play in Brooklyn again, and catcher Jocko Milligan thought a miner's lamp useful in Brooklyn for games after dark (S.L., 25 September 1889).

Winning helped as well. After defeating Louisville and Kansas City and taking heart from Icebox Chamberlain's return, the Browns traveled to Cincinnati for the supposed end of the season. However, Chris Von der Ahe was trying to arrange to play three postponed games with Philadelphia. If the Browns could beat Cincinnati, if Columbus could cause the Grooms some problems, then making up games with Philadelphia might give St. Louis a fifth consecutive Association pennant. Brooklyn suspected that Philadelphia had voted with the Browns on September 23 in return for some players in 1890. The scheduling arrangements seemed part of this deal (*Herald,* 4 October 1889). Rain fell in Cincinnati on October 12, but the news from Columbus was good.

Pitching again in cold weather, Bob Caruthers allowed Columbus five runs in the ninth inning to lose 7-5 to Lady Baldwin. Both teams argued vigorously throughout the game with Umpire Bob Ferguson, and Columbus players clearly indicated that they intended to give Brooklyn as much trouble as they had St. Louis. The loss decreased Brooklyn's lead to a mere one and one-half games. Rain canceled the Browns-Redlegs game again the next day, but Adonis Terry pitched one of the best games of his career by defeating Henry Gastright 2-1 in bitterly cold weather. Columbus patrons were so interested in the outcome of the pennant race that 6,000 sat in a strong northwest wind with the temperature below 45 degrees. Naturally, there were few hits, but both teams fielded very well despite the chill and sitting huddled in overcoats on the open, uncovered benches during the game. On the 14th, Silver King returned to strike out eight and defeat Cincinnati 5-1, but Terry out-pitched Baldwin 6-1 in Columbus. Unfortunately, Columbus shortstop Lefty Marr made four crucial errors, leaving the door open for later accusations by Von der Ahe that Marr had thrown the game. This was untrue, but combined with the activity of Brooklyn catcher Doc Bushong in Cincinnati on October 15, the American Association season concluded, consistently enough, with bitter, blustering recriminations.

Again trailing by two games, Chris Von der Ahe had arranged to play three postponed games in Philadelphia should his Browns defeat Cincinnati in a doubleheader on the 15th. Had St. Louis won all of those games, Brooklyn then would have had to make up its two postponed games with Columbus and Philadelphia. No one dared think of the rain-out between St. Louis and Brooklyn. Charles H. Byrne later indicated that he would have disputed Von der Ahe's rescheduling arrangements, but he took more practical steps at first.

Brooklyn catcher Doc Bushong had been injured in the July 4 doubleheader with St. Louis and had caught in only two games since. He had controversially acted as emergency, substitute umpire in the Brooklyn-Kansas City series at the end of August, and now he was to perform another important function. Byrne sent Bushong to Cincinnati to offer special incentives to the Cincinnati battery. The great young pitcher, Jim Duryea, and veteran catcher Jim Keenan were offered $100 apiece if they would defeat St. Louis. Thus, the one common factor in the League and Association pennant races was that they both ended in an atmosphere of what Henry Chadwick called open bribery. Whether Bushong's offer had anything to do with the outcome is debatable since the Browns fielded badly, and Jack Stivetts allowed eleven hits in an 8-3 loss. Icebox Chamberlain won the meaningless second game 2- 1, but the contentious Association season had mercifully ended. The name-calling did not. Arlie

Latham tried to have the last word by telegraphing Von der Ahe, "Mister Von der Ahe, come home and blame it on me" (*S.L.*, 23 October 1889).

Beneath the headline "Wolves", *The Sporting News* raved about "the bogus champions" from Brooklyn and charged that "they have won the place by Fraud, Bulldozing, and Bribery" (*S.N.*, 19 October 1889). Citing Bushong's monetary rewards to Duryea and Keenan as evidence of the Grooms' immoral behavior, Alfred Henry Spink compiled a list of wrongs: Columbus shortstop Lefty Marr had purposely fielded badly on October 14 to help Brooklyn, Charles H. Byrne had tried to secure umpires favorable to Brooklyn for home games, Baltimore favored Brooklyn, Byrne had tampered with Commy and other Browns' players by offering them high salaries, and so on. Other commentators regarded most of Spink's criticisms as what one would expect from a staunch supporter of the Browns. William Ingraham Harris, however, was equally concerned about Doc Bushong's assignment in Cincinnati.

Harris did not have the benefit of a Harvard degree as did William D. Sullivan ("Mugwump" in *Sporting Life*), but he had received a sound education from his mother as a youth and educated himself well thereafter. He was one of the most thoughtful sportswriters of his time and expressed intelligent opinions. At the conclusion of the American Association season, Harris decided to make an earnest protest against the practice by a team of offering monetary awards to its competitors' opponents. He cited the recent examples of what Boston, New York, and Brooklyn had done, regarding all of them equally guilty of wrongdoing. Then, like Henry Chadwick, Harris used strong terminology.

> What is all this bribery and betting going to lead to, or rather what has it and similar occurrences already led to? The inevitable result is to create suspicion...that money influences the result of ball games. (*S.L.*, 23 October 1889)

He knew that such suspicion was increasing because people asked him almost daily if baseball was really honest. Harris thought that both leagues should take action against any betting on games, noting that Brooklyn first baseman Dave Foutz had already wagered $100 on the Grooms to win the first World Series game. J.F. Donnolly also reported that the two managers, Jim Mutrie and Bill McGunnigle, had bet each other a suit of clothes on the series. Managers often wagered such items among themselves before the season and, sometimes, during an important series during the year. Still, William Ingraham Harris thought that gambling of any sort cast a cloud over baseball, and he took strong exception to the end of year "bribing-to-win". He thought that it must stop.

Another astute observer, Edward Cary, regarded baseball in its national and urban setting, emphasizing its general societal value, despite some minor failings. The day that the Association season ended, he wrote on the value of sports in the United States, particularly baseball.

The growth of athletics in this country during the past generation is an astonishing phenomenon. Except prize fighting, which then, as now, is carried on by gentlemen of Irish birth or extraction...every form of physical exercise that is susceptible of public exhibition has increased beyond all expectation....it is a matter of great national moment. There can be no doubt that the average American from twenty to thirty is far more given to exercise out of doors than he was thirty years ago, and that in consequence he is a much more capable person, intellectually as well as physically, and that the benefit of his exercise will accompany him through life and be transmitted to his children.

Professional sport seems to be the necessary complement, and perhaps the necessary drawback, of this extended and intensified amateur interest in sport, upon which it reacts very powerfully. There has never been anywhere anything comparable to the enthusiasm with respect to baseball, which pervades all the Northern States from Boston to Kansas City. In the West it is aided by a local rivalry keener than anything of which we in the East have any notion, and which makes the success of the local team as much a matter of local pride as the statistics of hog-killing, or the possession of the tallest building, or any other instance of the superlative degree.

Nothing could be better calculated to increase this feeling than the extraordinarily close finishes this year of the only two associations of professional players that can be fairly called national.

...the popularity of the game is likely to increase. It seems to us this is a public benefit. The stern moralist who objects to the sport would find it difficult to show that if the players were not playing they would be making better use of their faculties. The habitual spectators might indeed be more usefully employed, for a man sitting on a bench and yelling with delight or rage is not engaged in developing any of his organs except his lungs. Nevertheless, the interest thus shown by one class is shown by another equally numerous in taking wholesome and needful exercise. (*Times*, 15 October 1889)

Cary said that the close battles for first and third places in both leagues had kept eight major cities excited until the very end of the season. As he had earlier, Cary commended both leagues for their honorable play, and he lengthily upheld the honesty of the game. All of the questions about Arlie Latham's play from July to his second suspension seemed to have been forgotten or forgiven, not to mention the bribery at season's end (Also see *Herald*, 6 October 1889).

In St. Louis, of course, the gambling issue and Arlie Latham's actions received considerable attention. *The Sporting News* noted that Bob Caruthers had bet Dave Foutz $50 that he would win his World Series starts and agreed with Henry Chadwick and William Ingraham Harris that both leagues should halt such practices (*S.N.*, 3 November 1889). Despite these objections, Brooklyn and New York players bet on themselves to win the series (*S.L.*, 30 October 1889). Betting on the series was heavy in all major cities with New York and Brooklyn leading the way. Gambling and baseball, in one form or another, went hand in hand, and it was well into the twentieth century before major league baseball was forced to deal with the ramifications. In 1889, there were many diversions to draw attention from the questions raised by Harris, Chadwick, and Spink, not the least of which was the formation of The Players League after the World Series. However, St. Louis still had to deal with Arlie Latham.

Charlie Comiskey's role in the Latham affair is a bit difficult to assess. As late as October 3, Joe Pritchard reported that Commy was anxious to have Arlie off of the club and a week later, said that he would definitely not be with the Browns in 1890 (*S.L.*, 9, 16 October 1889). However, even before Brooklyn had won the pennant, Commy was making plans for a post-season western trip that included Latham, King, and Chamberlain on the team (*S.N.*, 12 October 1889). Perhaps Commy had decided that Arlie really did have a sore arm, as he claimed, and that this explained much of his poor play. Supposedly, Arlie had torn a muscle in his arm during a throwing contest with Doc Bushong during the mid-1880s (See Smith, *Baseball* 1970, 107). Yet, according to modern statistics, Arlie was a good fielding third baseman through 1891 (*Total Baseball* 1249). Commy also had grown tired of Von der Ahe's interference with the team and may have wished to restore some sort of order to his strife-torn team by mending fences with alienated players. This tactic seemed especially judicious considering the alternative for dissatisfied players offered by the Players League. Even though Commy had demanded both of Arlie's suspensions, as had Browns' players, it was an easy thing at the end of the season to allow others to blame most of the team's dissension on hot-headed Chris Von der Ahe. Commy had a reputation to protect as one of the best managers in the game, perhaps the best.

Various theories were advanced to explain the Browns' fall from the American Association throne. Joe Pritchard sensibly pointed to the Browns' losses to poor teams, particularly the three planned losses to Kansas City in May, although Brooklyn's main advantage was its better record against Philadelphia and Cincinnati. St. Louis also batted poorly during the last two months. Francis C. Richter complimented the Browns for their game battle despite Commy's managerial mistakes, the conflicts between Von der Ahe and the players, and dissension among some of the players. Richter decided that Von der Ahe's suspension-reinstatement process for supposedly suspicious player behavior largely refuted the suspicions. Essentially, Richter absolved Commy, commending him for his "skill and indomitable pluck," and placed most of the blame for the Browns' failure squarely on the shoulders of Chris Von der Ahe (*S.L.*, 23 October 1889). Commy's hand in the suspensions of Latham, King, and Chamberlain; his diatribe against Umpire Bob Ferguson in Columbus; and the slurs directed against Charles H. Byrne were largely written off by Richter. In a sense, Von der Ahe became a convenient scape-goat for analysts of the American Association's and the Browns' disintegration during 1889. He was such an easy, tempting target.

Alfred Henry Spink, Managing Editor of *The Sporting News*, zeroed in on Charles H. Byrne and the Brooklyn Bridegrooms, waging a bitter vendetta during the World Series and subsequent split within the American Association. His evaluation of the charges against Arlie Latham, however, was judicious and balanced. An admirer of Chris Von der Ahe despite his boorishness, Spink reached some sensible conclusions.

Even though Arlie stayed in St. Louis after the season ended, broke since he had not been paid since September 25, Browns' players had little sympathy for him because they still thought that his poor play had cost them the championship. Spink found one rationale for Arlie's behavior in the $1,500 debt owed by Latham to Von der Ahe at the beginning of the 1889 season. Arlie was angered at the manner in which Von der Ahe arranged for repayment-deductions from salary. Spink squarely faced the question of Arlie's having thrown games. He decided that Latham was not an accomplice but an associate of "gamblers who were betting heavily on games in which Latham was cutting a most important part" (*S.N.*, 19 October 1889). Commy had reported seeing Arlie with the gambler, Mr. Lynch, between games with the Bridegrooms on July 4. During the afternoon game, Arlie's three errors helped Brooklyn win. Because of this,

Commy and Von der Ahe decided to hire a detective to watch Arlie on and off the field. Latham and Lynch were "constantly together and they even passed nights in the same room. It was on the discovery of this evidence that Latham was laid off. Later, he was reinstated on the promise of good behavior and afterwards laid off again owing to the off color of his work." According to Spink, no one, including Von der Ahe, had actually charged Arlie with "crookedness," but "his comrades demanded that he be laid off and it was at their request that he was shelved." Of course, Commy was among those demanding Latham's suspension (*S.N.*, 19 October 1889).

By late October, Chris Von der Ahe seemed to have forgiven Arlie, pledging his intention to keep him on the Browns for 1890 despite the ill will felt towards Latham by his teammates (*S.N.*, 26 October 1889). Perhaps Vondy was influenced in this decision by all of the criticism directed at him during the season. Charged with irresponsible and unfounded accusations against Charles H. Byrne, Wheeler C. Wikoff, umpires, and eventually Arlie Latham, Von der Ahe probably realized that few people would have much patience with a lengthy investigation of the circumstances surrounding Arlie's suspensions. Vondy may also have agreed with Ren Mulford, *Sporting Life* correspondent for Cincinnati, that without Arlie, the Browns lacked an important ingredient. "The Browns, without Arlie Latham, seem to play just as good ball, but the club is like a menagerie minus the monkey cage-a circus parade without the steam calliope. There is no wit, no comedy on the lines, but just as much hard work" (*S.L.*, 23 October 1889). At any rate, by October 31, Vondy was even speaking well of Arlie, once more asserting his unwillingness to sell him at any price (*S.L.*, 6 November 1889).

While it is impossible to determine Arlie Latham's guilt or innocence in throwing games during 1889, it is possible to propose what may have happened between Arlie and his gambler associate. Latham could conceivably have told Mr. Lynch that he was dissatisfied with the way that Chris Von der Ahe was making him pay back his debt and that he had a sore arm which adversely affected his fielding. Encouraged by such confidences, Lynch could understandably have bet on the Browns' losing without Arlie's knowledge. Of course, Latham could have been given some of Lynch's winnings in return for his information, although this was never proven. Arlie needed money, and he may have been angry enough at Von der Ahe to try to make extra cash from someone else's bets. Commy, Von der Ahe, and his teammates were all extremely suspicious and very angry at Latham. However, as Latham often said during his suspensions, he had not received any money from anyone, and he had not thrown any games. In the absence of any other evidence, that must be the final word given the fact that Von der Ahe sought to sign him for 1890.

Curiously enough, Arlie played for Commy again in 1890 but not with the Browns. Both men jumped to the Chicago Players League team, and, as happened in 1889, Commy charged Arlie with throwing games. Latham was released, again pleading a sore arm, joined the National League Cincinnati team and delivered himself of this philippic against Commy: "As a captain he treats his men like an overseer in charge of a lot of street cleaners. When he opens his black and tan face to smile it means 'four more shovels of dirt, please,' or 'go run this errand for me' " (Latham file, NBL). After the Players League failed, Commy would return to manage one more year for Von der Ahe in St. Louis during 1891 and then conclude his managing career at Cincinnati with, fittingly enough, Arlie Latham at third base. From 1892-1894, Arlie fielded very badly, but Commy made no more charges about throwing games. Meanwhile, Chris Von der Ahe further demonstrated his renewed appreciation for Arlie by praising him during the 1890 season for putting "ginger" into the Chicago Brotherhood team. All of the charges and suspicions during the 1889 season were forgotten by Vondy as he began the long decline that would lead to his humiliating departure from baseball in 1898. After all, what was a little suspected gambling in a hot pennant race?

As the St. Louis Browns appraised the 1889 season and decided that Brooklyn was a greater malefactor than Arlie Latham, Brooklyn celebrated and excitedly began preparing to challenge the New York Giants. Charles H. Byrne breathed a long sigh of relief when he learned of the Browns' loss to Cincinnati on October 15. The possibility of yet another clash with Chris Von der Ahe and the American Association Board of Directors was thankfully averted. The malleable Association President Wheeler C. Wikoff would probably have allowed the Browns' makeup games to count in the standings, even though the Association Schedule Committee had agreed that the season should end on October 14. The problem was that the December, 1888 Association annual meeting had arranged for October 17 as the concluding date. Such matters would necessarily be taken up again in November at the 1889 yearly meeting. For the moment, Byrne could briefly savor his first pennant, and then his Bridegrooms could show the Giants how baseball was played.

Chapter Fourteen
Giants vs. Bridegrooms

Charles H. Byrne had traveled with his team for the last crucial seven games. He and the Bridegrooms did not hear of St. Louis' earlier loss to Cincinnati until they pulled into Jersey City in the late afternoon of October 15. Several hundred loyal cranks gleefully embraced the players while they danced and yelled themselves hoarse. On the ferry ride to Brooklyn, tugs, ferryboats, and assorted steam craft noisily saluted the new heroes. Ferdinand A. Abell, Charlie Ebbets, Henry Chadwick, and old baseball player Lipman Pike were among the celebrants who welcomed the Grooms home and guided them up Fulton Street in open carriages. Crowds lined both sides of the streets all the way to Washington Park while boys and young men accompanied the carriages on the dead run. Flags flew over City Hall and other public buildings, but the most heartfelt demonstration was arranged by the youngsters in the neighborhood of Washington Park. As the players and club officials arrived there, they lit a huge bonfire and strung a banner from two trees which pronounced "Brooklyns, Champions, 1890." A large crowd trooped to the ballpark for the concluding victory celebration which featured a fireworks display.

Amidst the pennant jubilation, Brooklyn eagerly looked forward to the World Series with the Giants. Even before the Grooms had won the pennant, enthusiastic Brooklyn cranks began wagering on their team despite the fact that the Giants were favored. Baseball analysts in New York, Brooklyn, and throughout the country had been predicting the strong possibility of a Giants-Bridegrooms World Series since the beginning of the year, so anticipation had been building for some time. The strong urban rivalry also enhanced the pre-series excitement, and the promotional hyperbole from both teams naturally attracted the public's interest. Of course, Jim Mutrie was confident of the Giants' chances.

"Brooklyn or the cream of all players in the American Association can't compare with the Giants," Mutrie said, echoing Buck Ewing's previous views (*Times,* 14 October 1889). The Giants' manager asserted that New York was superior to the Bridegrooms in all aspects of the game

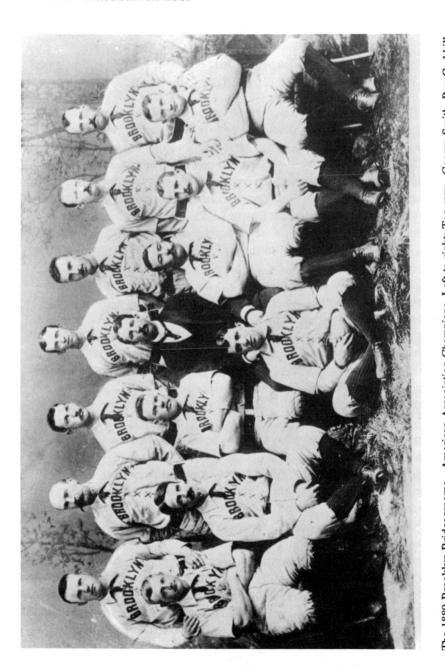

The 1889 Brooklyn Bridegrooms—American Association Champions. Left to right: Top row—George Smith, Pop Corkhill, Bill Terry, Dave Foutz, Darby O'Brien (Captain), Doc Bushong, Joe Visner, Bottom row—George Pinckney, Bob Caruthers, Hub Collins, Bill McGunnigle (Manager), Tome Burns, Bob Clark, Tom Lovett. Seated in front—Mickey Hughes and that Bob Caruthers was the only pitcher that stood a chance against Giant hitters. Mutrie was particularly critical of Brooklyn's catchers, correspondingly predicting that Ewing would easily stop the Grooms' running game. King Kelly went further than Mutrie in writing off Brooklyn's challenge by charging that even the lowly Washington Senators would be a good match for them. He effusively praised Buck Ewing, indicating that Ewing would insure a Giant victory: "There is only one great ball player in the country, and he is William Ewing....He is half of the New York Club....we shall never see his like again. He is to the average ball tosser...what the Statue of Liberty is to a toothpick, and I am proud to be his understudy" (*Times*, 14 October 1889).

Brooklyn President Charlie Byrne naturally disagreed with such views, noting that his team had played better in the pre-season series though losing two out of three to the Giants. Having served public relations, Byrne and Day quickly worked out the details for the best six of eleven game series. As they did so, betting became very brisk in Brooklyn and New York with the Giants becoming a slight favorite. Day and Byrne made sensible arrangements to enhance the quality of the series by arranging for two umpires, one from each league, and ascertaining that the series would end when either team won six games. In 1888, the Browns and Giants had played out all the games after the Giants had won, and attendance suffered greatly.

The Giants were undoubtedly the better team. They had five men who batted over .300 compared to Brooklyn's two, and they had greater pitching depth. True, the Grooms had a slight fielding edge, but their primary weakness was at catcher. Joe Visner was an erratic thrower, and Doc Bushong had not played for most of the season. Much pressure would be placed on Bob Clark.

Brooklyn's odds improved somewhat when Jim Mutrie unexpectedly approved John H. Gaffney to be one of the umpires. John Ward had actually fought with Gaffney a number of years ago, but still the Giants named him as the American Association umpire to work with the League's Thomas J. Lynch. Lynch hesitated to accept the assignment because he thought that he should be paid $800 rather than the $400 offered him. It was known that he might not appear before the second game on Saturday. With the opening game scheduled for October 18 in the New Polo Grounds, betting eventually worked out to $100-$85 in the Giants favor. Both cities were in a high state of excitement over the World Series widely predicted to be the best ever. John B. Day earnestly hoped for good weather and corresponding high attendance.

Friday the 18 dawned fair and bright, and over 8,800 cranks poured into the New Polo Grounds to watch the inaugural game of what would become one of the most intense rivalries in baseball history. Actually, the two teams had played each other in an 1886 post-season series plus the 1889 pre-season games. However, the 1889 World Series represented the beginning of serious competition between the Giants and Brooklyn. How fitting that the rivalry should begin in the most important World Series to that time. The cities of Brooklyn and New York had long been rivals, and the balanced crowd (approximately 3,000 came from Brooklyn) cheered almost every play. The noise was great enough that, at times, the coaches could barely be heard.

Probably because Adonis Terry was so well-rested and had pitched superbly at the end of the year, Bill McGunnigle chose him over Bob Caruthers for his opening game pitcher. Jim Mutrie started the great Tim Keefe, and the Bridegrooms demonstrated their disdain for all of the pre-series hoopla by hitting him hard for five runs in the first inning. Weak hitting Pop Corkhill unexpectedly batted in two of those runs, but Keefe settled down in the middle innings. Leading 6-2 after three innings, Brooklyn suffered the first of two key injuries when their great center fielder, Corkhill, hurt his back trying to catch Danny Richardson's long fly in the fourth. Unnerved, the Grooms' outfield made some key errors as the Giants chipped away and finally took a 10-6 lead with five runs in the seventh. To the consternation of Giants' cranks and Jim Mutrie, Brooklyn came back with two runs in their half of the seventh and then scored four in the eighth to win 12-10. Brooklyn supporters hollered as loudly as their lungs would permit while the Giants seethed over the unwillingness of the umpires to call the game because of darkness before the eighth inning ended.

The Bridegrooms possibly would not have won the game with normal light in the last inning, but they took great pride in their triumph and the showing of their catcher, Bob Clark. Although Ewing, Ward, and Roger Connor stole bases, Ward was thrown out at third twice and Ewing once. Brooklyn second baseman Hub Collins led all batters with a home run, two doubles, and a single as the Grooms impressed everyone with their hitting. William Ingraham Harris correctly predicted that Brooklyn's hitting would decline, noting that Giants' errors and misplays in the last inning were caused by darkness and greatly aided Brooklyn's victory. Brooklyn exulted nevertheless and hoped that Bob Caruthers could give them a two game edge the next day.

As had been expected, Tom Lynch did not appear for the first game, and Bob Ferguson was pressed into service. Because he was a life-long resident of Brooklyn, the Giants insisted that another umpire replace him for game two. The tardy Lynch teamed with Gaffney, and the proper balance was achieved. More than 16,100 people jammed Washington Park, the second largest crowd in its history. Crowds started arriving two hours before the game and assured standing room only in the outfield. Boston's Arthur Dixwell expressed astonishment at the packed grandstand and bleachers one hour before the game. A few young ladies attended, but the assemblage was primarily male with hundreds of young boys teetering on the top of the outfield fence.

Fast ball pitcher Cannonball Crane started for the Giants, and the Bridegrooms could only get four hits. The temperature was a near perfect 66 degrees, so Bob Caruthers was not hampered by cold weather. But the Grooms fielded wretchedly. Joe Visner was the main problem for Caruthers as he made three errors and threw so badly that the Giants stole seven bases. The normally dependable Germany Smith gave New York three runs with four errors at shortstop, and most of the crowd was disappointed by a 6-2 Giants' win. Buck Ewing demonstrated his great skill in the second inning when Hub Collins stole second with Pop Corkhill on third. Ewing faked a throw to second and then rifled the ball to Art Whitney at third to catch Corkhill. With Ewing on his game, the Giants could expectantly celebrate their pennant the next night, Sunday, October 20, at New York's Broadway Theatre. They had defeated Brooklyn's best pitcher, hitting him hard, and were certain that they would dispose of the Bridegrooms quickly.

James Barton Key, Manager of The Broadway Theatre, and two renowned vaudevillians, DeWolf Hopper and Digby Bell, had arranged an impressive benefit for the Giants. Over three thousand jammed in to honor their heroes with a large number of ladies included in the standing room only gathering. Ticket sales brought in $4,456, and it was thought that souvenir sales would increase the amount to be given the players to over $6,000. A long program of songs and recitations featured Maurice Barrymore and necessarily included Hopper and Bell doing "Casey at the Bat" and "Boy on the Left Field Fence." New York Mayor Hugh John

Grant was supposed to present the silk pennant to Manager Jim Mutrie and his team, but the chief crank, Hopper, had to fill in for the absent mayor. The only hitch in the proceedings occurred when the sign with Mutrie's slogan "We Are the People" nearly hit George Gore and Arthur Whitney on their heads as it was lowered. Unfazed, Jim Mutrie and John Ward gave brief acceptance and appreciation speeches to end the festivities. Bashful Buck Ewing declined to speak.

Unknown to all revelers at the benefit, they had chosen a good time for such activity since an early morning rain the next day made the New Polo Grounds too muddy for play. If any players had celebrated too much, they had an extra day to sleep off their partying. For some reason, Brooklyn Manager Bill McGunnigle decided that he would start little used Mickey Hughes on the 22nd. Buck Ewing was so certain that the Giants could solve Hughes that he confidently proclaimed that they would win.

Ewing's confidence seemed reasonable with well-rested Mickey Welch starting for the Giants, but the Grooms pounded him for eleven hits in an 8-7 victory. Over 5,100 cranks were entertained by a slugging match-eight doubles, one triple, and two home runs. Welch's surprising ineffectiveness was best measured by Pop Corkhill's home run in the fourth. Hank O'Day relieved in the sixth and shut out Brooklyn as the Giants began hammering Hughes. Jim O'Rourke's three run homer in the fifth made the score 8-5, but McGunnigle left Hughes in through the seventh. Some commentators thought that Umpires Lynch and Gaffney should have called the game because of darkness after the seventh inning. However, they allowed play to continue into the ninth when it was obviously too dark to play. They called the game in the top of that inning when the Giants had the bases loaded against Bob Caruthers and just one out.

Angry at having lost another close game, Jim Mutrie lashed out at Brooklyn players for delaying tactics that he compared to schoolboy antics. Ward and O'Rourke loudly criticized the umpires, but most writers thought that the Giants lost because of Welch's poor pitching. At Washington Park the next day, the hard feelings from the previous game boiled to the surface in the sixth inning.

With Adonis Terry pitching, Brooklyn had built a 7-2 lead through five innings against Cannonball Crane. The 3,000 plus cranks, which included many ladies, sensed another Brooklyn upset before the desperate Giants mounted a rally in the cold, windy weather. After three runs were in, Terry caught George Gore in a rundown between third and home, but Gore was hit by the ball. Umpire Gaffney said that Gore had deliberately impeded the ball's flight with his arm and called him out. The frantic Ewing let Gaffney have it with "anything but Sunday School language" (*Times*, 24 October 1889). Later in the inning, Ward singled Ewing to third and tried to steal second against Bob Clark. Clark faked a throw to second but then threw wildly past third in an attempt to catch Ewing. Buck raced home, and Ward streaked toward the plate as Darby O'Brien fired the ball to Clark. Third base coach Jim O'Rourke excitedly ran alongside Ward as he headed for home and was hit by O'Brien's throw. Gaffney decided that O'Rourke had interfered with the throw and sent Ward back to third.

All of the Giants kicked long and hard with Buck Ewing eventually issuing an ultimatum to Gaffney. "Mr. Gaffney, if you decide against us I will take my men from the field. You know perfectly well that Ward is entitled to his run. Gore, too, should have been allowed to score. I don't propose to be bulldozed any longer. One-sided umpiring has been the cause of our defeats, and it must stop right here" (*Times*, 24 October 1889). It is debatable that Ewing spoke in such a reasonable manner, but Gaffney's colleague, John Lynch, convinced him that the throw would not have beaten Ward anyway, so Gaffney changed his mind and allowed Ward's run. Naturally, the Bridegrooms then proceeded to kick long and hard but to no avail.

Over half an hour of valuable time was lost in all of the caterwauling, but Brooklyn was still allowed to bat in the last of the sixth despite the poor light. Pop Corkhill struck out, but second baseman Danny Richardson dropped Germany Smith's liner. Further evidence of the gathering dusk came when Ewing dropped Darby O'Brien's third strike. Hub Collins walked before Tom "Reddy" Burns hit "a murderous liner over Whitney's head" that carried into the crowd (*Herald*, 24 October 1889). Gaffney and Lynch then called the game to give the Grooms a 10-7 win. Shockingly, the underdog Brooklyn team led the Giants three games to one.

Cranks and newsmen complained about the unsatisfactory behavior of the players on both teams and the inability of the umpires to control the extended wrangling. While the Giants loudly blamed all of their losses on poor umpiring and Brooklyn's stalling tactics, they had fielded terribly in game four. Buck Ewing had a particularly bad day, allowing six stolen bases and two passed balls. Recognizing the need for some sort of understanding about the conduct of the players, Byrne and Day met with the umpires the next day before the fifth game. At first, John B. Day echoed Buck Ewing's views of the day before. "I want only what belongs to us....If the Brooklyns resort any longer to the dirty tactics that have characterized them in the games already played, and if the umpires continue to favor Brooklyn, the series will end with today's game. I will not allow my team to compete against a club that insists on playing dirty ball" (*Times,* 25 October 1889). Charles H. Byrne checked his temper enough to work out some sensible arrangements to prevent a repeat of game four. He may also have reminded Day that both teams had stalled and that Buck Ewing had "a first class reputation as a slow ball player" (*Herald,* 25 September 1889).

The following agreements were made to insure that the series could be played out in an orderly manner: 1. umpires decisions would be final and indisputable, 2. games could not be delayed on any pretext, 3. only the captain could "address" the umpires, 4. games would begin at 2:30 in Brooklyn and 2:15 in New York to enable a full nine innings to be played. With such laudable rationality prevailing, game five at Washington Park proceeded in a businesslike, gentlemanly way.

The cold and wind kept the crowd down to 2,900, and most of them were extremely disappointed by the poor showing of Bob Caruthers. Buck Ewing was suffering from sore hands after catching Crane's fast-balls the day before, so Big Bill Brown replaced him at catcher. California Bill hammered three hits, as did Arthur Whitney, in the Giants' 11-3 win over Brooklyn's supposedly best pitcher. Brooklyn cranks dejectedly called Caruthers a "bursted phenomenon" (*Herald,* 25 January 1889) as New York scored four runs in each of the third and fifth innings to put the game out of reach. The extent of Brooklyn's demoralization was obvious to all when Brown got a home run because Burns tried and failed to stop his grounder with his foot in the ninth inning. Caruthers had not done well in cold weather all year, and he seemed to let up against batters whom he thought were easier outs. Cannonball Crane, Danny Richardson, Whitney, and Brown collected ten of the Giants' twelve hits.

The major loss for Brooklyn was the muscle strain that Bob Clark suffered while running to first in the sixth inning. Doc Bushong replaced him, but neither he nor Joe Visner could be expected to control the Giants' base runners as Clark had. Despite Clark's serious injury, the Bridegrooms went ahead with their scheduled banquet at the Academy of Music Assembly Rooms on the evening of the 24th. The banquet had been arranged before the series began and coincided, before the rainout of the 21st, with the scheduled sixth game. It was as if Brooklyn either expected to lose to the Giants in six games or defeat them.

From a modern-day viewpoint, it seems highly irregular to schedule a banquet in the midst of a supposedly important "world championship." Of course, the Grooms had also played an exhibition game against the Baltimore Orioles the Sunday before at Ridgewood. However we might judge such activity, approximately two hundred people attended the banquet honoring the Brooklyn players and management for winning the 1889 Association pennant. This was a decidedly small scale celebration compared to the Giants' benefit, but a brass band provided music and others sang. Some Brooklyn city officials spoke briefly as did Henry Chadwick and Francis C. Richter. Amazingly, Charles H. Byrne allowed his players to remain well into the morning hours. Yet, the next day would find the Grooms and Giants playing the best game of the series.

Cold weather continued to discourage attendance as only around 2,500 cranks came to the New Polo Grounds for the crucial sixth game. They were handsomely rewarded for their pains. Adonis Terry and Hank O'Day dueled through eleven innings before the Giants won 2-1. Brooklyn could conceivably have won the game had they not made two stupid base running errors in the second inning when they scored their only run. Still, they led going into the ninth inning 1-0. Then, with two out, two strikes, and no one on base, John Montgomery Ward single-handedly turned the game and the series around.

In his book, Ward had defined the most important element in winning baseball. "It is the unseen influence that wins in the face of the greatest odds...Its real name is enthusiasm...Between two teams of equal or unequal strength the more enthusiastic will generally win. The field work may be slow and steady, but at the bat and on the bases there must be dash and vim"(Ward 137). With the Giants in danger of losing their fourth game, Ward superbly applied his theory. After singling past second baseman Hub Collins, he daringly stole second and third against the virtually helpless Brooklyn catcher, Joe Visner. Roger Connor then hit a savage bouncer past substitute shortstop Jumbo Davis, who had fielded well in place of Germany Smith. Apparently, Smith had celebrated too strenuously the night before and was too hung over to play. New York cranks threw hats, canes, and umbrellas in the air and shouted deliriously "Ward-Ward -Johnny-Ward!" (*Times*, 26 October 1889). Then they settled down for what they hoped would be a winning rally.

Two innings later, a Giants' substitute provided the spark. George Gore had a severe cold, so oft-injured Mike Slattery started in center field. He made two good catches in the top of the eleventh and, when the Giants batted, singled and stole second with one out. With two out, Ward hit a slow grounder to Davis. Slattery, a fast runner, tore around third as Davis fielded the ball rather slowly and threw to first. Ward barely beat the throw and when Dave Foutz, thinking that Ward was out, held the ball too long, Slattery scored the winning run ahead of Foutz' tardy throw to Visner. To Day's and Mutrie's great relief, the Giants had tied the series and were definitely favored to win it. Their championship flag of 1888 flapped triumphantly in the breeze as New York cranks rejoiced over their victory in one of the most exciting games played to that time. Everyone praised Ward's work at bat, on the bases, and in the field.

Because Bob Caruthers had pitched poorly in the fifth game, Manager Bill McGunnigle reasoned that Tom Lovett should start the seventh game. This logical strategy was also influenced by Caruthers' decreased effectiveness in cold weather, but everything backfired. Despite gloomy, overcast conditions and light rain, over 3,300 spectators attested to the great interest in the battle between Brooklyn and New York. Sadly for Brooklyn supporters, the Giants smashed seven hits and two home runs in the second inning as they built a 9-0 lead. Although Caruthers relieved Lovett in the fourth inning and held New York to six hits and two runs, the Grooms could only score seven runs against Cannonball Crane before Tim Keefe relieved in the seventh and shut them out. The Giants' 11-7 win was achieved despite a muddy, slippery field, liberally sprinkled with sawdust, and Crane's nine walks. The Giants were extremely confident as they looked forward to a day of rest before resuming the series on Monday the 28th.

With the World Series nearing its expected conclusion, tensions mounted over the question of how the National League and American Association owners would react to the players' revolt, still unannounced but widely predicted and discussed. The November 4 Brotherhood meeting in New York was supposed to provide definite information about the players' intentions for 1890. Expecting a revolt, Albert Goodwill Spalding said that he might seek injunctions against Chicago players who tried to play elsewhere in 1890 but would not say for certain what steps he would take. Chris Von der Ahe responded to charges that he was ruining the Browns with mismanagement by resurrecting his pet scheme for one big league of twelve teams. Von der Ahe thought that the large league, representing a combination of Association and League teams, would effectively challenge any Brotherhood plans for its own league. Spalding seemed unimpressed by Von der Ahe's plans, if indeed such existed, and Boston President Arthur H. Soden opposed any enlargement of the National League except for the inclusion of Cincinnati and Brooklyn.

The Bridegrooms' attendance record had National League owners greedily counting new revenues. Perhaps because of that consideration and in order to head off the players' revolt, Soden began openly speaking against classification as John B. Day had earlier (*Clipper*, 19 October 1889; *Herald*, 31 October 1889). As late as October 28, Day said that he did not think that a players' league would materialize even though stories circulated about the Presidency of the league being offered him. Such wishful thinking on Day's part was based on his generous treatment of New York players—large salaries, the best hotels, and first class travel on the road. (*Times*, 29 October 1889) How could his players, "my Giants" as Jim Mutrie called them, desert to a new league even if they deemed it to be in their better interests? He may also have just wanted to put off journalists for awhile longer so that he could savor the predicted victory over Brooklyn.

That Monday, on the muddy, slippery field of Washington Park, the Giants simply annihilated Brooklyn. With Cannonball Crane again pitching, New York pummeled Adonis Terry for nine runs in the first two innings and went on to win overwhelmingly, 16-7. The Grooms had been criticized for delaying Saturday's game with their incessant kicking, but they wilted quietly in this game.

The New York Herald reported a terrible story of child abuse next to the column about the Giants' drubbing of the Bridegrooms on the 28 (*Herald*, 29 October 1889). No comparison was intended, and no one may have noticed the proximity of the two stories, but Brooklyn obviously felt that it needed to reassert itself at the Polo Grounds. More than 3,000 cranks turned out to witness what everyone expected to be an easy Giants' victory. However, since Terry had only pitched four innings the day before, McGunnigle started him again, and he nearly matched his performance in game six.

Brooklyn scored two quick runs in the top of the first and maintained a 2-1 lead through five innings. In the last of the sixth, John Ward again became the catalyst for a rally. After singling and stealing second with the aid of Doc Bushong's poor throw, Ward later scored the tying run on Danny Richardson's sacrifice fly. The other hero of game six, Mike Slattery, singled and, again assisted by Bushong's bad throw, stole second in the bottom of the seventh with two outs. Clutch hitting Buck Ewing then struck out swinging, but the ball eluded Bushong. As that once worthy catcher frantically scrambled toward the grand stand, the swift Slattery scored all the way from second with the winning run.

Over fifty years before Mickey Owen, a fading Brooklyn catcher missed a crucial third strike in that team's first World Series. As they would do in so many series, Brooklyn died fighting when Captain Darby O'Brien tried to steal second with two outs in the ninth and failed. Hank O'Day once again completely stymied Brooklyn batters, allowing them only two hits after the first inning. So impressed was Boston's General Arthur Dixwell with the Giants' five-game sweep, after trailing three games to one, that he presented each Giants player with a diamond scarf-pin. The appreciative Giants boisterously cheered Dixwell and their beloved "boss rooter", saloon owner Nick Engel. The next day, they would try to help John B. Day accept reality.

Meeting at the New Polo Grounds club house, all New York players effusively praised Day, emphasizing that they had no grievances against him personally. They made it clear, however, that they were going to support the new players' league because they thought that they would benefit economically from it, and they opposed the business principles of the National League. When it came time to discuss dividing the series' profits, "there was a tinge of sadness in that parting that cast a gloom over the little gathering. The action of the managers and players spoke louder than words, and seemed to impress all present that it was to be a lasting one" (*Clipper*, 9 November 1889). Day tried to enliven the proceedings with an invitation to everyone for lunch at Barier's Casino. He also cheered the group with the news that after deducting $7,902.86 expenses from the gross series' receipts of $20,067.01, the Giants' share of the $12,164.15 profits would be $380.13 per man. Including the Broadway Theatre benefit take, each player was approximately $570 richer. To demonstrate their appreciation, the players presented Superintendent Arthur Bell with an $80 overcoat and ground keeper Pete Daily with a suit of clothes and an overcoat. Then everyone adjourned to the Casino for a sumptuous meal, band music, and an abundance of wine (*Herald,* 31 October 1889).

The Brooklyn team also gathered on the 30 at the Washington Park club house. They had nothing to be ashamed of since they had fought the Giants better than many people had expected them to do. William Ingraham Harris commended them for their fielding and "gallant, nervy game" (*S.L.,* 6 November 1889) but noted their obvious weaknesses in pitching, catching, and batting. However, had it not been for catcher Bob Clark's injury in game five, Pop Corkhill's bothersome spinal abscess caused by his tumble in game one, Germany Smith's absence in game six, and John Ward's magnificent performance, the Bridegrooms may have defeated the Giants. Charles H. Byrne said that he was well-satisfied on the whole with his team's play, and the Grooms demonstrated their affection for Bill McGunnigle by presenting Gunner with a gold watch chain and diamond-studded locket. Some of Captain Darby O'Brien's admirers had previously given him a medal with twenty-five diamonds, so, with their $389.29 per player from the World Series, Brooklyn players and their manager felt amply rewarded. The comedic O'Brien also received a pair of parrots to add to his growing menagerie.

Despite earlier comments about not managing for Brooklyn in 1890, McGunnigle was considering taking a team to the Pacific Coast for some winter exhibition games. Charlie Comiskey had already formed a team to visit California, so Gunner felt that profits could be made from extending their rivalry into the off-season.

On October 31, co-owners of the Giants and other friends gave Giants' President John B. Day a dinner at the Arena where they presented him with a handsome, solid silver punch bowl. Such awards were commonly distributed during the 1880s and 1890s, and since so few of these items have survived, one wonders what happened to them. Did family members of the players, managers and owners acquire these sports' heirlooms, or were they simply lost or auctioned off for purposes of retrieving the precious metal alone? In John B. Day's case, it would seem that he pawned most of his valuable acquisitions as the years progressed.

Even though he had lost money during the 1889 season according to his and Jim Mutrie's accounts, he still had $100,000 at the end of that year. After the costly war with the Players' League in 1890 and the ensuing battle with the American Association in 1891, Day found himself

$33,000 in the red (Allen, *Giants and Dodgers* 28). During the 1890s, Day was forced to resign the Presidency, sell all of his shares in the Giants, and return to his wholesale tobacco business. He managed briefly for the Giants in 1899 and was given the meaningless job of National League Chief of Umpires in 1900. Broken in spirit, Day experienced gradually declining health until, in 1923, he was discovered living as a pauper in lower Manhattan. Crippled after a paralyzing stroke in 1910, Day was found in 1923 without enough money for food and with his wife dying of cancer. Brooklyn President and owner Charles H. Ebbets got the National League to provide him with $1,200 annually. John B. Day died in January, 1925 after years of suffering, but in the fall of 1889, he was still fighting to hang on to his beloved team, his Giants (Reidenbaugh 28; Allen, *Giants and Dodgers* 116).

Jim Mutrie remained loyal to Day and the National League, doing his bit to rally the New York players in much the same manner as he promoted the Giants. Approached about joining the Players' League, Mutrie vowed that he would "stand by the old ship, no matter whether it sank or not. They are the people that have given us employment for the last eight years, and I for one will stick by them to death" (*Herald,* 1 November 1889). Years later, Chicago's great Manager, Adrian C. "Cap" Anson, echoed much the same feelings as those of his old rival Jim Mutrie. When approached by John Montgomery Ward late in the 1889 season about joining the players' revolt, Anson recalled "I felt bound in honor to stand by my friends, even if I sank with them, and at that time the skies did look remarkably dark..." (Anson 287).

Mutrie thought that any players league based on a cooperative plan with owners would face severe difficulties, among them, paying promised high salaries and expenses for new grounds. He also believed that the National League would be able to replace any revolting players with new, young ones. John B. Day had finally accepted the fact of a players' revolt. "Matters are taking such a shape now that I am rather inclined to think there is a very great deal in the [Brotherhood] scheme, and that the players are not bluffing, but actually intend to go into the business on their own hook. It is my opinion...that they are making a grand mistake and that their supporters will not stand by them" (*Herald,* 2 November 1889).

As things worked out during the 1890 season, the major reason for the Players' League failure was that predicted by Day. The new owners abandoned the new league, after just one season, primarily because they had incurred heavy losses. Day also lost heavily in 1890 by trusting National League assurances that League players could not legally play anywhere else in 1890. While some owners like Indianapolis' John T. Brush aggressively tried to lure players away from the Players' League, Day put his faith in the courts and did not exert himself much. Legal expenses and the hiring of many new players would cost him dearly (*Sporting Life's Official Baseball Guide*, 1891, 32). Early in November, 1889, angered over reports that many Giants had signed a lease for new grounds that would serve a New York Players' League team, Day used the same tactic that Al Spalding had, the threat of injunctions (*Herald*, 3, 4 November, 1889).

With good will fast diminishing among all owners and players, including Day and his Giants, National League players ended the suspense by throwing down the gauntlet on November 4, 1889. The most profitable season in baseball's history to that time concluded with the announcement of a players' revolt that would lead to two highly unprofitable seasons, the Players' League collapse, and an eventual consolidation of the American Association and National League. That consolidation, so often proposed by Chris Von der Ahe in the late 1880s, would prove a failure. Twelve teams in one large league meant that at least four cities lost interest in the pennant race very early in the season.

The 1890s were hard times for baseball players and owners. But the National League players had high hopes for an end to being treated like underlings when they met in New York on November 4, 1889. They had gained the financial support of an impressive number of capitalists in eight major cities with the undeniably necessary assistance of Albert L. Johnson. However, the great Giants' shortstop, John Montgomery Ward, was their President and leader. He was their spokesman on November 4. He hurled everything back at the National League owners, like Albert Goodwill Spalding and John T. Brush, with a vengeance. This was war.

Chapter Fifteen
The Players' League

Representatives of the National League Brotherhood of Professional Base Ball Players met for six hours in the afternoon of November 4 at New York's Fifth Avenue Hotel. Afterwards, Ward read a prepared statement to the assembled press. It was no less dramatic for the fact that its essence had been publicized since September. Couching his words in a libertarian context, Ward placed the players on the side of justice and natural rights. "There was a time when the League stood for integrity and fair dealing-today it stands for dollars and cents....Men have come into the business from no other motive than to exploit it for every dollar in sight....Players have been bought, sold and exchanged as though they were sheep instead of American citizens....now we are in shape to go ahead next year under new management and new auspices. We believe that it is possible to conduct our national game upon lines which will not infringe upon individual and natural rights" (*Clipper*, 9 November 1889). Throughout his statement, Ward concentrated on the injustice of player sales and the reserve rule though he had thrice previously recognized the value of the latter (see Ward 30-2; Spalding 271; Voigt 157-58; Seymour 224; Bass 64-5) and agreed that players sometimes profited from their sale. In this Manifesto, however, the owners were portrayed as comparable to the strongest trust, arbitrary, and un-American. In tried and true American tradition, Ward implied, the players were finally standing up for their rights.

After reading the Manifesto, Ward addressed the group of reporters and players. Reviewing the manner in which the Brotherhood representatives had tried to meet with Albert G. Spalding in June, 1889 and been rejected, Ward reminded everyone that the major concern of the players was "to promote and elevate our national game by every honorable means" (*Clipper*, 9 November 1889). No mention of players' monetary interests clouded either the Manifesto or Ward's brief comments. This was to be a war fought for idealistic, worthy purposes-rights and justice. Al Spalding could play that game as well as anyone and by November 21, he,

John B. Day, and John I. Rogers of the Phillies had composed a reply to the Brotherhood Manifesto. The National League was pure. It had an "untarnished record of fourteen years," stood "for the honesty and integrity of Base Ball," had insured players "the dignity of [their] profession and the munificent salary...guaranteed while playing," and had rescued the game from corrupt players who controlled the game before 1876 (Spalding 273). Where did truth, honor, justice, and the American way reside in baseball? Why, with the National League, of course, said Albert Goodwill Spalding as he girded for this most serious challenge to his autocratic will.

So the propaganda war was well underway even before the Players' League could officially organize in December 1889. It would not abate until the players were abandoned by their financial backers in the fall of 1890. Not surprisingly, Albert Spalding was a master of using the newspapers for his particular purposes since he had early recognized that news reporting, even when highly critical, was essential for good attendance (Spalding 528). Spalding shrewdly manipulated the news throughout the 1890 season, effectively check-mated the players' early advantage, and he won.

After defeating the Players' League, Spalding went on to make millions more in his burgeoning sporting goods business and gradually withdrew from baseball. John B. Day, Chris Von der Ahe, and Charles H. Byrne all lost large amounts of money in the following years. Day and Von der Ahe lost everything while Byrne managed to hang on until his death in January 1898. They all paid a heavy price for following Spalding's lead in beating down the players and the American Association. But, of course, they had themselves primarily to blame for their future declines. John B. Day had paid insufficient heed to the Polo Grounds issue during the 1888-1889 off-season for health and business reasons. He had trusted New York's aldermen to provide him with necessary space, and they had failed him. Caroming from park to park cost him dearly in construction expenses and revenues lost from low attendance. Similarly, once the player's revolt was a certainty, Day put his trust in John I. Rogers' and Al Spalding's legal remedies. Too late, he sought other players as he watched legal expenses mount. Eventually, John B. Day would have to solicit loans from fellow League owners with the aforementioned result. Von der Ahe and Byrne ended the 1889 season with one last fight and a parting of the ways which would greatly harm both. Their bitter, personal feud could not be resolved amicably, and organized baseball was adversely affected for the next decade because they could not settle their disputes within the American Association that they had built.

On November 13, the National League and American Association owners convened their annual meetings at the same Fifth Avenue Hotel which had hosted the earlier Brotherhood gathering. In the Association meetings, the venomous relationship that had developed during the season between St. Louis and Brooklyn became of immediate importance. The Grooms' World Series loss to the Giants had been applauded by the Browns, Brooklyn was accused of treachery in their victories, and "Byrne and his dirty crew" were objects of ridicule in St. Louis (*S.N.*, 26 October, 3 November 1889). Rightfully angered by such unrelenting hatred, Charles H. Byrne was appalled by the organized resistance to him and his influence at the annual meeting.

Chris Von der Ahe had recruited the support of Louisville, Columbus and Philadelphia owners in opposing Byrne's policies regarding the division of gate receipts and his choice of a new President. With Cincinnati, Kansas City and Baltimore taking Byrne's side, the ensuing deadlock was only broken when he decided that he would accept the National League's invitation to join them. Cincinnati's owner Aaron S. Stern left with Byrne, and the National League owners cheerily drank to Arthur H. Soden's toast: "I know that I voice your sentiments and those of our friends, the gentlemen of the press, in welcoming Brooklyn and Cincinnati to the League and wishing them prosperity among their new associates" (Allen, *Giants and Dodgers* 20-21).

While Von der Ahe initially denounced Stern and Byrne as deserters at the same time that he expressed pleasure over their resignations from the Association, he must have realized that the loss of Cincinnati and Brooklyn severely weakened the Association. Brooklyn's large attendance helped all the teams in its league, and the heated, established rivalries with St. Louis, Columbus, Baltimore, and Philadelphia encouraged many cranks to attend games just to watch old enemies have at it. Conversely, National League owners eagerly awaited the crowds that Brooklyn could attract even though John B. Day originally opposed Brooklyn's entry (Rice 54). Possibly worried about Brooklyn competing too effectively for the greater New York baseball audience, Day could not influence his fellow owners much since his financial situation was precarious. He also saw the wisdom of bringing in a franchise which could draw people so well, and the New York-Brooklyn rivalry was a natural.

So with the Players League attracting the National League's now undivided attention and with the American Association beginning to disintegrate, everyone concerned with baseball had reasons to neglect the important issues that had emerged during the 1889 season. The worthwhile discussions that questioned gambling for one's own team or of offering premiums to other players to encourage the defeat of a rival team were overlooked as owners, players, and newsmen concentrated on the players' revolt and the coming conflict. The long-standing problems between Chris Von der Ahe and his players which resulted in the thrown games in Kansas City, accusations about Arlie Latham's gambling associations, and the suspensions and finings of Latham, Silver King, and Icebox Chamberlain were never investigated by the American Association as it fought for simple survival. Charlie Comiskey never had to answer for his patently false accusations against Umpire Bob Ferguson nor those hurled at Charles H. Byrne by him, Von der Ahe, and *The Sporting News.* Byrne's relationship to Association umpires was not investigated.

In this moment of great crisis in both major leagues, highly questionable practices of the past season could not be seriously assessed because organized baseball, although seriously divided, needed to present a proper image to the public. Spalding knew the importance of a righteous front, and his opponents tried to imitate his example. On that, all of the actors could agree. Thus, the chorus lauding the honesty and integrity of the national game swelled to include even those who had responsibly criticized aspects of baseball during the 1889 season. The most important among those composing what would become organized baseball's litany of hypocrisy was Francis C. Richter, *Sporting Life's* editor.

At the banquet honoring the Brooklyn team on October 24, Richter was asked to comment about the reasons for the popularity of baseball. After all that had happened during 1889, what did this intelligent man cite as one of the major reasons for the outpouring of public interest? The honesty of the game. Honest it was not, but honest it must be in order to present the best face to the public. The baseball flag, the pure, honorable image of the national game, was being invented and raised by 1889 despite evidence that all was not well. It would require another period of growth and expansion before the gambling issue was squarely faced after 1919. But, since no human institution, and certainly not a professional sport, is ever wholly free from corruption, baseball would again have to deal with gambling and other, greater problems in the late twentieth century. We should not be surprised that gambling and baseball have been so closely associated in recent years. They were from the beginning.

Epilogue

Professional baseball went into decline for a decade after 1889. Some of the players adapted to the changed conditions and played well into the 1890s. Many simply dropped out of baseball when owners began cutting salaries after the American Association died following the 1891 season. Others retired gracefully after long, successful careers, and some met untimely deaths.

Among the New York Giants, President John B. Day and Jim Mutrie experienced the most troubled times. For the two original Giants, their sun began setting soon after 1889. Desperate for funds, Day was forced to fire Mutrie after the 1891 season because a new co-owner, Edward B. Talcott, demanded that another manager be hired. If Day had not fired "Truthful Jim", Talcott may have withdrawn his financial support (Allen, *Giants and Dodgers* 28). Mutrie managed a minor league team in Elmira for part of 1892, but retired in mid-season and went back to New York to haunt the newspaper sports offices (S.N., 27 January 1938). About thirty years later, Giants' owner Charles A. Stoneham discovered that the proud, nearly blind old man was scraping together a living by serving as a gatekeeper at the Polo Grounds. Stoneham decided that the first Giants' manager, at age seventy, did not deserve such a menial occupation and provided him with a "pension that eased the years that were left" (Allen 116).

Thus enabled, Jim Mutrie lived until defeated by cancer in 1938 and was treated to seven more Giants' pennants under John McGraw's and Bill Terry's management. Though suffering from poor health, John B. Day possibly knew of Stoneham's charitable act and probably approved of it. Tardily aided with a pension from the National League after 1923, Day died in 1925, a little over forty years after becoming involved with the sport that whittled away most of his fortune earned in the wholesale tobacco business. At his death, Day was praised for his ability to attract the "better citizens" of New York to the Polo Grounds and for his loyalty to the National League, even in the face of financial disaster during 1890. Still, he died penniless (Day file, NBL; *S.N.,* 5 February 1925).

Captain Buck Ewing played for a few more years but with diminished skills compared to those he demonstrated in the 1880s. After managing

Mickey Welch—Pictured in his 1888 uniform, Welch trailed only John Clarkson in winning percentage during 1889. He was third in ERA, wins, and complete games. Photo credit National Baseball Library, Cooperstown, N.Y.

Cincinnati for five years in the late 1890s, Buck returned to Andrew Freedman's Giants but retired in 1900 in poor health. Ewing had reportedly made $65,000 during his playing career with the Giants and invested it well. When he died from Bright's disease in 1906, he left his family with property valued at over $60,000 (Ewing file, NBL; *S.L.*, 27 October 1906).

Close friends Roger Connor and Danny Richardson played in the National League until the mid-1890s, returned to their home areas in Connecticut and New York, and died in old age. One of the best second basemen during the 1880s, Richardson became a successful department store owner in Elmira. Connor played in the Connecticut League from 1898 to 1903, finally retiring from baseball at age forty-six. When Connor died, he was extolled as the Giant with the "benignant air and rolling gait...more of a country squire than a professional ball player" (*S.N.*, 15 January 1931). Connor, Ewing, Keefe, and Welch were all remembered as highly popular with New York's sporting public, and the 1889 Giants were then regarded as unsurpassed in their recognized fame (*S.N.*, 15 January 1931).

Light-hitting third baseman Arthur Whitney left major league baseball after 1891, worked as a sporting goods salesman (drummer) for his brother's company, and subsequently, for many years represented A. G. Spalding & Bros. before his death in 1943 (*S.N.*, 26 August 1943).

The great pitching duo, Mickey Welch and Tim Keefe, had been like brothers during their years in New York. After 1889, Welch remained loyal to the Giants for the remaining three years of his career, but Keefe spent most of his concluding years with Philadelphia once the Players' League collapsed. Differences regarding the players' revolt did not diminish their friendship, and Welch wistfully recollected Keefe's skills and character to sportswriter Joe Vila when Keefe died in 1933 (Keefe file, NBL). By that time, "Smiling Mickey" had returned to New York and become the recipient of one of John McGraw's last charitable acts. Like Dan Brouthers before him, Welch worked as a Polo Grounds bleacher entrance attendant until his death in 1941. It was the least that should have been done for the Giant pitcher who had started the first game at the oldest Polo Grounds, had requested only the privilege not to pitch two days in succession, and had remained loyal to Day and the Giants through 1892 (*S.N.*, 7 August 1941).

John Montgomery Ward played and managed for Brooklyn and the

Giants through the mid-1890s, then retired from baseball and became a successful New York City lawyer. A defender of players' rights in the 1890s and early 1900s and business manager of Brooklyn's Federal League team in 1914, Ward later became chief counsel for the National League and also represented John McGraw. Because of baseball politics and his wide-ranging knowledge, Ward gained some support for the presidency of the National League in 1909 and served briefly as Boston Braves' President in 1912 (Lowenfish 68-69; *S.N.*, 14 March 1964). An excellent golfer and a vigorous, active outdoorsman all his life, Ward died of pneumonia, contracted while hunting in Georgia, in 1925. Only a few weeks before, he had participated in ceremonies at New York's old Broadway Central Hotel, which began the National League's golden jubilee year. There the old shortstop and players' advocate spoke effectively about the Brotherhood War causes and the resultant benefits for baseball and the players. Francis C. Richter once more recounted the 1889-1890 strife when he learned of Ward's death (*Times,* 5 March 1925; *S.N.,* 12, 19 March 1925).

Jim O'Rourke also practiced law, as a graduate of Yale Law School, and worked in various baseball capacities after retiring as a major league player in 1893. Astoundingly, this superbly conditioned man actually played in a Giants' game, at catcher, as late as 1904 when he was fifty-two. Presumably reinvigorated, "Orator Jim" continued to play for and manage a minor league team in Bridgeport, Connecticut until he was fifty-five. From the time, as a young boy in knickers, he had first attracted attention by competing with returning Civil War veterans, he simply could not get baseball out of his system. He tried umpiring in 1894 but soon plunged into baseball's organizational realm, becoming President, Secretary, and Treasurer of the Connecticut State League by 1897.

Noted for tremendous vocal volume and vague rhetorical flourishes, O'Rourke earned notoriety in minor league gatherings which rivaled his reputation as a player. He "stood six feet and more, [actually only 5' 8"] deep of chest and straight of shoulder, with bushy brows and an eye like a searchlight. His upper lip was decorated with a fierce gray mustache. When he arose to speak, tossed his great mane of gray hair, stamped his foot and grasped the back of his chair,...brave indeed was the man who would combat his ideas in a league meeting..." (*S.N.,* 16 January 1919).

Highly opinionated, O'Rourke insisted until he died that he was one of the greatest catchers, that the Boston team of the early 1870s was the equal of any since, that George Wright and Ross Barnes matched any modern players, and that Harry Wright initiated the hit and run in the early 1870s. Perhaps because he was becoming a bit of a bore or, more likely, because of his domineering manner, Orator Jim was edged out of baseball when his Eastern Association merged with another league in 1915. Charles C. Spink averred that O'Rourke was crushed by the development, broke off relations with his life-long friend Tim Murnane (Murnane became President of the new league), and proclaimed that baseball "had no gratitude in its makeup."

He continued his law practice, and in 1968, his youngest daughter, Edith Hanke, recalled that "he was the kind of lawyer who was too kind-hearted to charge a fee to anyone in modest circumstances" (S.N., 2 October 1968). Like Ward, he died suddenly from pneumonia in 1919. O'Rourke had maintained a life-long pride in never taking a drink or using tobacco and regarded his $100,000 estate as proof of the value of hard work and clean living. Yet he praised Hoss Radbourn as one of the greatest pitchers of all time without noting his bingeing habits. If he could not forgive baseball, he could forgive much within its fraternity.

Despite Cap Anson's testimony to George Gore's drinking problems (Anson 115), Gore played for two and one-half more years before retiring. After working on the New York police force, Gore lived in Nutley, New Jersey and died at the Masonic Home in Utica, New York in 1933. A good hitter and capable of brilliant defensive work (S.N., 21 September 1933), Gore would probably have been a serious candidate for the Hall of Fame if he had been a more consistent fielder and if he had not incurred the wrath of Albert Goodwill Spalding for supposed poor discipline.

According to Charles C. Johnson Spink, the other member of the 1889 Giants' outfield, "Silent Mike" Tiernan, should be in the Hall of Fame. An excellent hitter, runner and a brilliant fielder, Tiernan acquired his nickname because he disliked publicity and played in a reserved, quiet manner. Employed by the Giants throughout his thirteen year career, which began at age twenty in 1887, Tiernan died of tuberculosis in 1918, shortly before the armistice ending World War I. He had escaped from public scrutiny years before and, still vigilant in protecting his privacy, had entered Bellevue Hospital under an assumed name (S.N., 14 November 1918).

World Series hero Hank O'Day pitched only one more year in the Players' League, lost his effectiveness, and finished in the minor leagues by 1893. He then began umpiring and worked his way into the National League crew in 1895. Fellow umpire and National League President John A. Heydler recalled when O'Day died of heart trouble in 1935 that "he was an umpire and nothing else. He wanted to be nothing else" (*S.N.*, 7 November 1935). This single-minded determination was particularly helpful for O'Day after he gained unwanted notoriety for his part in the 1908 Merkle game between Chicago and New York. Mercilessly heckled for years afterwards by New York fans, O'Day worked as an umpire until 1927 except for two one year stints as a manager.

At his death, Frederick G. Lieb praised O'Day for his courage, baseball knowledge and skill in calling balls and strikes. However, O'Day also developed a reputation for defining taciturnity. He was capable of sitting in complete silence for hours at his closest friend's home. Rarely attending the theatre or movies, reading little else except sports news, ignoring pool or billiards, O'Day fashioned a bleak life-shell in which "baseball was his only life and interest and he kept that to himself" (Lieb).

Another part-time but valuable contributor to the Giants' 1889 world championship, catcher Willard "Big Bill" Brown, died of tuberculosis in 1897, only three years out of major league baseball. Brown had not only adequately spelled Buck Ewing at catcher, for he had loosened up teammates with his practical jokes during the tight 1889 pennant race (Brown file, NBL). John Ward's substitute at shortstop and pitcher when Keefe, Welch, and Crane were sidelined, Gil Hatfield, eventually became a bank teller in hometown Hoboken and died of heart disease in 1921 (*S.N.*, 2 June 1921).

The most tragic end for all of the Giants' players was that suffered by Ed "Cannonball" Crane. Unable to shake his drinking habits acquired on the Spalding world tour, the hard-throwing right-hander became a mediocre pitcher, failed as an umpire, and drifted out of baseball. Trying to cope with depression, Crane died in 1896 after taking an overdose of chloral hydrate, a drug then commonly used to treat depression but which was lethal in large amounts. Cannonball Crane was only 34 (Crane file, NBL).

Like Crane, Boston's great pitchers, John Clarkson and Hoss Radbourn, did not go gently into the dark night. Radbourn won twenty games in 1889 but had been widely criticized by Boston sportswriters for his drinking. He pitched only two more years in the major leagues, during which time his "uniform only was pitching...the physique of the original

Rad was there no more" (Sullivan 99). Hoss then invested in a Bloomington, Illinois saloon, billiard room, and sportsman's resort. After losing an eye in a shooting accident, Radbourn's health declined rapidly. He died of paresis in 1897, leaving a widow and one son (*S.L.*, 13 February 1897; *Clipper*, 13 February 1897). The clinical definition of paresis describes a psychosis caused by extensive destruction of brain tissue, resulting from the latter stages of syphilis.

John Clarkson stayed with Boston's National League team during the 1890 season, supposedly because his wife convinced him to do so (Tip O'Neill file, NBL). Even after his 620 inning, seventy-three game marathon season of 1889, Clarkson had two more good years. However, at the first sign of arm trouble in 1892, Boston's owners dispatched him to Cleveland where he gave the youthful Cy Young the benefit of his considerable pitching knowledge. Retiring from baseball after 1894, John Clarkson operated a cigar store in Bay City, Michigan until 1902.

Increasingly troubled with a nervous disorder, Clarkson was confined in the Eastern Michigan Asylum for the Insane at Pontiac, Michigan until the summer of 1908. Then, sufficiently recovered, he lived with his father in Winthrop, Massachusetts until contracting double pneumonia and dying in 1909. In his last days, "he seemed to have no memory at all for things of today, but talked clearly and lucidly of matters connected with his past" (Jacob C. Morse, S.L., 13 February 1909).

Radbourn's and Clarkson's widely admired catcher, Charlie Bennett, lived into old age even though he lost both of his legs in an 1894 railroad accident. Undoubtedly aided in his incapacity by his ability to endure pain, Bennett still needed creative diversions and decided to paint china with his battered hands. He was eventually honored by having the Detroit Tigers' first baseball park named after him (*S.N.*, 31 March 1906, 4 April 1968; Alexander, *Cobb* 32). The fact that he, the only catcher of the 1880's and 1890's compared to Buck Ewing, has not been considered for the Hall of Fame indicates modern baseball's ignorance of the late nineteenth century game. Bennett's alternate from 1886 through 1893, Charlie Ganzel, succumbed to cancer in 1914 (*S.L.*, 18 April 1914).

Boston first baseman Dan Brouthers bounced around among six more teams before he retired from the National League after 1896. Durable Dan competed in the minor leagues through the 1905 season and, like Jim O'Rourke, played for the 1904 pennant-winning Giants as an old man. John McGraw later helped "Big Dan," one of his teammates on the 1894

Baltimore Orioles, get jobs as a Giants' scout, ticket taker, and press gate keeper at the Polo Grounds. The old slugger lived until 1932 in relatively comfortable circumstances before dying of heart disease (*S.N.*, 8 August 1932).

Boston's superb utility man, Hardie Richardson, played only three more years. A line drive hitter who was compared to Chicago Cubs' Riggs Stephenson when he died in 1931, Richardson was one of the most well-disciplined players of his time (S.N., 22 January 1931). An excellent fielder, a clutch hitter, and one of the best players of his era, he earned the nickname "Old True Blue."

Popular, steady third baseman Billy Nash played with Boston's pennant winners of 1891-93 and was still going strong at age thirty in 1895. Then Boston's owners discovered the great Jimmy Collins, five years Nash's junior, and peddled Nash to Philadelphia where he ended his career in 1898. Later a health official in East Orange, New Jersey, Nash was victimized by a heart attack in 1929 (*S.N.*, 21 November 1929).

Nash lived into old age, but young, hard-drinking Michael Joseph "Kid" Madden did not. The slight, five foot seven pitcher left the majors after the 1891 season, played for some minor league teams and died of consumption in 1896, age twenty-nine. A widow and three children survived him (*S.N.*, 21 March 1896).

The other members of Boston's 1889 support cast, second baseman Joe Quinn, shortstop Pop Smith, center fielder Dick Johnston, and left fielder Tom Brown, all lived to be old men, but only Quinn and Brown played through the next decade. When Johnston died of throat cancer in 1934, old-timers asserted that he had been "the perfect defensive outfielder," even better than Tris Speaker, Ty Cobb, or Max Carey (*S.N.*, 12 April 1934). Brown, one of the best base stealers of his time and a good fielder, played for five more teams after 1889, finishing as player-manager of the lowly Washington Senators in 1898. Like many retired players, he tried umpiring for awhile but soon became involved in business pursuits. Tom Brown died in Washington at age 67 (*S.N.*, 3 November 1927). The popular Joe Quinn held down second base for Boston's 1891-92 champions before being displaced by Bobby Lowe in 1893. After 1901, Quinn joined his father-in-law's undertaking business and prospered until his death in 1940 (*S.N.*, 21 November 1940). Except for the fact that he outlived his Beaneater teammates, Quinn's other claim to fame was spelling Heinie Reitz at second base on Baltimore's 1896 pennant winners.

Mike "King" Kelly still possessed much fame at the end of 1889, but he neither played nor lived for many years after.

The King jumped to the Players' League in 1890, captained the Boston team to the pennant, and added considerably to his mythology during that year. When Albert Goodwill Spalding tried to lure Kelly back to the National League with a huge salary, Kelly turned it down because he "couldn't let the boys down" (Spalding 293-97). Something of Spalding's inconsistency is demonstrated by the fact that he later produced a maudlin account of Kelly turning down his $10,000 offer to desert, praised it as an example of how players remained loyal to each other in 1890, and preceded the whole by quoting Henry Chadwick's attack against the Players' League recruitment of players through "a system of terrorism peculiar to revolutionary movements" (289-97).

Kelly also gained fame in 1890 by substituting at catcher ("Kelly now catching" were the immortal words) while a foul pop fly, which would have eluded the Boston catcher on the field, was still in the air. Kelly made the catch, eventually causing rule makers to make certain that such actions could not happen again. Because the inventive Kelly left baseball soon after 1890, they neglected their oversight for a number of years. At least three different accounts of Kelly's "substitution" exist, but since an eyewitness account identified Morgan Murphy as the catcher, and since Kelly and Murphy played together only in 1890 (except for four games with Boston's American Association team in 1891), it is probable that Kelly's most famous trick was perpetrated only four years before he died (Kelly file, NBL; See Kaese 42 for an alternative identification for the catcher and the year).

Ricocheting among three teams in 1891, Kelly finally settled with his old National League employers in Boston. He achieved obesity in 1892, hit below .200 for the first time in his life, and was shunted off to the Giants. New York's owners thought that Kelly would still have some crowd appeal, but he could only struggle through twenty games in 1893, his last major league season. Rapidly becoming an embarrassment to those who cared for him, the King caused men to turn away when he attempted to entertain with recitations of "Casey at the Bat" in bars, and he was an object of ridicule with the Allentown, Pennsylvania minor league team. He died, after contracting pneumonia, in November, 1894, age thirty-six. Surely, it is one of the ironies of that time that two of best-conditioned athletes, Jim O'Rourke and John Montgomery Ward, and one of the worst,

King Kelly, suffered death from one of the two great equalizers of the era.

Asa Bordages, sportswriter for *The New York World- Telegram*, later wrote a popular account of Kelly's life which has since been pillaged, plagiarized, and quoted by many. Alfred P. Cappio penned the most thoughtful treatment of Kelly for the Passaic County Historical Society in 1962. Cappio thought that Kelly's major support came from young boys and men from the working class, though his popularity was widespread among all kinds of cranks. Many adult admirers condoned his drinking and fighting and deeply resented sportswriter' criticisms of his off-field escapades. But Kelly paid a high price for entertaining the multitudes in his incomparably hedonistic style. While difficult to separate fact from fiction when assessing the King's life, it is known that he died virtually penniless although he had earned an estimated $250,000 during his career. The recipient of a fine home in Hingham from adulatory Boston supporters, Kelly mortgaged it, eventually lost it, and hocked everything of value that he had ever received. General Charles H. Taylor, publisher of the *Boston Globe*, had awarded him with a medal for stealing eighty-four bases in 1887. Twenty years later, a Boston baseball fan discovered the relic in a New York pawn shop, from whence it eventually made its way to Cooperstown (Kaese 44-5).

After his death, Kelly's widow, the former Agnes Headifen of Paterson, New Jersey, was forced to live in the home of Umpire John Kelly, one of the King's many drinking chums. Cleveland street car magnate and premier supporter of the Players' League, Albert L. Johnson, reportedly sent her $100 monthly for a time, but Agnes' primary means of support was her work as a seamstress. Two years before her death in 1937, and after relating the way that she would often accompany her husband in his nocturnal tours, she remembered him simply as "an overgrown kid" (Cappio, *"Slide Kelly, Slide": The Story of Michael J. Kelly*). At least five thousand people filed past his body as it lay in state at Boston's Elks Hall in November, 1894. Thousands more filled the streets outside St. James Church during his memorial service. As Kelly would have wished, you could have told your mother about it.

James A. Hart, the Boston manager who had gently tried to partially tame Mike Kelly's free spirit, journeyed to England and Scotland during the spring of 1890 to promote baseball and possibly open up some new markets for Albert Spalding's sporting goods business. Upon his return, he became Secretary of Spalding's club, worked through the Players' League crisis, and rose to President of the Chicago White Stockings after Spalding resigned that post in 1891. Always complimentary of Kelly, Hart never managed again after 1889 and became part of the enlarged National League which established management's dominance over the players. The 1890s and competition from the American League after 1900 dimmed his zeal somewhat, and by 1905, Hart decided to sell his interest in the Chicago Cubs to Charles W. Murphy (Brown, 46). The Cubs were just one year away from their most successful era. Hart invested his capital well and at the time of his death from heart failure in 1919, was President and a large stockholder of Chicago Gravel Company and "other substantial interests" (*S.N.*, 24 July 1919). He outlived Spalding by four years.

Boston's owners, Arthur H. Soden, William H. Conant, and James B. Billings, recruited superior players after 1889 and won five pennants during the 1890s, though the 1891 flag was clouded by questions concerning deliberately thrown games (Tiemann, *Baseball Research Journal* (1989) 2-5). When the American League lured away some of their best players, the wealthy trio sold the Beaneaters to George B. Dovey, from St. Louis, after the 1906 season (*S.N.*, 8 December 1906).

St. Louis' manager, Charles Albert Comiskey, pledged his loyalty to Chris Von der Ahe and the Browns until January, 1890, when he broke with his obstreperous boss over whether or not Pete Sweeney should be retained for 1890. Vondy wanted to hire Sweeney. Commy did not. Long afterwards, Commy claimed that he had jumped to the Players' League "to be on the level with the boys" (Axelson 112), probably hoping to benefit tangentially from the sentimental publicity surrounding King Kelly's rejection of Al Spalding's bribe. Most likely, Commy left St. Louis because he could not abide further interference with the management of the Browns from Von der Ahe. The latter's son, Edward, had infuriated Commy with his meddling in 1889, but Commy's primary complaint was with Chris Von der Ahe's increasing intrusions (Sullivan 234-39; *S.N.*, 29 January 1890). Returning to his home town, Commy managed the Chicago Players' League team in 1890 but did not do well. Arlie Latham accompanied him, the two tangled over the same issues that had surfaced in 1889, and Latham was let go. Commy suffered a badly broken little finger and never could settle the petty disputes between Association and League players on the Chicago team (*S.N.*, 1 November 1890). Jimmy Ryan, an ex-White Stocking outfielder on the team, opined that Commy was too easy on him. Arlie Latham undoubtedly did not agree.

When the Players' League collapsed, Commy came back to Von der Ahe for the concluding American Association campaign. At the 1891 season's end, he resisted Vondy's attempt to lower his 1892 salary from $6,000 to $5,000 and accepted Cincinnati's offer (Comiskey file, NBL). Commy managed the Redlegs for three years, married Nan Kelly in 1892, and came under the influence of Cincinnati owner John T. Brush. For someone so concerned about "the boys," Commy developed a close relationship with the man who had devised the 1889 classification system that helped cause the 1890 National League players' revolt. He grew to respect Brush's business methods, which were notoriously parsimonious in regard to players' salaries. A prime example of Commy's regard for his new boss concerned an old nemesis, Arlie Latham. Arlie had landed in Cincinnati after leaving Commy and Chicago in 1890. Commy uttered no more complaints about him, apparently agreeing with Brush that "his flow of humor in coaching and 'kidding' brought much enjoyment to spectators..." and should be kept "long after he deteriorated as a player because of his drawing power as a comedian and humorist" (*Times,* 6 February 1909).

However, Commy grew restive in the huge, twelve-team National League structure foisted on the public after 1891. So when Byron Bancroft Johnson, a young Cincinnati sportswriter and one of John T. Brush's severest critics, asked his help in creating the Western League, Commy left Cincinnati and became the owner-manager of the St. Paul team from 1895 through 1899 (Allen, *100 Years of Baseball* 134-39).

When the huge National League sank of its own weight and reduced to eight teams after 1899, Johnson and Commy organized the new American League in 1900-1901. As President and owner of the Chicago White Sox, Commy ultimately became a millionaire. His teams won four pennants and two world series during the new league's first two decades. Taking Brush as his model rather than the lavishly spendthrift Von der Ahe, Commy gained a reputation for tight-fisted salary negotiations. (Asinof, passim) Such stinginess partially explained the infamous 1919 world series. Thirty years after he had angrily questioned the relationship between Arlie Latham and his gambling friend, Charles Albert Comiskey was again brought face to face with gambling's effect on baseball. Did he recall, while anguishing over what to do about Manager Kid Gleason's reports that some of his players were throwing games, his essentially amoral approach to baseball in the spring of 1889? "I go on the field to win a game by any hook or crook. It is the game we are after, not reputations as society dudes" (*S.N.*, 27 April 1889). The man who urged his players to "turn a trick" whenever the opportunity arose if they could get away with it must have been haunted by such advice as he learned of the supposedly unthinkable "tricks" that Chick Gandil, Eddie Cicotte, Lefty Williams, Happy Felsch, Fred McMullen, Swede Risberg, Joe Jackson, and Buck Weaver either arranged or approved by their silence. Embittered thereafter, Charlie Comiskey died in 1931. The stadium that he built in 1910 was torn down after the 1990 baseball season.

While Charlie Comiskey's fortunes waxed profusely following 1889, Chris Von der Ahe's waned dramatically. From 1881, when he became a majority stock holder of the St. Louis Baseball Association, through 1889, Von der Ahe made over $500,000 in baseball, built whole blocks of houses on Grand and St. Louis Avenues, and was one of the most publicized men in the United States. Profligate and a supreme egotist, just one measure of his need for adulation was the mass produced 1887 ladies day satin kerchief, featuring the champion Browns with Vondy's own Falstaffian visage smack in the middle. Squandering $30,000 to transport the Browns to the 1888 World Series (Axelson 63-4) after losing some money in the real estate collapse of the late '80s, Vondy was ill prepared for the horrendous 1890 season. With most of his players deserting to the Players' League, he spent heavily to save his own team and to prop up the American Association. Von der Ahe must have rued the day that he forced his two crowd- pleasing rivals, Cincinnati and Brooklyn, out of the Association, but he never admitted it. The 1891 war with the National League further depleted Vondy's treasury, but he thought that inclusion in the new twelve-team National League, a concept proposed by him as early as 1887, would be his salvation (Von der Ahe file, NBL).

It was a disaster particularly for Von der Ahe and his Browns. Never finishing above ninth place, Chris attempted to lure crowds to the park with entertainment gimmicks such as hiring Arlie Latham as manager for a few days in 1896. On occasion Von der Ahe would desperately install himself as manager, but, as John J. McGraw later recalled, "after awhile, he was more pathetic than funny, even to us players...he didn't know field strategy or opposing weaknesses" (Mrs. McGraw 65). A lawsuit initiated by Mark Baldwin in 1890 dragged through eight years, when Vondy was kidnapped by private detectives and forced, with the National League's aid, to settle the claim. The 1890's severe depression and two divorces diminished his resources still more, and then, on April 16, 1898, a fire destroyed Sportsman's Park at Vandeventer and Natural Bridge Avenues as 4,000 spectators panicked. Many were trampled and burned, resulting in an overwhelming number of lawsuits. The entire grandstand, club offices, and Vondy's saloon burned with all of his personal effects, including the treasured trophies from the 80's. "That night his friends thought the man would go mad" (Lieb, *Cardinals* 20).

His numerous creditors and bondholders plus the National League forced Von der Ahe out of baseball in 1899. On March 14, 1899, G. A. Gruner, a prominent St. Louis lumber dealer representing Vondy's creditors, bought the ballpark and franchise at public auction for $33,000 (S.L., 18 March 1899). Two old St. Louis cronies, Commy and Tom Loftus, attended the auction but did not bid. Later in the year, magnates Frank De Haas and Stanley Robison purchased the franchise and kept it in the League. Sued by his son as the century concluded, Vondy eventually failed in his attempts to revive his old saloon business. Ever optimistic, as late as 1906, Von der Ahe was hoping to get back into baseball with profits from his saloons. It was not to be. In 1908, the Cardinals and Browns played a benefit game for him. Living on those proceeds and the reported charity of Charlie Comiskey, suffering from cirrhosis of the liver and dropsy, this lonely, reclusive man died in June, 1913. Commy made certain that he received a proper funeral and was buried in St. Louis' Bellefontaine Cemetery beneath the statue that he had commissioned of himself during the halcyon days of the '80s. The Browns players of that era served as pallbearers (Von der Ahe file, NBL).

Two Browns of 1889, talented Alabaman Charlie Duffee and Yank Robinson, succumbed to tuberculosis in 1894. After eleven years of carousing and playing baseball, Robinson died in St. Louis at the home of his friend, Patsy Tebeau. He left only $770 to be divided between Tebeau and his brother in Cleveland, Ohio (Robinson file, NBL). Shortstop Shorty Fuller hung on with the Browns through 1891 and then escaped to the Giants, playing until 1896. Fearful of dying from tuberculosis, the disease that had claimed four members of his family, Fuller "dropped out of sight and seemingly waited the coming of death." As he had feared, Fuller died of consumption in 1904 (*Cincinnati Enquirer,* 13 April 1904; *S.L.,* 23 April 1904). Toad Ramsey pitched only one more year in the majors, bounced around in the minors for awhile, went back to bricklaying and tending bar for his brother in Indianapolis, and drank diligently until his death from pneumonia in 1906 (Smith, 1970 54-5; *S.L.,* 7 April 1906).

Silver King's pitching skills declined after 1891, the year that he achieved his top salary of $5,000 with Pittsburgh, and he also had difficulty adjusting to the increased pitching distance in 1893. Leaving baseball for two years, King was lured back by Washington in 1896. When National League owners imposed a $2,400 salary limit after the 1897 season, King, who had made $4,000 with Washington that year, sensibly called it quits. Never again entering a major league baseball park, he returned to brick contracting in St. Louis, married Stella Loring in 1900, had four children, retired comfortably at age 57 and lived until gallstones and appendicitis at seventy (King file, NBL; *S.N.,* 26 May 1938).

Icebox Chamberlain eventually joined Commy in Cincinnati but was finished by 1894. The other member of the Browns' pitching staff, Happy Jack Stivetts, stuck with Von der Ahe through 1891 and then had a rollicking time with the Boston Beaneaters for the next seven years. Praised by Kid Nichols as one of the best pitchers of his time, Stivetts hurt his arm in 1897 and quit in 1899. Both he and Chamberlain lived to be fairly old (Stivetts file, NBL). Nat Hudson fared well in hometown Chicago after leaving Von der Ahe and baseball in mid-season of 1889, living until 1928 (*S.N.,* 22 March 1928). Jim Devlin played in the minor leagues for eight years after St. Louis released him, dying at the young age of 34 in 1900 (*S.N.,* 29 December 1900).

Commy's two big catchers, Jocko Milligan and Jack Boyle, played until the early and late 1890s respectively and then repaired to their home cities of Philadelphia and Cincinnati. "Honest Jack" died after a long illness in 1913, but his two sons had developed a vaudeville act in order to support them and their mother (Ren Mulford, Jr., *S.L.,* 18 January 1913). Jocko died ten years later.

Stellar outfielders Tip O'Neill and Tom McCarthy played only one more year together in St. Louis, during 1891. Tip followed Commy around through 1892, when he became ill in Cincinnati and sat out the last six weeks of the season. The thirty-four year old Canadian had been plagued by malarial attacks as early as 1889 and retired from baseball after 1892. A life-long bachelor, Tip moved to Montreal to live with his mother and two brothers. He operated a saloon and restaurant, lumbered some, and umpired a bit in the minors before dying suddenly from heart disease in 1915 (O'Neill file, NBL; *S.N.,* 6 January 1916).

Joe Visner and his partner in front of their bar in Rochester, N.Y.—mid 1980s. Photo credit Richard L. Smith

Joe Visner—Despite his throwing problems, Visner batted well in 1889 and hit 8 homeruns. From July 1, 1889,

Joe Visner after he left baseball. Photo credit Richard L. Smith.

Tom McCarthy surprisingly stayed with Von der Ahe until the American Association folded. He then had his greatest years with the Boston teams of 1892-95, when he teamed with Hugh Duffy to create the famous "heavenly twins". While in Boston, McCarthy perfected the art of faking the failure to field a ground ball so that he could throw an advancing runner out, faking a catch so that he could short-hop the ball to force a runner at a base, and pretending not to catch a ball, then catch it, and double a runner off of a base. He averaged twenty-six assists in nine of his seasons. His "tricks" inspired the infield fly and tag up rules. Finishing at Brooklyn in 1896, Mac scouted some for Cincinnati and Boston but spent most of his later years coaching baseball at Dartmouth, Holy Cross, and Boston College before he died in 1922. Boston friends had tardily arranged for a benefit game prior to his death, so the $5,000 proceeds were instead given to his daughters (McCarthy file, NBL; *S.N.*, 17, 24 August 1922). The Clown, Arlie Latham, outlived them all.

Walter Arlington Latham cut the same sort of figure in Cincinnati during the mid-1890s as he had in St. Louis, substituting a red necktie "with his shirt-collar standing up" as he played third or coached (*Times,* 6 February 1909). However, he fielded horribly and was essentially finished after 1895. Actually umpiring for the National League in 1899-1900 and again in 1902, Arlie also toiled as an arbiter in the International, Southern, New York State, Interstate, and Sally Leagues (*Complete Baseball,* Spring, 1951, 80). Scouting briefly for Brooklyn at the turn of the century, occasionally appearing in minor stage shows, and working at whatever came along, Arlie rather fortunately landed with McGraw as third base coach for the Giants in 1909. Giants' outfielder Fred Snodgrass recollected that he was a terrible coach, and few players warmed to his renowned sense of humor (Alexander, *McGraw* 143-144).

Finished with coaching after 1912, Arlie embarked for England. When World War I broke out, he became involved in organizing a baseball league there and again took his turn at umpiring. Arlie stayed in London for eighteen years, eventually resorting to checking hats at the Savoy. Making his way back to the United States, Arlie lived well past his ninety-second birthday employed as the press box custodian at the Polo Grounds and Yankee Stadium. In that capacity, "the freshest man on earth" told and retold stories that no one else could refute, praised Joe Dimaggio as the greatest player ever, and occasionally leveled criticism at his old boss, Charlie Comiskey (Latham file, NBL; *S.N.*, 10 December

1952).

In Brooklyn, Charles H. Byrne struggled through the 1890s and never again made as much money in baseball as he had in 1889. The high-salaried Bridegrooms won the National League pennant in 1890, but attendance declined because of the battle with the Players' League. Five major league teams had competed for public attention in the New York metropolitan area during 1890. With old rivalries and familiar teams wholly disrupted, many cranks simply stayed away from the ballparks. The World Series with the American Association's rejuvenated Louisville Colonels concluded in a tie because of bitterly cold weather. Gleaning no financial benefits from the Series, Byrne and Abell faced the 1891 season with losses of $25,000.

When the Players' League disbanded, former National League and American Association players were allowed to return to their respective leagues. In Brooklyn, the players' team, The Wonders, merged with the Bridegrooms. Byrne and Abell also asked George W. Chauncey, the primary financial backer of the Wonders, to invest in their franchise. Chauncey did so but insisted that John Montgomery Ward replace Bill McGunnigle as the Grooms' manager and that the team play its home games at Eastern Park in East New York. Byrne and Abell agreed to Chauncey's conditions, demonstrating that they sorely needed his capital. So Bill McGunnigle was fired after winning two consecutive pennants in two separate leagues. Byrne had praised his manager at the close of the 1890 season as "clever and hardworking" and complimented him for his kind treatment of players. Clearly, he would not have let McGunnigle go if he had not been under extreme financial pressure.

Ward did fairly well for Byrne, bringing the Wonders up to second and third places in the split season of 1892. The ex-Giant was not that happy in Brooklyn, however, and Byrne sold him to the Giants after 1892. Dave Foutz then managed until his Fillies, as the team was sometimes called, sank to tenth in 1896.

By 1897, Charles H. Byrne took less interest in his team because he had become seriously ill. Acquiring the designation "The Napoleon of Baseball," Byrne had worked unceasingly since 1891 to make Brooklyn a winner again. He was one of the prime movers in the reconstruction of the twelve team National League during the fall of 1891, another unprofitable year. Despite financial worries, he labored day and night for many weeks to help resolve the numerous conflicts that arose during the consolidation meetings with the American Association. The work must have been particularly stressful since Byrne had previously been an opponent of such a large league.

Eastern Park did not draw crowds, and poor attendance combined with mediocre teams brought more financial setbacks for Byrne and Abell. His health deteriorating, Byrne relinquished much of his work as President to Charles Hercules Ebbets and visited Virginia Hot Springs twice during the summer of 1897. A lifelong bachelor, Byrne died in January, 1898. His brother-in-law, Joseph J. Doyle, had retired from baseball in 1889, leaving control of the Bridegrooms with Byrne and Abell. When Doyle died in 1906, the last remaining contact of Brooklyn's first President with the team was his brother, William G. Byrne. The latter died in 1932, after forty-two years as custodian of the press gate at Washington Park and Ebbets Field (Byrne file, NBL; *S.L.*, 13 January 1906).

From 1887, Charles H. Byrne had served on baseball's Board of Arbitration and shown special concern for the welfare of the minor leagues. With his legal background, he was a prominent baseball legislator and particularly helpful in rules discussions. This concern over rules had contributed greatly to the feud with St. Louis Browns' owner Christopher Von der Ahe in 1889. Feeling that he had to leave the American Association because of Von der Ahe's opposition, Byrne virtually insured its failure with his departure. Neither Byrne nor Von der Ahe fared well in the expanded National League. The great paradox of Charles H. Byrnes' baseball career was that he actually harmed his team and baseball because of irreconcilable differences with another man, Chris Von der Ahe, who also devoted his life to the game albeit in a decidedly different manner. At the time of Byrne's death, Von der Ahe was on the verge of losing everything that he had invested in baseball.

And what of Bill McGunnigle? One of the true characters in late nineteenth century baseball, Gunner developed quite a reputation for his ability to steal opposing teams' signs. He also devised ingenious methods to signal his own players. Supposedly the first to wave a scorecard from the bench, the nervous McGunnigle thought it equally useful to give signs by tapping bats together. Occasionally, he would signal players with a hat, sometimes using two simultaneously. He even concocted a scheme to signal batters which pitch to expect by using an underground electrical device. Wise electricians counseled against the plan, and his players dissuaded him from using an outfield advertising sign for the same purpose (Allen, *Giants and Dodgers* 25-26). Despite such idiosyncrasies, McGunnigle was exceptionally devoted to his players and their overall welfare.

Nonetheless, Byrne released him after 1890 because of financial pressures. McGunnigle returned to his home state of Massachusetts and managed the Brockton team for half a season before finishing up with Pittsburgh in the National League. He managed successfully at Brockton and Lowell during the next two years but decided to leave baseball for a time to try the shoe business. Lured to Louisville for the last half of the 1896 season, Gunner then gave up baseball for good and settled in Brockton. Like so many other baseball men, he contracted tuberculosis and died in 1899, leaving a widow and several children. Francis C. Richter remembered him as "loyal, genial, generous to a fault...a kindly man who always had an encouraging word and helping hand for the struggling youngsters of the profession" (*S.L.*, 18 March 1899).

Three of McGunnigle's players from 1889 and 1890 preceded him in death. Promising young second baseman Hub Collins never fully recovered from head injuries received in a horrendous, on-field collision with Tom Burns in July, 1891. With both players chasing a short fly at top speed, the locomotives that ran near Eastern Park prevented their hearing the other's warnings. Collins' concussion disabled him for the remainder of that season, and he died of typhoid fever in the spring of 1892 (*S.N.*, 25 July 1891, 28 May 1892). Captain Darby O'Brien, who had entertained cranks by occasionally leaping in the air to break up a double play or racing towards home as third base coach to draw a throw that would advance runners, contracted tuberculosis in 1892 and went home to Peoria, Illinois to die in 1893 (*Herald*, 16 June 1893). The inveterate gambler, Dave Foutz, died rather unexpectedly from an asthmatic condition in 1897.

Variously called "Scissors," "Hunkidori Boy," "His Needles " and "The Human Hairpin," Foutz may have lived improvidently because he realized that he would not live long and chose to enjoy life while he could. Gaining a reputation for drinking and gambling through the night as a minor league player in Bay City, Michigan, Foutz curtailed his drinking after he married Minnie Glocke in 1889 but maintained his wagering habits. Always popular among his teammates, Foutz was tabbed by Charlie Byrnes to manage Brooklyn from 1893 through 1896. His Fillies finished in the middle of the twelve-team National League the first three years and then sank to tenth. Foutz was judged to be too lenient with the players, and in his last year, they constantly violated the "rules". However, his poor health and family concerns were the primary reasons for his resignation after the 1896 season.

Two years prior to his death, Foutz had contracted a severe cold which developed into pneumonia. His wife nursed him back to health, but she suffered what was then described as a nervous collapse and was committed to an asylum for a time. Although his wife recovered somewhat, Foutz was understandably never the same devil-may-care individual that he had once been. Upon learning of his former manager's death, Charles H. Byrne dropped everything and hastened to Baltimore to attend to Foutz's funeral arrangements. Both Byrne and Foutz had been members in the Brooklyn Elks, and Byrne enlisted the aid of the Baltimore organization for the funeral. The man who had been a target of humorous remarks for years because of his peculiar appearance was, at the end, the recipient of sincere respect and admiration (Tiemann and Rucker 47; *S.N.*, 13, 20 March 1897; *S.L.*, 13 March 1897).

Catcher Bob Clark played sparingly for two seasons after 1890, returned to his home town of Covington, Kentucky, and died there of chemical burns in 1919. George "Germany" Smith played impressively at shortstop through 1898, mostly with Cincinnati. The gifted shortstop, so soon forgotten after the turn of the century, also suffered a violent death. Smith had managed Altoona in the Tri-State League before becoming a railroad crossing watchman. He died in 1927 after being struck by a skidding automobile just as he left his watchman's gate (Clark and Smith files, NBL; *S.N.*, 8 December 1927).

Albert John "Doc" Bushong appeared in very few games in 1890 and retired from the game. Unlike many players of that period, Doc had been preparing for another career by acquiring a dental degree from the University of Pennsylvania in 1882 and studying dentistry in Bordeaux, France during the 1883 and 1884 off-seasons. A pioneer of the padded catcher's glove and catching primarily with one hand, Bushong held rather bizarre views about the reason for good vision. He thought that mustaches aided eyesight, blaming the lack of one for having broken a finger from a pitched ball in 1887. Needing no knowledge of eyesight for his dental practice, Doc prospered with offices in South Brooklyn and Hoboken, New Jersey. Always in good condition and a temperate man, Bushong died of cancer in 1908 (Bushong file, NBL; Tiemann and Rucker 23).

Doc's cycling partner, "Adonis" Bill Terry, helped Brooklyn win the 1890 pennant with his pitching and outfield play. Leaving Brooklyn after 1891, Terry pitched for three more National League teams before finishing with Ban Johnson's new minor league in Milwaukee. After 1898, he worked for the Milwaukee organization until he died of pneumonia in 1915 (*S.L.*, 6 March 1915). Terry's physical opposite, Tom Lovett, had two good years in Brooklyn, winning thirty games in 1890. Criticized for his dull, phlegmatic personality by New York writers in 1889, Lovett was characterized by one paper as a "neat looking fat boy" (*Herald*, 5 September 1889). Because of such press, but most likely because he objected to a lower salary, Lovett held out for the entire 1892 season. He tried to come back in 1893-94, but the increased pitching distance caused him to fail. One day in March, 1928, he fell unconscious on a street in his home town of Providence, Rhode Island and died at age 64 (*S.N.*, 29 March 1928). Mickey Hughes never did recover from the sore arm that he developed early in 1889 but lived into old age after leaving baseball in 1890.

Extremely shy third baseman George Pinckney left Brooklyn after 1891 and was out of major league baseball in two years. A mediocre fielder, Pinckney could not stick when his hitting declined. From 1886 through 1889, he played in every game for Brooklyn and was known as the iron man of his era. Returning to Peoria, where he and his old chum Darby O'Brien had begun their baseball careers, Pinckney died of pneumonia in 1926 (*Tribune*, 3 November 1889; *S.N.*, 18 November 1926). John Stewart "Pop" Corkhill, one of the best center fielders during the 1880s, bruised his heel in 1890 and retired after being severely beaned with Pittsburgh in 1892 (*S.N.*, 14 April 1921). Pop had invested wisely in Philadelphia area real estate and lived well until his death in 1921. Tom "Reddy" Burns played impressively with Brooklyn through 1894, retired from baseball after 1897, and lived comfortably from his employment with the Borough of Brooklyn until his death in 1928 (*S.N.*, 22 November 1928). Such unremarkable lives are refreshing in a way, considering the tribulations of many players, but catcher-outfielder Joe Visner chose a different path.

Few people, especially the baseball players of the 1880s, experienced the odyssey upon which Joseph Paul Visner embarked after 1889. A prominent figure in the Bridegrooms' pennant drive during that year, Visner complained afterwards that there were "cliques among the players that rendered things disagreeable all around" (Visner file, NBL). He became the only Brooklyn player to jump to the Players' League. Son of a French fur trapper, named George Vezina, who had married a full-blooded Chippewa woman and was once attacked and left for dead because of a conflict over furs, Visner may have experienced some prejudice because of what then would be regarded as "half-breed" status. He also resented the strong criticism of his catching during the 1889 World Series and wished to take advantage of the higher salary offered by the Pittsburgh Players' League team. Visner continued to hit well in 1890 but still had trouble in the field. After playing briefly for Washington and St. Louis during the final year of the American Association, he left the majors.

He then played for a series of minor league teams, Rochester being one of them, gradually becoming disenchanted by owners' inability to pay salaries. Joe had played with Rochester in 1885, after dislocating his shoulder with the Association Baltimore team, and met his future wife, Willemena "Minnie" Wurtz. Her Dutch immigrant parents owned a hotel there and may have helped the Visners open a bar in the mid-1890s. Visner and another baseball player named Buckley operated the Baseball Exchange until the latter alienated Joe by trying to cheat him out of the proceeds. Drifting to St. Louis, Joe Visner learned that he had inherited 400 acres of land on the White Earth Indian Reservation in northern Minnesota With a growing family, the prospect sounded promising, so the Visners repaired to Minnesota, where Joe had been born in 1859 or 1862.

By 1907, they were supporting nine children and Joe, at age forty-five, found it increasingly difficult to accept the rather sedentary life of the reservation. He decided to embark on a fur-trapping expedition in Canada with his oldest son Paul. The next year, Paul returned to the reservation without his father. Joe Visner, for reasons that will never be known, had abandoned his family. Moving back to Rochester with her parents, Minnie Visner and her children did not see her husband again until 1937. Then Joe Visner appeared in Rochester and simply said: "I'm home."

Working as a fur-trapper, cabinet maker, knife sharpener, and general handy-man, Joe Visner spent thirty years wandering across Canada and the United States on his bicycle. One of his grandchildren in Rochester remembered that he read the Bible every evening, dozed off in the process, sharpened knives with powerful hands that displayed multiple broken fingers, and enjoyed eating fried kidneys. After about a year, he abruptly left again and was not heard from until he appeared at his eldest daughter's house near the White Earth Reservation. There he stayed for the last four years of his life, dying at age ninety-two in 1954. The last Bridegroom had come home (Interview with Richard L. Smith, October 6, 1990; Telephone conversations with Lawrence P. Smith, 10, 19 May 1992; Lawrence P. Smith, The Genealogy of Marie Catherine Visner 4-13).

The man whom Visner caught in 1889, Robert Lee "Parisian Bob" Caruthers, had begun his career exotically enough. After winning forty games for Vondy in 1885, he accompanied his catcher Doc Bushong to France where he dickered for a higher salary. Thus, the nickname. Even though he suffered from malaria in 1887, he still pitched well but was blamed by Von der Ahe for the World Series loss to Detroit. Sold to Brooklyn, Caruthers again won forty games in 1889 although he did not pitch well in the Series. Coming from a wealthy family in Chicago, Caruthers often threatened to quit baseball in order to get a better salary. One of the highest paid players in the game, he reportedly earned $5,500 in 1888. A control pitcher unconcerned with strikeouts, Caruthers again pitched well in 1890 but played most of the last half of the season in the outfield because of Pop Corkhill's injury. A slight but muscular man, he faded a bit in 1891, jumped to St. Louis the next year, labored in the minors for three years, and then retired. His brother's hardware business in Chicago satisfied him for only a short time. Catching on as an umpire, Parisian Bob was working in the Three-I League when he suffered a nervous collapse in 1911 and died in Peoria, age forty-seven, three years after John Clarkson. A good umpire when not inebriated, Caruthers died from the effects of years of dissipation. Both Caruthers and Clarkson had led their leagues in pitching during 1889 (Caruthers file, NBL; *S.N.,* 10 August 1911; *S.L.,* 12 August 1911; Tiemann & Rucker 26).

So the players of 1889 lived and died in all manner of ways. In that pivotal year, a few of them, such as John Montgomery Ward and Tim Keefe, realized that they were performing during a crucial time. Most of them lived and played for the moment. Who are we to blame them? They lived during a time when death and life walked hand in hand through the United States' countryside and cities. Tuberculosis was a painful and deadly killer. Why would not most players, then, "live high" while they could and pay little heed to long-term, financial planning? Owners often operated on the same basis, as witness Chris Von der Ahe. However, they all played the game with an intensity, vigor, inventiveness, and a sense of joy that is often absent in the modern era. They played in a year that brought baseball's first exciting expansion decade to an end and ushered in a decade of decline.

Many of the problems that have plagued the game since were featured in 1889. It was the a fulcrum on which baseball turned through 1919. *Sporting Life's* J.F. Donnolly called the infamous September 7 Brooklyn-St. Louis game "a lobster-Frankenstein nightmare." Applied to the entire season, most of the players and owners would have said "Amen," toasted the thought, and laid odds on when it might happen again. They played the game.

Works Consulted

Archival Resources

Microfilms of Henry Chadwick's Diaries, Volume 14, and Scrapbooks, Volume 2, National Baseball Library, Cooperstown, New York.

Player, Manager, and Owner files cited in the notes, National Baseball Library, Cooperstown, New York.

Newspapers

New York *Clipper*, 1888-1889.

New York Daily Tribune, 1889.

New York Herald, 1889.

New York Times, 1889.

Sporting Life, 1889.

Sporting News, 1889.

Personal Communications

Noesen, Father Jerry. Telephone interview. 28, 29 April 1992

Smith, Lawrence P. Telephone interview. 10, 19 May 1992

Smith, Richard. Personal interview. 6 October 1990.

Smith, Richard L. Telephone interview. 18 May 1992

Books

Alexander, Charles C. *John McGraw*. New York: Viking Penguin, 1988.

_____. *Ty Cobb*. New York: Oxford UP, 1984.

Allen, Lee. *The Giants and the Dodgers: The Fabulous Story of Baseball's Fiercest Feud* New York: Putnam's, 1964.

_____. *One Hundred Years of Baseball*. New York: Bartholomew House, 1950.

Anson, Adrian C. *A Ball Player's Career*. Chicago: Era, 1900.

Asinof, Eliot. *Eight Men Out: The Black Sox and the 1919 World Series*. New York: Holt, 1963.

Avrich, Paul. *The Haymarket Tragedy*. Princeton: Princeton UP, 1984.

Axelson, Gustav. *"COMMY": The Life Story of Charles A. Comiskey*. Chicago: Reilly, 1919.

Barth, Gunther. *City People: The Rise of Modern City Culture in Nineteenth-Century America*. New York: Oxford UP, 1980.

The Baseball Encyclopedia. 8th ed., New York: Macmillan, 1990.

Benson, Michael. *Ballparks of North America.* Jefferson: McFarland, 1989.

Betts, John Rickards. *America's Sporting Heritage: 1850-1950.* Reading: Addison Wesley, 1974.

Breen, Matthew P. *Thirty Years of New York Politics.* New York: Polhemus, 1899.

Brody, David. *Steelworkers in America: The Nonunion Era.* Cambridge: Harvard UP, 1960.

Broeg, Bob. *Redbirds: A Century of Cardinal Baseball.* St. Louis: Rivers City, 1981.

Brown, Henry Collins, ed. *Valentine's Manual of Old New York.* No. 7, New Series, 1923. 126-137.

Brown, Warren. *The Chicago Cubs.* New York: Putnam's, 1946.

Cappio, Alfred P. *"Slide, Kelly, Slide": The Story of Michael J. Kelly.* Passaic County Historical Soc., 1962.

Dexter, Charles, ed. *Dodgers' Victory Book, 1942.* New York: W. & H., 1942.

Dickson, Paul, ed. *The Dickson Baseball Dictionary.* New York: Avon Books, 1991.

Dubofsky, Melvyn. *Industrialism and the American Worker, 1865-1920.* Arlington Heights: AHM, 1975.

Durant, John. *The Dodgers.* New York: Hastings, 1948.

Dworkin, James B. *Owners Versus Players: Baseball and Collective Bargaining.* Boston: Auburn, 1981.

Eckel, John C., and Frank Connelly, eds. *The Universal Baseball Guide.* New York: Rand, 1890.

Fitzgerald, Ed., ed. *The Book of Major League Baseball Clubs: The National League.* New York: Grosset & Dunlap, 1955.

Foner, Eric. *Reconstruction: America's Unfinished Revolution 1863-1877.* New York: Harper, 1988.

Goldstein, Warren. *Playing for Keeps: A History of Early Baseball.* Ithaca: Cornell UP, 1989.

Gordon, David M., Richard Edwards, and Michael Reich. *Segmented Work, Divided Workers.* Cambridge: Cambridge UP, 1982.

Graham, Frank. *The Brooklyn Dodgers.* New York: Putnam's, 1945.

_____. *The New York Giants.* New York: Putnam's, 1952.

Grayson, Harry. *They Played the Game.* New York: Barnes, 1944.

Grob, Gerald N. *Workers and Utopia: A Study of Ideological Conflict in the American Labor Movement: 1865-1900.* Northwestern UP, 1961.

Guttmann, Allen. *A Whole New Ball Game.* Chapel Hill: North Carolina UP, 1988. 58-63.

_____. *Sports Spectators.* New York: Columbia UP, 1986. 111-113.

Gutman, Herbert G. *Work, Culture and Society in Industrializing America.* New York: Knopf, 1976.

Hammack, David C. *Power and Society: Greater New York at the Turn of the Century*. New York: Russell Sage, 1982.

Hardy, Stephen. *How Boston Played: Sport, Recreation, and Community, 1865-1915*. Boston: Northeastern UP, 1982.

Hart, Rollin Lynde. *The People At Play*. Boston: Houghton, 1909. 279-317.

History of Cooperation In The United States. Johns Hopkins Univ. Studies in Historical and Political Sciences, Vol. VI. Baltimore: Guggenheim, 1888.

Holli, Melvin G., and Peter d'A. Jones, eds. *Biographical Dictionary of American Mayors*. Westport: Greenwood, 1981.

Holmes, Tommy. *Baseball's Great Teams: The Dodgers*. New York: Macmillan, 1975.

_____. *Dodger Daze and Knights*. New York: McKay, 1953.

Kaese, Harold. *The Boston Braves*. New York: Putnam's, 1948.

Keith, Harold. *Oklahoma Kickoff*. Norman: University of Oklahoma UP, 1978 ed.

Kelly, Mike. *"Play Ball": Stories of The Ball Field*. Boston: Emery, 1888.

Leitner, Irving. *Baseball: Diamond in the Rough*. New York: Abelard-Schuman, 1972.

Levine, Peter. *A. G. Spalding and the Rise of Baseball: The Promise of American Sport*. New York: Oxford UP, 1985.

Lieb, Frederick G. *The Baseball Story*. New York: Putnam's, 1950.

_____. *The St. Louis Cardinals*. New York: Putnam's, 1947.

_____. *The Story of the World Series*. New York: Putnam's, 1965.

Lowenfish, Lee and Tony Lupien. *The Imperfect Diamond*. New York: Stein, 1980.

Lowry, Philip J. *Green Cathedrals*. Cooperstown: Soc. for American Baseball Research, 1986.

Mack, Connie. *My 66 Years in the Big Leagues*. Philadelphia: Winston, 1950.

McFarlane, Paul, ed. *Daguerreotypes of Great Baseball Stars*. St. Louis: The Sporting News, 1981.

McGraw, John J. *My Thirty Years in Baseball*. New York: Boni, 1923.

McGraw, Mrs. John J. and Arthur Mann, eds. *The Real McGraw*. New York: McKay, 1953.

McNeill, George E., ed. *The Labor Movement: The Problem of Today*. Boston: Bridgman, 1886.

Montgomery, David. *The Fall of The House of Labor: The workplace, the state, and American labor activism, 1865-1925*. New York: Cambridge UP, 1987.

Moreland, George C. *Balldom: "The Britannica of Baseball"*. New York: Balldom, 1914.

Mrozek, Donald J. *Sport and American Mentality, 1886-1910*. Knoxville: University of Tennessee UP, 1984.

The New York Clipper 1891 Annual. New York: Frank Queen, 1891.

Okrent, Daniel, and Harris Lewine, eds. *The Ultimate Baseball Book*. Boston:

Houghton, 1984.

Orem, Preston D. Baseball, *From the Newspaper Accounts, 1888, 1889*. Altadena: n.p., 1966-1967.

Palmer, Harry Clay, ed. *Athletic Sports in America, England and Australia*. Chicago: Hubbard Brothers, 1889.

———. *Stories of the Base Ball Field*. New York: Rand, 1890.

Patten, William, and J. Walker McSpadden, eds. *The Book of Baseball*. New York: Collier, 1911.

The Players' National League Official Guide. 1890.

Porter, David L., ed. *Biographical Dictionary of American Sports: Baseball*. New York: Greenwood, 1987.

Powderly, Terence V. *Thirty Years of Labor: 1859 to 1889*. Columbus: Excelsior, 1890.

Reach's Official American Association Baseball Guide. 1890.

Reidenbaugh, Lowell. *One Hundred Years of National League Baseball*. St. Louis: The Sporting News, 1976.

Rice, Damon. *Seasons Past*. New York: Praeger, 1976.

Richter, Frances, ed. *The Sporting Life's Official Baseball Guide and Hand Book of the National Game*. Sporting Life, 1891.

———. *Richter's History and Records of Baseball*. Philadelphia: Richter, 1914.

Riess, Steven A. *City Games: The Evolution of American Urban Society and the Rise of Sports*. Urbana: University of Illinois UP, 1989.

Ritter, Lawrence. *The Glory of Their Times*. Rev. ed., New York: Morrow, 1984.

Rodgers, Daniel T. *The Work Ethic in Industrial America 1850-1920*. Chicago: University of Chicago UP, 1978.

Roff, Elwood A. *Baseball and Baseball Players*. Chicago: Roff, 1912.

Ross, Steven J. *Workers On The Edge: Work, Leisure, and Politics in Industrializing Cincinnati, 1788-1890*. New York: Columbia UP, 1985.

Rosenzweig, Roy. *Eight Hours for What We Will: Workers and Leisure in an Industrial City, 1870-1920*. New York: Cambridge UP, 1983.

Seymour, Harold. *Baseball: The Early Years*. New York: Oxford UP, 1960.

———. *The People's Game*. New York: Oxford UP, 1990.

Smith, Myron J. *Baseball: A Comprehensive Bibliography*. Jefferson: McFarland, 1986.

Smith, Robert. *Baseball*. New York: Simon, 1947, 1970.

Somers, Dale A. *The Rise of Sports in New Orleans, 1850-1900*. Baton Rouge: Louisiana State UP, 1972.

Spalding, Albert G. *America's National Game*. New York: American Sports, 1911.

Spalding's Official Base Ball Guide. 1890.

Spink, Alfred H. *The National Game*. St. Louis: National Game, 1910.

Stagg, Amos Alonzo. *Touchdown!*. New York: Longmans, 1927. As told to Wesley Winan Stout.

Sullivan, Ted P. *Humorous Stories of The Ball Field*. Chicago: Donohue, 1903.

Tiemann, Robert L. and Mark Rucker, eds. *Nineteenth Century Stars*. Soc. for American Baseball Research, 1989.

Thorn, John, and Pete Palmer, eds. *Total Baseball*. New York: Warner Books, 1989.

Tuohey, George V., compiler. *A History of The Boston Baseball Club*. Boston: Quinn, 1897.

Tutko, Thomas, and William Bruns. *Winning is Everything and Other American Myths*. New York: Macmillan, 1976.

Voigt, David Quentin. *American Baseball, Volume I: From Gentleman's Sport to the Commissioner System*. Norman: University of Oklahoma UP, 1966.

_____. *Baseball: An Illustrated History*. University Park: Pennsylvania State UP, 1987.

Wallop, Douglass. *Baseball, An Informal History*. New York: Norton, 1969.

Ward, John Montgomery. *Base-Ball: How to Become a Player with the Origin, History, and Explanation of the Game*. Philadelphia: Athletic, 1888.

Ware, Norman J. *The Labor Movement in The United States, 1860-1895: A Study in Democracy*. New York: D. Appleton, 1929.

Articles:

Adelman, Melvin L. "Baseball, Business and The Work Place: Gelber's Thesis Reexamined," *Journal of Social History*. Winter 1989: 285-301.

Akin, William E. "Bare Hands and Kid Gloves: The Best Fielders, 1880-1899." *Baseball Research Journal*. (1981): 60-65.

Bass, Cynthia. "The Making of a Baseball Radical." *The National Pastime*. Fall 1982,   Vol. 2, No. 1: 63-65.

Betts, John Rickards. "Sporting Journalism." *American Quarterly V*. Spring 1953: 39-56

Egenriether, Richard. "Chris Von der Ahe: Baseball's Pioneering Huckster." *Baseball Research Journal*. (1989): 27-31.

Fullerton, Hugh. "The Fellows Who Made the Game." *Saturday Evening Post*. CC April 21, 1928: 18-19, 184-188.

Gelber, Steven M. "Working at Playing: The Culture of the Workplace and the Rise of Baseball." *Journal of Social History*. XVI Summer 1983: 3-32.

Hardy, Stephen. "Entrepreneurs, Organizations, and the Sport Marketplace: Subjects in Search of Historians." *Journal of Sport History*. Vol. 13, Spring 1986: 14-33.

Holst, David L. "Charles Radbourne: The Greatest Pitcher of the Nineteenth Century." *Illinois Historical Journal*. LXXXI Winter 1988: 255-268.

Irwin, Will. "Baseball: An Historical Sketch." *Collier's*. XLIII May 8, 15, June 5, 12, 1909: 12-13, 32-34; 14-15, 26-30; 11-12, 25-26; 11, 31-33.

Latham, Arlie. "My 75 Years in Baseball." *Complete Baseball*. Spring 1951: 10,

76, 80.

Lamoreaux, David. "Baseball in the Late 19th Century: The Source of Its Appeal." *Journal of Popular Culture*. XI Winter 1977: 597-613.

Lowenfish, Lee. "The Later Years of John M. Ward." *The National Pastime* Fall 1982, Vol. 2, No. 1: 67- 69.

Murdock, Eugene C. "The Pre-1900 Batting Stars." *Baseball Research Journal* (1973): 75-78.

New York Times. Article on the consumption of alcohol in the United States. July 12, 1889: 3.

Shaw, William Bristol. "Cary, Edward." in Allen Johnson and Dumas Malone, eds., *Dictionary of American Biography*. III New York: Charles Scribner's Sons, 1929, 1958: 554-555.

Somers, Dale A. "The Leisure Revolution: Recreation in the American City 1820-1920." *The Journal of Popular Culture*. V Summer 1971: 113-139.

Spalding, Albert G. "Baseball." *Cosmopolitan*. VII (1889): 603 ff.

_____. "Baseball Then and Now." *Baseball Magazine*. II January 1909): 7-10.

Sullivan, Dean A. "Faces in the Crowd: A Statistical Portrait of Baseball Spectators in Cincinnati, 1886-1888." *Journal of Sport History*. Vol. 17 Winter 1990: 354-365.

Tiemann, Robert L. "The Forgotten Winning Streak of 1891." *Baseball Research Journal*. (1989): 2-5.

Voigt, David Q. "Out With The Crowds: Counting, Courting and Controlling Ball Park Fans." in Peter Levine, ed., *Baseball History 2*. Westport: Meckler, 1989: 92-129.

Von Bories, Philip. "Requiem For A Gladiator." *Baseball Research Journal*. (1983): 147-157.

Ward, John Montgomery. "Notes Of A Base-Ballist." *Lippincott's Monthly Magazine*. XXXVIII August 1886: 212-220.

_____. "Is The Base-Ball Player A Chattel?." *Lippincott's Monthly Magazine*. XL August, 1887: 310-319.

_____. "Our National Game." *The Cosmopolitan*. V October 1888: 443-455.

Weir, Hugh C. "The Real Comiskey." *Baseball Magazine*. XII February 1914: 21-28.

Highly-Paid Players In 1889

The National League:

Player	Team	Salary
Buck Ewing	New York	$5,000
Fred Dunlap	Pittsburgh	$5,000
Dan Brouthers	Boston	$4,700
Tim Keefe	New York	$4,500
John Ward	New York	$4,250
Hardie Richardson	Boston	$4,200
King Kelly	Boston	$4,000
Hoss Radbourn	Boston	$4,000
Arthur Irwin	Philadelphia-Wash.	$4,000
Jim O'Rourke	New York	$3,500
Roger Connor	New York	$3,500
Deacon White	Pittsburgh	$3,500
Jack Rowe	Pittsburgh	$3,500
Ned Hanlon	Pittsburgh	$3,100
Cannonball Morris	Pittsburgh	$3,000
Pud Galvin	Pittsburgh	$3,000
Billy Nash	Boston	$3,000
Jimmy Ryan	Chicago	$3,000
Ned Williamson	Chicago	$3,000
Fred Pfeffer	Chicago	$3,000

(Source: *Spalding's Baseball Guide, ... 1890,* pp. 19-20. White and Rowe were paid at a $500/month rate and also received $1,500 each for transferring from Buffalo to Pittsburg. Orem, p. 383, said the Philadelphia payroll was between $45,000-$50,000 for 1889.)

The American Association:

Player	Team	Salary
Bob Caruthers	Brooklyn	$5,000
Charlie Comiskey	St. Louis	$5,000
Tom Lovett	Brooklyn	$4,000
Mark Baldwin	Columbus	$3,500
Arlie Latham	St. Louis	$3,200
Silver King	St. Louis	$3,200
Jocko Milligan	St. Louis	$3,000
Dave Foutz	Brooklyn	$3,000
George Pinckney	Brooklyn	$3,000
Doc Bushong	Brooklyn	$3,000
Jack Boyle	St. Louis	$2,800
Yank Robinson	St. Louis	$2,700
Tip O'Neill	St. Louis	$2,600
Joe Visner	Brooklyn	$2,400

(Sources: *Spalding's Baseball Guide, ... 1890,* p. 21; Caruthers and King files, NBL; Orem, pp. 383-384, 390, 443; *Sporting Life,* 4/3, 10, 24/89. Seymour, p. 117, notes that American Association teams generally paid lower salaries than the National League. Brooklyn and St. Louis paid the highest salaries in the Association.)

National League 1889

POS	Player	AB	BA	HR	RBI	PO	A	E	DP	TC/G	FA
New York 1B	R. Connor	496	.317	13	130	1265	32	30	68	10.1	.977
W-83 L-43 2B	Richardson	497	.280	7	100	332	416	53	60	6.4	.934
Jim Mutrie SS	M. Ward	479	.299	1	67	229	319	68	38	5.7	.890
3B	A. Whitney	473	.218	11	59	160	265	57	27	3.7	.882
RF	M. Tiernan	499	.335	11	73	179	19	23	2	1.8	.896
CF	G. Gore	488	.305	7	54	239	21	41	5	2.5	.864
LF	J. O'Rourke	502	.321	3	81	165	18	22	2	1.6	.893
C	B. Ewing	407	.327	4	87	524	149	45	10	7.4	.937
P	M. Welch	156	.192	0	12	13	59	4	2	1.7	.947
P	T. Keefe	149	.154	0	8	10	78	8	3	2.0	.917
C	W. Brown	139	.259	1	29	138	38	32	3	5.6	.846

Pitcher	G	IP	W	L	SV	ERA
M. Welch	45	375	27	12	2	3.02
T. Keefe	47	364	28	13	1	3.31
C. Crane	29	230	14	10	0	3.68
H O'Day	10	78	9	1	0	4.27

National League 1889

POS	Player	AB	BA	HR	RBI	PO	A	E	DP	TC/G	FA
Boston 1B	D. Brouthers	485	.373	7	118	1243	58	35	78	10.6	.974
W-83 L-45 2B	Richardson	536	.304	7	79	246	310	46	44	7.0	.924
Jim Hart SS	J. Quinn	444	.261	2	69	67	167	38	19	4.3	.860
3B	B. Nash	481	.274	3	76	205	274	50	25	4.1	.905
RF	K. Kelly	507	.294	9	78	155	24	32	4	1.9	.848
CF	D. Johnston	539	.228	5	67	267	22	26	6	2.4	.917
LF	T. Brown	362	.232	2	24	169	13	20	1	2.2	.901
C	C. Bennett	247	.231	4	28	419	74	23	9	6.3	.955
C	C. Ganzel	275	.192	1	43	13	87	4	19		.927
P	J. Clarkson	262	.154	2	23	10	172	8	8	3.2	.885
SS	P. Smith	208	.259	0	32	138	170	32	23	5.5	.890

Pitcher	G	IP	W	L	SV	ERA
J. Clarkson	73	620	49	19	1	2.73
O. Radbourn	33	277	20	11	0	3.67
K. Madden	22	178	10	10	1	4.40

Batting And Base Running Leaders

Batting Average		Slugging Average		Home Runs	
D.Brouthers, BOS	.373	R. Connor, NY	.528	S. Thompson, PHI	20
J. Glasscock, IND	.352	J. Ryan, CHI	.516	J. Denny, IND	18
M. Tiernan, NY	.335	D. Brouthers, BOS	.507	J. Ryan, CHI	17
F. Carroll, PIT	.330	M. Tiernan, NY	.501	R. Connor, NY	13
B. Ewing, NY	.327	S. Thompson, PHI	.492	H. Duffy, CHI	12

Total Bases		Runs Batted In		Stolen Bases	
J. Ryan, CHI	297	R. Connor, NY	130	J. Fogarty, PHI	99
J. Glasscock, IND	272	D. Brouthers, BOS	118	K. Kelly, BOS	68
R. Connor, NY	262	C. Anson, CHI	117	T. Brown, BOS	63
S. Thompson, PHI	262	J. Denny, IND	112	M. Ward, NY	62
M. Tiernan, NY	248	S. Thompson, PHI	111	J. Glasscock, IND	57

Hits		Base on Balls		Home Run Percentage	
J. Glasscock, IND	205	M. Tiernan, NY	96	S. Thompson, PHI	3.8
J. Ryan, CHI	187	R. Connor, NY	93	J. Denny, IND	3.1
H. Duffy, CHI	182	P. Radford, CLE	91	J. Ryan, CHI	3.0
D. Brouthers, BOS	181	C. Anson, CHI	86	D. Farrell, CHI	2.7
Van Haltren, CHI	168				

Runs Scored		Doubles		Triples	
M. Tiernan, NY	147	K. Kelly, BOS	41	W. Wilmot, WAS	19
H. Duffy, CHI	144	J. Glasscock, IND	40	R. Connor, NY	17
J. Ryan, CHI	140	J. O'Rourke, NY	36	J. Fogarty, PHI	17
G. Gore, NY	132	S. Thompson, PHI	36	M. Tiernan, NY	14

Pitching Leaders

Winning Percentage		Earned Run Average		Wins	
J. Clarkson, BOS	.721	J. Clarkson, BOS	2.73	J. Clarkson, BOS	49
M. Welch, NY	.692	J. Bakely, CLE	2.96	T. Keefe, NY	28
T. Keefe, NY	.683	M. Welch, NY	3.02	M. Welch, NY	27
O. Radbourn, BOS	.645	C. Buffinton, PHI	3.24	C. Buffinton, PHI	27
C. Buffinton, PHI	.614	T. Keefe, NY	3.31	P. Galvin, PIT	23

Saves		Strikeouts		Complete Games	
B. Sowders, BOS, PIT	2	J. Clarkson, BOS	284	J. Clarkson, BOS	68
B. Bishop, CHI	2	T. Keefe, NY	209	H. Staley, PIT	46
M. Welch, NY	2	H. Staley, PIT	159	D. O'Brien, CLE	39
		C. Buffinton, PHI	153	M. Welch, NY	39
		C. Getzein, IND	139		

Fewest Hits/9 Innings		Shutouts		Fewest Walks/9 Innings	
T. Keefe, NY	7.66	J. Clarkson, BOS	8	P. Galvin, PIT	2.06
M. Welch, NY	8.16	P. Galvin, PIT	4	H. Boyle, IND	2.26
J. Clarkson, BOS	8.55	Hutchinson, CHI	3	O Radbourn, BOS	2.34
C. Crane, NY	8.65	E. Beatin, CLE	3	F. Dwyer, CHI	2.35

Most Strikeouts/9 Inn	A. Rusie, IND	J. Clarkson, BOS	620
T. Keefe, NY	4.36	H. Staley, PIT	420
5.17	E. Healy, CHI, WAS	C. Buffinton, PHI	380
C. Crane, NY	4.35	H. Boyle, IND	379
5.09	**Innings**	**Games Pitched**	

	W	L	PCT	GB	R	OR	2B	3B	HR	BA	SA
New York	83	43	.659		935	708	207	77	53	.282	.394
Boston	83	45	.648	1	826	626	196	53	43	.270	.363
Chicago	67	65	.508	19	867	814	184	66	79	.263	.377
Philadelphia	63	64	.496	20.5	742	748	215	52	44	.266	.362
Pittsburgh	61	71	.462	25	726	801	209	65	42	.253	.351
Cleveland	61	72	.459	25.5	656	720	131	59	25	.250	.319
Indianapolis	59	75	.440	28	819	894	228	35	62	.278	.377
Washington	41	83	.331	41	632	892	151	57	25	.251	.329
					6203	6203	1521	464	373	.264	.359

	SB	E	DP	FA	CG	BB	SO	ShO	SV	ERA
New York	292	437	90	.920	118	523	542	6	3	3.47
Boston	331	413	105	.926	121	413	497	10	4	3.36
Chicago	243	463	91	.923	123	408	434	6	2	3.73
Philadelphia	269	466	92	.915	106	428	443	4	2	4.00
Pittsburgh	231	385	94	.931	125	374	345	5	1	4.51
Cleveland	237	365	108	.936	132	519	435	6	1	3.66
Indianapolis	252	420	102	.926	109	420	408	3	2	4.85
Washington	232	519	91	.904	113	527	388	1	0	4.68
	2087	3468	773	.923	947	3612	3492	41	15	4.02

American Association 1889

	POS	Player	AB	BA	HR	RBI	PO	A	E	DP	TC/G	FA
Brooklyn	1B	D. Foutz	553	.277	7	113	1371	33	30	65	10.7	.979
W.93 L-44	2B	H. Collins	560	.266	2	73	385	410	61	56	6.2	.929
Bill	SS	G. Smith	446	.231	3	53	182	417	67	37	5.6	.899
McGunnigle	3B	G. Pinckney	545	.246	4	82	183	278	53	19	3.7	.897
	RF	T. Burns	504	.304	5	100	139	23	14	5	1.6	.920
	CF	P. Corkhill	537	.250	8	78	317	35	19	8	2.7	.949
	LF	D. O'Brien	567	.300	5	80	255	14	28	5	2.2	.906
	C	J. Visner	295	.258	8	68	198	72	40	7	5.8	.871
	C	B. Clark	182	.275	0	22	275	86	54	4	7.8	.870
	P	B. Caruthers	172	.250	2	31	29	95	4	4	2.3	.969
	P	A. Terry	160	.300	2	26	24	86	4	2	2.8	.965

Pitcher	G	IP	W	L	SV	ERA
B. Caruthers	56	445	40	11	1	3.13
A. Terry	41	326	22	15	0	3.29
T. Lovett	29	229	17	10	0	4.32
M. Hughes	20	153	9	8	0	4.35

American Association 1889

	POS	Player	AB	BA	HR	RBI	PO	A	E	DP	TC/G	FA
St. Louis	1B	C. Comiskey	587	.286	3	102	1225	45	39	71	9.8	.970
W-90 L-45	2B	Y. Robinson	452	.208	5	70	305	333	81	53	5.4	.887
Charlie	SS	S. Fuller	517	.226	0	51	240	459	67	46	5.5	.913
Comiskey	3B	A. Latham	512	.246	4	49	197	249	59	22	4.4	.883
	RF	T. McCarthy	604	.291	2	63	229	38	32	11	2.1	.893
	CF	C. Duffee	509	.244	15	86	296	43	23	7	2.7	.936
	LF	T. O'Neill	534	.335	9	110	264	12	19	3	2.2	.936
	C	J. Boyle	347	.245	4	42	378	108	27	11	6.4	.947
	C	J. Milligan	273	.366	12	76	370	105	34	7	7.7	.933
	P	S. King	189	.228	0	30	19	91	5	2	2.1	.957
	P	Chamberlain	171	.199	2	31	15	67	7	0	1.7	.921

Pitcher	G	IP	W	L	SV	ERA
S. King	56	458	33	17	1	3.14
Chamberlain	53	422	32	15	1	2.97
J. Stivetts	26	192	13	7	1	2.25

Batting And Base Running Leaders

3Batting Average		Slugging Average		Home Runs	
T. Tucker, BAL	.372	H. Stovey, PHI	.527	H. Stovey, PHI	19
B. Holliday, CIN	.343	B. Holliday, CIN	.519	B. Holliday, CIN	19
T. O'Neill, STL	.335	T. Tucker, BAL	.484	C. Duffee, STL	15
D. Lyons, PHI	.329	T. O'Neill, STL	.478	J. Milligan, STL	12
D. Orr, COL	.327	D. Lyons, PHI	.469	D. Lyons, PHI	9
				T. O'Neill, STI	9

Total Bases		Runs Batted In		Stolen Bases	
H. Stovey, PHI	293	H. Stovey, PHI	119	B. Hamilton, KC	117
B. Holliday, CIN	292	D. Foutz, BKN	113	D. O'Brien, BKN	91
T. Tucker, BAL	255	T. O'Neill, STL	110	H. Long, KC	89
T. O'Neill, STL	255	L. Bierbauer, PHI	105	H. Nicol, CIN	80
D. Orr, COL	250	B. Holliday, CIN	104	A. Latham, STL	69

Hits		Base on Balls		Home Run Percentage	
T. Tucker, BAL	196	Y. Robinson, STL	118	H. Stovey, PHI	3.4
B. Holliday, CIN	193	J. McTamany, COL	116	B. Holliday, CIN	3.4
D. Orr, COL	183	M. Griffin, BAL	91	C. Duffee, STL	2.9
T. O'Neill, STL	179	B. Hamilton, KC	87	J. Keenan, CIN	2.0

Runs Scored		Doubles		Triples	
M. Griffin, BAL	152	C. Welch, PHI	39	L. Marr, COL	15
H. Stovey, PHI	152	H. Stovey, PHI	37	M. Griffin, BAL	14
D. O'Brien, BKN	146	D. Lyons, PHI	36	H. Stovey, PHI	14
B. Hamilton, KC	144	T. O'Neill, STL	33	O. Beard, CIN	14

Pitching Leaders

Winning Percentage		Earned Run Average		Wins	
B. Caruthers, BKN	.784	J. Stivetts, STL	2.25	B. Caruthers, BKN	40
Chamberlain, STL	.681	J. Duryea, CIN	2.56	S. King, STL	33
S. King, STL	.660	M. Kilroy, BAL	2.85	Chamberlain, STL	32
J. Stivetts, STL	.650	G. Weyhing, PHI	2.95	J. Duryea, CIN	32
T. Lovett, BKN	.630	Chamberlain, STL	2.97	G. Weyhing, PHI	30

Saves		Strikeouts		Complete Games	
T. Mullane, CIN	5	M. Baldwin, COL	368	M. Kilroy, BAL	55
		M. Kilroy, BAL	217	M. Baldwin, COL	54
		G. Weyhing, PHI	213	G. Weyhing, PHI	50
		Chamberlain, STL	202	S. King, STL	47
		S. King, STL	188	B. Caruthers, BKN	46

Fewest Hits/9 Innings		Shutouts		Fewest Walks/9 Innings	
J. Stivetts, STL	7.18	B. Caruthers, BKN	7	B. Caruthers, BKN	2.10
G. Weyhing, PHI	7.66	M. Baldwin, COL	6	J. Conway, KC	2.42
A. Terry, BKN	7.87	F. Foreman, BAL	5	S. King, STL	2.46
F. Foreman, BAL	7.91	M. Kilroy, BAL	5	T. Lovett, BKN	2.55

Most Strikeouts/9 Inn		Innings		Games Pitched	
J. Stivetts, STL	6.71	M. Baldwin, COL	514	M. Baldwin, COL	63
M. Baldwin, COL	6.45	M. Kilroy, BAL	481	M. Kilroy, BAL	59
A. Terry, BKN	5.13	S. Kings, STL	458	S. King, STL	56
J. Sowders, KC	5.06	G. Weyhing, PHI	449	B. Caruthers, BKN	56

	W	L	PCT	GB	R	OR	2B	3B	HR	BA	SA
Brooklyn	93	44	.679		995	706	188	79	48	.263	.365
St. Louis	90	45	.667	2	957	680	211	64	58	.266	.370
Philadelphia	75	58	.564	16	880	787	239	65	43	.275	.377
Cincinnati	76	63	.547	18	897	769	197	96	52	.270	.382
Baltimore	70	65	.519	22	791	795	155	68	20	.254	.328
Columbus	60	78	.435	33.5	779	924	171	95	36	.259	.356
Kansas City	55	82	.401	38	852	1031	162	77	17	.254	.328
Louisville	27	111	.196	66.5	632	1091	170	75	22	.252	.330
					6783	6783	1493	619	296	.262	.354

	SB	E	DP	FA	CG	BB	SO	ShO	SV	ERA
Brooklyn	389	421	92	.928	120	400	471	10	1	3.61
St. Louis	336	438	100	.925	121	413	617	7	3	3.00
Philadelphia	252	465	120	.921	130	509	479	9	1	3.53
Cincinnati	462	440	121	.926	114	475	562	3	8	3.50
Baltimore	311	536	104	.907	128	424	540	10	1	3.56
Columbus	304	497	92	.916	114	551	610	9	4	4.39
Kansas City	472	611	109	.900	128	457	447		2	4.36
Louisville	203	584	117	.907	127	475	451	2	1	4.81
	2729	3992	855	.916	982	3704	4177	50	21	3.84

Afterword

Now that all is ready, now that the second proofing is completed, the title is chosen and the manuscript mailed to the printers, there is yet more history to tell.

Daniel Pearson, whom I have always known as Pop, died on January 2, 1993. I would love to have watched him sign the first copies of this book for his friends and family, and turn carefully the many pages of this dream fulfilled. Pop was a baseball crank by the age of 10. He made his brothers, Richard and Eddie, wash their hands before he would let them enjoy a look at his baseball mags. His father Everett made the grave error of creasing one of the prized magazines during an intense read—an error Pop promptly corrected by tucking it under his arm, walking back over to Liscum's Drugstore and switching it for a new one. Jackie Robinson was Pop's first hero, and he kept his first copy of *The Jackie Robinson Story* always close at hand on his shelf. When Sarah and I were less than 10 he introduced us to our own heroes under the '76 globe and the palms at Dodger Stadium. We held our breath, cheered and roared watching Guerrero, Smith, Dusty, and the Penguin, Lopez, Russell, Garvey, Yeager, Welch and Reuss work their magic on the field. After Grandma Pearson died, we dug out from the back of one of her attic cubbyholes a dusty shoebox, and opened the lid to find the baseball card collection Pop had instructed his mom to throw away when he started college. That dusty box renewed his zeal for collecting the cards and stirred up vivid memories of his first heroes. Not long after, Nanny (Janice Knight) gave him *Shoeless Joe* to read, which inspired Pop to prepare his own field of dreams. These chapters are the fruit of his field, this book the harvest of his dreams.

I have spent hours this past week poring over the books and papers he kept in his desk and in other places in the house, searching for keys to my questions concerning his death. I am searching still, but I did find a single paper of my own among his, an essay I wrote for a History department Senior Seminar course in college. I argued that the historian becomes, in the process of his or her research and writing, a creator and translator not only of history, but also of his or her self. This view I had gleaned from Pop, as he introduced me to history. I think that is why he kept the paper among his own. He hoped to set

233

the voices of the major league baseball players of the 1880's free on the following pages, and to let them tell their story with their feet. I know that during the months of research and writing for this book, he set free a part of himself—maybe the same part of himself that always wanted to play first base for the Dodgers—, and he found his own story, his history, mingled with the experiences of those nineteenth-century owners, players, sportswriters and fans.

I hope that you who read *Baseball in 1889* discover new heroes on the playing fields and among the people rooting in the stands of the Beaneaters, the White Stockings, the Redlegs and the Bridegrooms. And I want to tell you something too, Pop. I promised you once I would take you out to Crown City Brewery to celebrate the publication of this book and to toast all the bases King Kelly never touched. That celebration is on hold for a while, now. But I will not forget.

Peace,
Rachel Pearson
daughter of the author